PHILOSOPHY'S BIG QUESTIONS

PHILOSOPHY'S BIG QUESTIONS

COMPARING BUDDHIST AND WESTERN APPROACHES

EDITED BY

STEVEN M. EMMANUEL

Columbia University Press   *New York*

Columbia University Press
Publishers Since 1893
New York   Chichester, West Sussex
cup.columbia.edu

Copyright © 2021 Columbia University Press
All rights reserved

Library of Congress Cataloging-in-Publication Data
Names: Emmanuel, Steven M., editor.
Title: Philosophy's big questions : comparing Buddhist and
 Western approaches / Steven M. Emmanuel.
Description: New York : Columbia University Press, [2021] |
 Includes bibliographical references and index.
Identifiers: LCCN 2020050812 (print) | LCCN 2020050813 (ebook) |
 ISBN 9780231174862 (hardback) | ISBN 9780231174879
 (trade paperback) | ISBN 9780231553612 (ebook)
Subjects: LCSH: Buddhism and philosophy. | East and West. |
 Philosophy, Comparative.
Classification: LCC BQ4040 .P455 2021 (print) |
 LCC BQ4040 (ebook) | DDC 181/.043—dc23
LC record available at https://lccn.loc.gov/2020050812
LC ebook record available at https://lccn.loc.gov/2020050813

Cover design: Milenda Nan Ok Lee
Cover image: *Buddha's Life Events Portrayed in the Āryāstasahasrikā
Prajñāpāramitā Sūtra* (*The Perfection of Wisdom in 8,000 Lines*).
Manuscript cover, gold on neel patra paper. 1511 CE, Nepal.
From the Collection of the Royal Library, Copenhagen

CONTENTS

Foreword vii
LEAH KALMANSON

Acknowledgments xiii

Abbreviations xv

Editor's Introduction 1
STEVEN M. EMMANUEL

1 How Should We Live? 23
Happiness, Human Flourishing, and the Good Human Life
STEPHEN J. LAUMAKIS

2 What Is Knowledge? 58
Knowledge in the Context of Buddhist Thought
DOUGLAS DUCKWORTH

3 Does Reality Have a Ground? 79
Madhyamaka and Nonfoundationalism
JAN WESTERHOFF

4 Can Consciousness Be Explained? 97
Buddhist Idealism and the "Hard Problem" in Philosophy of Mind
DAN ARNOLD

5 Is Anything We Do Ever Really Up to Us?   129
Western and Buddhist Philosophical Perspectives on Free Will
RICK REPETTI

6 Why Do Bad Things Happen to Good People?   164
"And None of Us Deserving the Cruelty or the Grace":
Buddhism and the Problem of Evil
AMBER D. CARPENTER

7 How Much Is Enough?   205
Greed, Prosperity, and the Economic Problem of Happiness:
A Comparative Perspective
STEVEN M. EMMANUEL

8 What Do We Owe Future Generations?   250
Compassion and Future Generations: A Buddhist Contribution
to an Ethics of Global Interdependence
PETER D. HERSHOCK

Concluding Remarks   275
STEVEN M. EMMANUEL

For Further Reading and Study   287
Contributors   293
Index   297

FOREWORD

LEAH KALMANSON

Definitions of philosophy are notoriously contested, but an investigation into the "big questions" must be one of the most frequent of them. Presumably, these are foundational questions about existence, reality, and human life that cannot help but obsess us—we who find ourselves, here in the first half of the twenty-first century, still uncertain about the nature of our own consciousness, the origins of our universe, or what happens after we inevitably die.

The present collection by Steven M. Emmanuel brings together a group of experts to guide readers through a series of the big questions via Buddhist and Western approaches. Buddhist philosophy dates back to the teachings of Siddhārtha Gautama in the sixth or fifth century BCE. Its rich history developed over the subsequent centuries in diverse stages and produced multiple schools and branches of inquiry. The scholarly practices and methods of Buddhist philosophy are perhaps exemplified by the famed monastic university of Nālandā, said to be founded in India as early as the fifth century BCE, flourishing from the fifth to the thirteenth centuries CE, and attracting students and patrons from Korea to Indonesia. Several of the important philosophers discussed in this volume—including Nāgārjuna (c. 150–250),

Dignāga (c. 480–540), and Dharmakīrti (c. 600–660)—are affiliated with it. To this day, its scholarly traditions persist at the Buddhist universities of Tibet, with the current Dalai Lama considering himself a member of the Nālandā lineage.[1]

We might say that Nālandā is indeed a pivotal institution in the history of world philosophies, in that it trained several of the most influential translators of Sanskrit texts into Chinese, including Xuanzang (602–664) and Yijing (635–713). The reception of Sanskrit-language materials in China undoubtedly marks one of the most important cross-cultural exchanges in philosophy. Despite linguistic and grammatical barriers that render certain conventions of Sanskrit and literary Chinese simply incommensurable to each other, Buddhist philosophy made an indelible impact on China, both intellectually and culturally. Many of the texts and thinkers discussed in the present volume had a direct or indirect influence on the scholarly renaissance of the Song dynasty (960–1279), known in English as "neo-Confucianism," another pivotal episode in the history of philosophy and a focal point in my own research.

All that said, this accounting of philosophical historiography is perhaps at odds with another common description of philosophy—that is, that it began in Greece, a special discovery of Socrates (d. 399 BCE), who from out of the mix of superstition and sophistry emerged with a unique vision for the "love of wisdom" and the disciplinary methods for practicing it. Is there not a fundamental tension between the idea that philosophy engages foundational (and presumably widespread) questions of shared human concern and the coincident claim that it is the unique discovery of a small group of ancient scholars in a single Greek city-state? I cannot help but see an uncomfortable evolutionary picture being painted here. Is the implication not that the Greeks were more advanced? That the emergence of philosophical thought is evidence of the pace of a people advancing along some developmental trajectory? As one historian of philosophy says in 1865, in a comment that reflects widespread beliefs about the philosophical narrative that grew increasingly entrenched over the nineteenth century: "No Asian people . . . has lifted itself to the heights of free human contemplation from which philosophy issues; philosophy is the fruit of the Hellenic spirit."[2]

We should pause here to note that the myth of Greek origins has been thoroughly debunked by philosophers and intellectual historians through careful and responsible research and argumentation. The previous quote is not unknown—it is taken from historian Peter K. J. Park's 2013 book *Africa, Asia, and the History of Philosophy*, which is featured prominently in online platforms such as the *Chronicle of Higher Education*, discussed at length in various philosophy blogs, and reviewed by numerous academic journals.[3] Before this, in the 1990s, Robert Bernasconi documented that the theory of Greek origins surfaced only in the early nineteenth century, and he charged philosophy with the "paradox of parochialism," or the apparent conflict between the idea that philosophy is fundamentally about universal claims and the idea that it is culturally Greek by birth.[4] In this same decade, Emmanuel Chukwudi Eze was discussing the role of racial theories in shaping the understanding of reason and rationality during the Enlightenment.[5]

In support of such work, Park's 2013 intellectual history presents a wealth of detailed evidence that the narrative of philosophy's Greek origins emerged only around the same time that a newly minted pseudoscience of race in Europe first allowed the Greeks to be called "white" and first proposed that a capacity for reasoning might be race-based. Prior to the development of this particular racial classification schema, if we look at various histories of philosophy written in Europe between the 1500s and

1800s, we will find over twenty that either attribute the origins of philosophy to a non-Greek source (such as Egypt or India), or that survey multiple philosophical traditions originating in different areas, including (to name just a few) Persia, Ethiopia, China, and, in one case, Canada (by which the author meant the indigenous peoples of the Americas).[6]

I am confident that very few philosophers today actively subscribe to the explicit theory of racial essentialism that undergirds notions such as the "Hellenic spirit" cited previously. And, in increasing numbers, we philosophers are growing worried that our curriculum and our canon indeed implicitly transmit this outdated mode of essentialist thinking to students via the form and content of standard academic tracks in philosophy departments. For example, the curricular requirements for a philosophy major and minor most often include a "history of philosophy" series that recapitulates nineteenth-century historiography from ancient Greece to modern Europe. Our course catalogs, to give another example, reflect familiar categories that are the products of European philosophy's disciplinary schema, such as metaphysics, ethics, logic, and epistemology. When we send students to graduate school, they learn to discuss their specializations in terms of this intellectual history and these disciplinary categories. When they enter the job market, they generally are answering ads seeking specialists similarly defined by this history and categorization.

Imagine for a moment an undergraduate philosophy department shaped by different terms and categories (here borrowed from my own areas of specialization). Instead of "ancient" and "modern" philosophy, students have taken classes in "Han-dynasty" and "Song-dynasty" philosophy—the appropriate historical markers for discussing important moments in Chinese intellectual history. Instead of analytic philosophy and continental philosophy, students have been exposed to the "teachings of awakened ones" (*fofa* 佛法) and the "lineage of scholars" (*rujia* 儒家)—that is, "Buddhism" and "Confucianism"—reflecting two of the major competing approaches in China to the big questions that obsess us humans. Finally, instead of being taught the difference between "epistemology" and "ethics" (a line that is hard to draw in Chinese discourse), students have been taught to distinguish "*li*-studies" (*lixue* 理學) from "*xin*-studies" (*xinxue* 心學), two major disciplinary methodologies that emerged during the Song era. It goes without saying that any student trained in this way would be unrecognizable to the vast majority of philosophy graduate programs and hiring committees.

As this illustrates, the cultural homogeneity of mainstream philosophy is held in place at a structural level via the terminological choices that determine everything from our academic specializations, to the titles of our books and journals, to the curricular requirements for our majors and minors. Those with concerns about diversifying the canon (and there is an entire blog series at the website of the American Philosophical Association on this issue)[7] must walk a line between the desire to intervene in hegemonic practices and the need to remain visible and understandable within the mainstream academic discipline. Our experiences at this often-fuzzy border require constant negotiations.

In a situation such as this, a book on philosophy's big questions that skillfully negotiates Buddhist and Western approaches is indispensable. Books like this one give all of us the kinds of tools we need to approach content outside our areas of specialization and bring that content into our classrooms. Buddhist philosophy speaks to us and our students with existential urgency. This book manages the task of expressing Buddhism's big questions in the tradition's own terms, via its own methodologies, and in a way that communicates inclusively, inviting readers to make connections to their immediate lives and experiences. Emmanuel and the impressive set of scholars gathered in this collection help us all appreciate the richness of a pluralistic philosophy where supposedly old questions still manage to surprise and inspire.

NOTES

1. Dalai Lama (Tenzin Gyatso), Khonton Peljor Lhundrub, and Jose Ignacio Cabezon, *Meditation on the Nature of Mind* (Somerville, MA: Wisdom, 2011), 15–16.
2. Quoted in Peter K. J. Park, *Africa, Asia, and the History of Philosophy* (Albany: State University of New York Press, 2013), 4. Park quotes Friedrich Michelis.
3. Carlin Romano, "The Toxic History of Philosophy's Racism," *Chronicle of Higher Education*, September 8, 2014, https://www.chronicle.com/article/the-toxic-history-of-philosophys-racism/.
4. Robert Bernasconi, "Philosophy's Paradoxical Parochialism: The Reinvention of Philosophy as Greek," in *Cultural Readings of Imperialism: Edward Said and the Gravity of History*, ed. Keith Ansell-Pearson, Benita Parry, and Judith Squires (New York: St. Martin's, 1997), 212–26.
5. Emmanuel Chukwudi Eze, "The Color of Reason: The Idea of 'Race' in Kant's Anthropology," in *Postcolonial African Philosophy: A Critical Reader*, ed. Emmanuel Chukwudi Eze (Malden, MA: Blackwell, 1997), 103–40.
6. Park, *Africa, Asia, and the History of Philosophy*, 70–77.
7. The blog series is searchable by the tag "Diversifying the Canon." See *Blog of the APA*, https://blog.apaonline.org/tag/diversifying-the-canon/.

ACKNOWLEDGMENTS

First, I would like to express my sincere gratitude to the outstanding group of scholars who contributed their energy and expertise to this project. As always, it is a privilege to be able to collaborate with like-minded people who are dedicated to promoting a greater understanding of the Asian philosophical traditions. There are, of course, different schools of thought regarding the best way to achieve the goal of globalizing the philosophy curriculum. Although I have benefited from a great many conversations with colleagues on this subject, I am particularly indebted to Bronwyn Finnigan for her insightful feedback on the somewhat unconventional approach taken in this volume.

Next, I would like to extend a heartfelt thanks to Wendy Lochner at Columbia University Press for taking on this project and for the very helpful suggestions that she provided at critical stages along the way. I am also grateful to Lowell Frye, Milenda Lee, Kathryn Jorge, and the entire production team at Columbia University Press for the marvelous job they did in preparing this volume for publication.

Finally, I want to thank my wife, Henriette, and my sons Dan, Nick, and Marcus for their patient support, for their cheerful encouragement, and for being a constant source of happiness in my life. This book is lovingly dedicated to them.

ABBREVIATIONS

AN	*Aṅguttara Nikāya*
DN	*Dīgha Nikāya*
MN	*Majjhima Nikāya*
MP	*Milindapañha*
SN	*Saṃyutta Nikāya*

PHILOSOPHY'S BIG QUESTIONS

EDITOR'S INTRODUCTION

STEVEN M. EMMANUEL

Given the breathtaking advances made in the natural sciences over the last four centuries, it is perhaps understandable that some philosophers should wonder why their own discipline has not made more progress than it has. After all, writes David Papineau, "philosophers still struggle with many of the same issues that exercised the Greeks. What is the basis of morality? How can we define knowledge? Is there a deeper reality behind the world of appearances?"[1] The problem is not that philosophy has failed to produce any good answers to these questions, but that it has not produced any definitive answers to them: "When it comes to topics like morality, knowledge, free will, consciousness and so on," says Papineau, "the lecturers still debate a range of options that have been around for a long time."

Some would argue that a good deal of progress has been made, even though it may not seem so due to the kinds of problems that engage the attention of philosophers and the methods they use to investigate them. Philosophy grapples with difficult questions that cannot be settled by empirical evidence alone. Although science can tell us a great deal about the biochemical and physiological factors that contribute to human well-being, it cannot resolve deep disagreements about how we ought to live or what constitutes a just distribution of goods in society. By the same token, contemporary investigations in neuroscience and cognitive psychology have contributed much to our understanding of the human mind by shedding light on the neural correlates of mental phenomena. "But even here," notes David Chalmers, "these sciences seem to have left the big questions—the problems of consciousness and intentionality, of mental causation and free will—wide open."[2] This is the case not merely because there are gaps in our scientific knowledge of the world, but because philosophical inquiry is driven by a curiosity that reaches beyond the results of observation and experimentation. As J. L. Schellenberg explains:

> Philosophy wants to know if nature, which science explores, is the whole of reality, or whether there's something more. Tracing, with science, the innumerable causal pathways associated with our behaviours, philosophy wants to know whether these leave room for me to really be free and deserve praise or blame for my behaviour. And if there are truths about how things *ought* to be as well as scientific truths about how things are, what are they and how are they discovered?[3]

To arrive at answers to these questions, philosophers use the tools of intuition, conceptual analysis, and argumentation. Philosophical progress is possible because this process of critical reasoning forces us to be more rigorous and precise in our thinking—it clarifies our understanding of a problem by defining key terms, making careful distinctions, and subjecting our assumptions to critical scrutiny.

One by-product of this reasoning process, however, is that it leaves ample room for disagreement. Indeed, as Chalmers points out, one of the main reasons why philosophers struggle to build consensus is that "arguments for strong conclusions in philosophy (unlike science and mathematics) almost always have premises or inferences that can be rejected without too much cost."[4] This is not to deny that philosophers are working toward a better understanding of problems and solutions. Indeed, adds Chalmers, "many new philosophical methods have been developed and many old methods have been refined, in order to help reach philosophical conclusions."[5] These include linguistic analysis, phenomenological reflection, feminist critique, cross-cultural inquiry, and even the use of experimental methods designed to shed light on our intuitions about morality and free will.[6] Yet while all these approaches have led to progress in the form of new insights, arguments, and conclusions, there has not been a collective "convergence to the truth" on the big questions of philosophy.[7]

To be clear, Chalmers does not equate philosophical progress with convergence to the truth. There are, he concedes, "many values that can be realized through philosophy," and also "many ways of advancing and realizing those values."[8] For instance, progress can simply mean gaining greater understanding of the issues underlying the big questions, or exploring "new views and new areas of philosophical space that we had not even conceived of earlier."[9] Historically, philosophy has also been associated with a kind of moral or spiritual progress—the cultivation of a better, happier, more fulfilling life. For Socrates, this meant engaging in a process of self-examination that led to wisdom and virtue. Yet even the Socratic ideal of the examined life was based on a commitment to the pursuit of truth and knowledge. For Chalmers, as for many contemporary philosophers who work in the analytic tradition, convergence to the truth is important because agreement is a requirement for knowledge, and where sufficient disagreement exists, nobody can be said to know the truth.

Not surprisingly, the question of whether and to what extent we may ever hope to achieve consensus on any of philosophy's big questions is itself a matter of disagreement. Many are pessimistic about the prospects. Peter van Inwagen, for instance, sees disagreement in philosophy as both "pervasive and irresoluble," while Colin McGinn speculates that we may simply lack the cognitive capacity to solve philosophical problems and establish true philosophical theories.[10] But as Chalmers views the situation, it is not unreasonable to suppose that we might eventually arrive at a greater degree of convergence on at least some of philosophy's big questions:

> We may need to develop new methods, increased discipline, new sorts of insights, and perhaps there will need to be a conceptual revolution or two, but none of this will lie outside human capacity. It may turn out that there is a curve of increasing philosophical sophistication such that past a certain point on the curve, major progress is possible.[11]

In the meantime, our best option is simply to keep doing philosophy as well as we can, trying to "come up with those new insights, methods, and concepts that might finally lead to us answering the questions."[12]

A similar optimism is expressed by Schellenberg, who suggests that we may still be in the earliest days of philosophical history—that the past 2,500 years of thinking on the most difficult problems is perhaps just a first step. At this preliminary stage, disagreement is not only to be expected, but actively encouraged:

> The right orientation will require bringing our positions into friendly conversation with the positions of disagreeing others in as many human configurations as possible. Disagreement can be

made to work for us: its purpose is to expand our imaginations and to enlarge and improve, for everyone, the body of available evidence.... It is astonishing that anyone should think philosophy could get very far before having done this.[13]

According to this view, allowing a greater diversity of voices and cultural perspectives to enter into the conversation deepens the well of philosophical insight, thereby increasing the chances of making the kind of progress that we should like to see.

It is in this spirit that the present volume looks to the seminal figures and texts of the Buddhist tradition for fresh insight into some of philosophy's big questions. The study is divided into eight chapters, each one focusing on a particular set of philosophical issues and concerns that have engaged the attention of thinkers in different times and cultures. These include basic concerns about happiness and the good life, the nature and scope of human knowledge, the ultimate structure of reality, the nature of consciousness, the relation between causality and free will, the pervasiveness of human suffering, and the conditions for a just and flourishing society.

Western and Buddhist thinkers approach their respective inquiries in different ways, both in terms of their motivating concerns and in the concepts and methods they employ. There is a natural temptation in cross-cultural discussions of this sort to want to gloss over such differences—to distill from the rich tradition of Buddhist thought some version of "what Buddhists think about *x*" that conforms, more or less, to our own ideas about what it means to inquire into *x*. But such an exercise would be neither useful nor informative for the purposes at hand. Although Buddhist thinkers have had a lot to say about the nature of consciousness and the problem of human suffering, for instance, their contributions cannot be appreciated properly if we are forced to view them through the narrow lens of what Western philosophers call "the mind-body problem" or "the problem of evil." Fostering a genuinely cross-cultural dialogue demands that we engage Buddhist thought on its own terms—that we allow the Buddhist texts to challenge the familiar ways in which Western philosophers have framed their inquiries.

It is important to note, in this connection, that the questions that appear in the chapter titles in this volume are intended only to situate the discussion in the philosophical territory under investigation. In other words, they function primarily as *topic* questions.[14] This allows the contributors the freedom to show where and how the philosophical interests of Buddhist and Western thinkers intersect and inform each other, while paying close attention to the distinctive ways in which they articulate and answer big questions. For instance, the topic question posed in the final chapter—"What Do We Owe Future Generations?"—provides a useful point of entry into an age-old question about the extent of our ethical obligations to others and the kinds of beings to whom we are responsible. Because the formulation of that question in intergenerational terms is a relatively recent development in Western thought, one might suspect that we are simply posing a "Western" question and seeing what Buddhist thinkers have to say about it. In reality, though, the intergenerational perspective is deeply embedded in Buddhist thought. The chapter's discussion reveals that for Buddhist thinkers, the ethical question about our obligations to future generations is closely connected to metaphysical arguments concerning the nature of the self and the practice of compassion. But it also shows how one important strand of Buddhist thinking on that question intersects with a contemporary Western attempt to formulate a theory of global social justice based on compassion.

In a similar fashion, each chapter in this volume sets out to create a cross-cultural discussion that expands and enriches our philosophical perspective, thereby opening up new possibilities for thinking about old questions. Indeed, one of the great benefits of this approach lies in the discovery that there are other conceptual and methodological strategies for thinking about philosophical problems, and that these may produce new and unexpected kinds of questions and answers. Furthermore, the engagement with Buddhist thought reminds us that philosophy has a practical as well as a theoretical dimension—that the pursuit of wisdom aims not only to understand the world but to know how to live in it. In this way, the cross-cultural perspective provides a valuable opportunity to reflect on the practice of philosophy itself.

In addition to promoting a greater diversity of cultural voices and perspectives, there are two other ways in which this study seeks to be more inclusive. First, while many collections of this kind focus on topics in philosophy of language, epistemology, logic, and metaphysics, this book pays ample attention to concerns related to ethics, social and political philosophy, and the philosophy of religion. Second, the reader will find here a variety of approaches to doing comparative philosophy. As this is one of the more striking features of the volume, a few words of explanation are in order.

There has been a great deal of pushback in recent years against a traditional approach to cross-cultural study—one that restricts itself to the comparative task of pointing out similarities and differences between divergent philosophical traditions. Various reasons are given for rejecting this approach, but the most serious of these seems to be that merely comparing traditions fails to advance the conversation in any meaningful way. As Jay L.

Garfield declares in the introduction to his book *Engaging Buddhism: Why It Matters to Philosophy*:

> We needed comparative philosophy at an earlier stage of cultural globalization when it was necessary to juxtapose different philosophical traditions in order to gain an entrée and in order to learn how to read alien traditions as philosophical. But now we can safely say, "been there; done that." I therefore take it for granted that the days when "comparative philosophy" was the task are over, and a different methodology is necessary at this stage of philosophical practice.[15]

What the critics of the comparative approach wish to see is a more robust form of engagement that seeks to *incorporate* the resources of the Buddhist tradition in our own thinking about philosophical problems—an approach that Mark Siderits calls "fusion philosophy." Succinctly put, fusion philosophy is the "serious and sustained effort to use elements from one tradition to solve problems arising in another."[16] By placing the emphasis squarely on problem-solving, he consciously aligns this approach with the analytic tradition of philosophy and the narrower conception of progress presupposed by it.

While Garfield agrees with the general approach outlined by Siderits, he prefers not to think of it in terms of a "fusion" of traditions, but rather as creating cross-cultural dialogue.[17] In the case of the Indian Buddhist philosophers, says Garfield, such a dialogue is possible because

> they engage with questions and problems in which we are interested, sharing enough common ground for us to understand what they have to say, and contributing enough that is new that we have some reason to listen to it. They invite us to inhabit a new

philosophical horizon, different enough from our own to set new questions and new phenomena in relief, but familiar enough that many of them will be recognizable as philosophical puzzles and insights... That is the nature of real dialogue.[18]

Moreover, a fruitful interchange of this sort promises to enrich both traditions, as each can draw on the wealth of conceptual and methodological resources available in the other in order to solve philosophical problems. In practice, however, there has been a tendency among Western philosophers interested in Buddhist thought to be rather selective about what they engage with, focusing only on those elements that they identify as properly "philosophical," and therefore relevant to the kinds of discussions we find in mainstream Western philosophy journals. The worry, of course, is that by bracketing certain concepts and issues—mainly soteriological ones—that are central to Buddhism, we may be letting the West set the agenda for philosophical inquiry. This would seem a less open and respectful kind of engagement than the one that we should aspire to have.

It would seem, then, that there is still something to be said for comparative philosophical discussions that consciously attempt to place the ideas, theories, and methods of another tradition in their proper historical and cultural context. This would include elements that a Western thinker might not deem *philosophically* relevant (e.g., Buddhist teachings on karma and rebirth), but are nevertheless important for understanding how certain problems arose for thinkers in that tradition, or why the various answers they proposed would make sense to them.[19] Indeed, we should imagine that some amount of this type of work is necessary in order to move skillfully within the thought-world of another culture. Viewed in this way, it seems unwise to try to draw too sharp a distinction between "comparative" and "cross-cultural" philosophy, or for that matter to equate philosophical progress with an analytical method aimed solely at solving problems. After all, as noted earlier, there are different values that can be realized through philosophy, and one of the benefits of engaging the Buddhist tradition is that it provides us with an opportunity to reflect on how we conceive of philosophical practice.

The latter point is particularly important in terms of the task of globalizing the philosophy curriculum—an area in which a great deal of thoughtful work remains to be done. To this end, we should bear in mind that the needs of a first- or second-year philosophy student are different from those of a graduate student or nonspecialist scholar. The undergraduate who would benefit from a comparative survey of Western ethical theories surely can also benefit from a discussion that lays out the various philosophical positions advanced by Buddhist and Western thinkers, with a view to illuminating important points of contrast and convergence. We should hasten to add that *comparing* these positions can be done in a rigorous and respectful way that expands the possibilities for thought and imagination and shows us philosophically different ways of seeing the world and being in the world.

A key premise of this study is that the work of globalizing the philosophy curriculum is not well served by insisting on only one way of introducing culturally diverse voices into the conversation. The reader will find a variety of approaches presented here. For instance, some chapters offer comparative expositions of key ideas and theories in ethics and epistemology, while others engage with complex arguments in Buddhist metaphysics and philosophy of mind, with the goal of drawing out their implications for contemporary debate. Some chapters situate their discussion in the systematic writings of Buddhist philosophers, while others work primarily with canonical sources, gleaning from those texts key insights that are brought to bear on a range of issues in social and political thought and philosophy of religion. While some chapters aim to expand the options for thinking about their questions or to clarify and refine major concepts, others present detailed expositions of Buddhist theories that either have no parallel in the West or challenge our thinking on a topic in fundamental ways.

What follows is a brief overview of the philosophical terrain to be covered.

HOW SHOULD WE LIVE?

The teachings of the historical Buddha (Siddhārtha Gautama) have a clear soteriological focus—to elucidate the causes of suffering and to articulate a path of practice that leads to liberation from that suffering. In this sense, one might suppose that the Buddha is better thought of as a religious or spiritual teacher than as a philosopher. Yet there is an undeniably philosophical dimension to the Buddha's teachings, for the project of liberation described therein depends on gaining a certain kind of knowledge or insight concerning the true nature of reality. The metaphysical views at the heart of the teachings are elaborated in various discourses by means of key concepts such as impermanence, dependent origination (i.e., all phenomena arise within a nexus of causes and conditions), and nonself. These concepts, together with the contemplative methods that lead to a direct awareness of the realities described by them, would become the focus of rigorous philosophical analysis by later Buddhist thinkers—in particular the Indian philosophers of the first millennium CE.[20] But as Matthew Kapstein notes, while some of these thinkers were deeply interested in the "technical aspects of truth and knowledge," their efforts were never entirely removed from "the overarching Buddhist interest in the contours of the good life—that is, the life directed to realizing the peace, insight, and compassion whose highest exemplar was always considered to be the Buddha himself."[21]

In the opening chapter, Stephen J. Laumakis provides a broad historical framework for understanding the connection between theory and practice in Western and Buddhist philosophy. He sets up this comparative discussion by briefly reviewing three paradigmatic Western approaches to the "good human life." But rather than trying to explain the Buddhist approach in terms of this Western framework, Laumakis situates the Buddhist understanding of the good life in its native intellectual and historical context. While some common ground is shared by the two traditions, a fundamental difference emerges in the way that Buddhism integrates the wisdom or insight of one who sees things as they really are with the compassion of one who understands and responds appropriately to the suffering at hand. The difference between the two traditions is most clearly evident in the way that Buddhism integrates a metaphysical understanding of the world with a practice of mental and moral training that not only informs our understanding of how we should live, but also provides the motivation to do so.

WHAT IS KNOWLEDGE?

Knowledge, as Douglas Duckworth reminds us, is "a slippery subject." Any attempt to define knowledge with precision is immediately complicated by the fact that there are various kinds of knowledge and ways of knowing. To frame his comparative discussion, Duckworth draws mainly on the writings of two key figures in the Mahāyāna tradition—Dignāga (sixth century) and Dharmakīrti (seventh century), whose detailed analyses of perception and inference are examined alongside the epistemological views of prominent Western philosophers of the twentieth century.

One of the most distinctive features of Buddhist epistemology is that it includes sources of knowledge that go beyond the five senses. In addition to sense perception, Dharmakīrti describes three other sources: mental perception, self-awareness, and what he calls "yogic perception." The latter, which can be achieved only through the intensive practice of meditation, is particularly important for understanding the Buddhist path to liberation, as it yields a special kind of knowledge—a transformative insight that changes how we see and act in the world.

DOES REALITY HAVE A GROUND?

Jan Westerhoff takes up a perennial question in metaphysics concerning the ultimate structure of reality. Western and Buddhist philosophers alike have thought deeply on the question of whether reality has an underlying foundation. A car, for instance, might be said to depend for its existence on the various parts that make it up—the engine, drivetrain, wheels, and so on. But these parts in turn depend on smaller parts that make them up, which depend on still smaller parts, and so on. The question naturally arises as to whether this chain of ontological dependence terminates in some ultimately basic parts, which, having no parts themselves, serve as the foundation or ground that supports the whole. In the Western tradition, it has generally been assumed that some form of foundationalism is required to make sense of reality. Although some early Buddhist philosophers reached a similar conclusion, others suggested a radically different possibility (namely, that there is no underlying foundation). This view was advanced by the second-century Indian philosopher Nāgārjuna, one of the founders of the Madhyamaka school of Buddhism, who argued that nothing in the world—neither persons nor objects—exists as an ontologically independent reality. Westerhoff lays out the main arguments for this position, evaluates its consistency, and concludes with a discussion of the implications of nonfoundationalism for a Buddhist theory of truth.

CAN CONSCIOUSNESS BE EXPLAINED?

In this chapter, Dan Arnold takes up a vexing problem in philosophy of mind commonly known as the "hard problem" of consciousness. David Chalmers frames the basic question as follows:

> How can we explain why there is something it is like to entertain a mental image, or to experience an emotion? It is widely agreed that experience arises from a physical basis, but we have no good explanation of why and how it so arises. Why should physical processing give rise to a rich inner life at all? It seems objectively unreasonable that it should, and yet it does.[22]

While science can give us objective, third-person explanations of the neurophysiological processes underlying conscious mental events, these explanations inevitably fail to capture the qualitative aspect of a subject's first-person experience—what it feels like *for* the subject. Indeed, the felt quality of that subjective experience is so different from the physical structures and events described by science that it is hard to understand how phenomenal consciousness could arise at all.

Arnold sheds fresh light on this question by calling attention to a parallel problem that arose for philosophers in the Yogācāra school of Mahāyāna Buddhism. Although these thinkers were reductionists, they were also idealists. Dharmakīrti, for instance, defended the Buddhist doctrine of rebirth by rejecting the physicalist claim that consciousness arises from the body or that it ontologically depends on the body. But both Dharmakīrti and his predecessor, Dignāga, faced serious difficulties in providing a coherent account of the occurrence and content of mental cognitions. Arnold's reading of these Buddhist idealists reveals a more conceptually basic problem concerning consciousness—one that has less to do with "what kind of *stuff* experience is made of" than with how or whether we can reconcile first- and third-person perspectives on cognitive events.

IS ANYTHING WE DO REALLY UP TO US?

Are we really free when we choose to do one thing rather than another? Was it really possible for us to have chosen differently, or is the feeling that we could have done otherwise merely an illusion? Is it possible that our choices are really determined by factors beyond our control—that nothing we do is really up to us?

Rick Repetti begins by examining some of the main arguments that Western philosophers have made against free will. The first two are standard arguments showing how determinism and indeterminism undermine the claim that our choices are up to us. A third argument shows how our choices may be manipulated in various ways (without our knowledge) that render them unfree in a manner akin to determinism. The final argument focuses on the mental state of an agent at the moment of choice. As the argument goes, this state of mind is the most recent in a long sequence of mental states, each one conditioned by the previous one, together with other factors such as heredity and experience. But because no choice is ever made in an unconditioned mental state, we cannot be said to be free in the sense required to be morally responsible for our actions.

With these arguments in hand, Repetti turns to considering a variety of Buddhist perspectives—some skeptical, some optimistic—on the problem of free will. What is especially noteworthy about the Buddhist approach is the reductionist view of persons that informs the Buddhist outlook. The view of nonself might at first glance seem to present a serious problem for a Buddhist understanding of agency. However, Repetti suggests that not only is an "agentless agency" philosophically tenable, but it may form the basis of a powerful counterargument to Western skeptics of free will.

WHY DO BAD THINGS HAPPEN TO GOOD PEOPLE?

The "problem of evil," as it is commonly presented in the philosophical literature, poses a challenge to traditional theism. Briefly stated, the problem is whether it is possible to reconcile the existence of a supremely good, all-knowing, and all-powerful God with the presence of evil in the world. Why would a just and benevolent God allow the innocent to suffer? According to the evidential version of this argument, the sheer volume of undeserved suffering in the world makes it highly unlikely that God exists, while a stronger, logical version of the argument purports to demonstrate that the presence of such suffering logically precludes the existence of God.

The problem of evil is not just for theists, however, for the undeserved suffering that it describes is problematic in its own right. This secular version of the problem is rooted in our need for there to be some sense of proportion between the moral quality of our actions and the consequences that follow them. A world in which the wicked flourish and the virtuous often suffer offends our sense of justice and robs us of any good reason for acting in a principled way. In order "to act in the world and to value and care," explains Amber Carpenter, "we must be able to hope that there is a fair and measured arrangement possible in the world, not to see that evident in our daily lives *just is* the problem of evil. This is a problem of evil that we all have, regardless of our theistic convictions."

Carpenter examines this nontheistic problem of evil in light of the Buddhist analysis of suffering and the doctrine of karma. Her discussion illuminates important assumptions underlying both the Western and Buddhist approaches. On Carpenter's reading of the Pāli canonical texts, suffering does not appear to present for Buddhists the kind of problem that it does for Western thinkers. The Buddhist approach focuses squarely on the *fact* of suffering and the causes that give rise to it. From a karmic perspective, the categories of guilt and innocence, justice and desert not only fail to provide an adequate explanation for suffering but also are symptomatic of the kind of confusion that gives rise to suffering in the first place. According to this understanding, no one is ultimately to blame for the fact that ignorance "sets people against each other and makes them callous or incognizant of the suffering that their actions cause." The more aware we are of the nature of our predicament, "the more urgently we want to interrupt this self-perpetuating process, to eliminate suffering by eliminating the causes of suffering."

HOW MUCH IS ENOUGH?

Chapter 1 of this book frames the general question of what it means for an individual to live well and be happy. In chapter 7, we turn our attention to the social and political dimensions of that question as we explore the conditions for a flourishing and happy society. The first part of the discussion calls attention to a major shift in Western thinking about greed that began in the seventeenth century and culminated in the writings of the eighteenth-century philosopher Adam Smith. In his seminal *Wealth of Nations* (1776), Smith presented a classic defense of the free market system, arguing that the constant striving of individuals to better their own condition is the engine that drives economic growth and prosperity in society.

Smith was well aware of the costs of such a system—not least the social and psychological ills of inequality, selfishness, inauthenticity, anxiety, and indifference to the misery of the poor. He also noted how the relentless pursuit of wealth disrupts the tranquility and contentment that are key to happiness. Many scholars have pointed to the paradoxical implications of Smith's analysis: it would appear that the prosperity required for a flourishing and happy society—one in which *everyone* is able to enjoy a reasonable level of material security and comfort—depends on a kind of economic activity that undermines individual happiness.

A similar problem is addressed in a number of early Buddhist canonical texts, in which the Buddha speaks to the benefits and the dangers of wealth acquisition as it pertains to happiness. These texts describe an ennobling form of economic activity that not only is compatible with moral and spiritual growth, but also promotes the conditions for a peaceful, prosperous, and happy society. What we find here is an account of economic progress that values economic freedom while posing a robust challenge to the valorization of greed in Western libertarian accounts of prosperity.

WHAT DO WE OWE FUTURE GENERATIONS?

Finally, chapter 8 extends the traditional discussion about social justice by considering the consequences of our present actions for those living in the distant future. In the face of unprecedented global challenges such as climate change, argues Peter Hershock, the "extension of justice concerns to include future generations can no longer be seen as a purely academic exercise; it has become a global ethical imperative." But what would an ethic of global justice look like? Could such a theory be morally and politically compelling enough to motivate collective action on behalf of future generations?

One promising approach, suggested by Martha Nussbaum, attempts to construct a global ethics of social justice around the "social emotion" of compassion. She argues that compassion generates the kind of "breadth and depth of ethical vision" that is necessary to gain moral and political traction, insofar as it involves the recognition of an undeserved suffering in others that we would not want to experience ourselves. In this way, compassion serves as an effective motivation to build institutions that guarantee all citizens certain core capabilities, including, among other things, the freedom to enjoy a healthy life, with opportunities to develop the mind, to make emotional connections with others, and to exercise some control over the political and material conditions of one's life.

Hershock is skeptical of the prospects for Nussbaum's "capabilities" approach. For political and economic systems that seek to achieve social justice by securing the capabilities of individuals to act in their own interests might not encourage "the depth of partnership" required to address global problems like climate change. As an alternative, Hershock draws on the distinctive conceptual resources of Mahāyāna Buddhism—in particular, the all-inclusive "great compassion," or *mahākaruṇā* of the bodhisattva—to propose an "irreducibly relational" account of global social justice in which all beings are seen as "intergenerational beings."

NOTES

1. David Papineau, "Is Philosophy Simply Harder Than Science?," *Times Literary Supplement*, June 1, 2017.
2. David J. Chalmers, "Why Isn't There More Progress in Philosophy?," *Philosophy* 90, no. 1 (2015): 24.
3. J. L. Schellenberg, "Philosophy's First Steps," *Aeon*, April 10, 2018. Italics in original.
4. Chalmers, "Why Isn't There More Progress in Philosophy?," 25.
5. Chalmers, 22–23.
6. Chalmers, 23.
7. Chalmers, 6.
8. Chalmers, 14.
9. Chalmers, 13.
10. Peter van Inwagen, "Freedom to Break the Laws," *Midwest Studies in Philosophy* 28 (2004), 332; Colin McGinn, *Problems in Philosophy: The Limits of Inquiry* (Oxford: Wiley-Blackwell, 1993), chap. 1.
11. Chalmers, "Why Isn't There More Progress in Philosophy?," 31.
12. Chalmers, 31.
13. Schellenberg, "Philosophy's First Steps."
14. Here, I follow Daniel Stoljar, who distinguishes between the topics or subject matter of philosophical inquiry and the specific questions that philosophers in different times and places have asked about those topics. See Daniel Stoljar, *Philosophical Progress: In Defence of a Reasonable Optimism* (New York: Oxford University Press, 2017), 12.

15. Jay L. Garfield, *Engaging Buddhism: Why It Matters to Philosophy* (New York: Oxford University Press, 2015), 3.
16. Mark Siderits, *Personal Identity and Buddhist Philosophy: Empty Persons* (New York: Routledge, 2003), 1.
17. Garfield, *Engaging Buddhism*, 3.
18. Jay L. Garfield, "Two Truths and Method," in *The Moon Points Back*, ed. Koji Tanaka, Yasuo Deguchi, Jay L. Garfield, and Graham Priest (New York: Oxford University Press, 2015), 251–52.
19. For a discussion of the dangers involved in studies that selectively ignore the soteriological elements in Buddhist thought, see John Powers, "Compassion and Rebirth: Some Ethical Implications," in *A Companion to Buddhist Philosophy*, ed. Steven M. Emmanuel (West Sussex, UK: Wiley-Blackwell, 2013), 221–37. In this essay, Powers argues that the Mahāyāna conception of the bodhisattva's task is incoherent without rebirth.
20. The prominent figures and texts of this tradition, sometimes referred to as the "Golden Age" of Buddhist philosophy, have attracted a large amount of the attention of Western philosophers.
21. Matthew Kapstein, "'Spiritual Exercise' and Buddhist Epistemologists in India and Tibet," in *A Companion to Buddhist Philosophy*, ed. Steven M. Emmanuel (West Sussex, UK: Wiley-Blackwell, 2013), 271.
22. David J. Chalmers, *The Character of Consciousness* (New York: Oxford University Press, 2010), 5.

BIBLIOGRAPHY

Chalmers, David J. *The Character of Consciousness*. New York: Oxford University Press, 2010.

Chalmers, David J. "Why Isn't There More Progress in Philosophy?" *Philosophy* 90, no. 1 (2015): 3–31.

Emmanuel, Steven M., ed. *A Companion to Buddhist Philosophy*. West Sussex, UK: Wiley-Blackwell, 2013.

Garfield, Jay L. *Engaging Buddhism: Why It Matters to Philosophy*. New York: Oxford University Press, 2015.

McGinn, Colin. *Problems in Philosophy: The Limits of Inquiry*. Oxford: Wiley-Blackwell, 1993.

Papineau, David. "Is Philosophy Simply Harder Than Science?" *Times Literary Supplement*, June 1, 2017.

Schellenberg, J. L. "Philosophy's First Steps." *Aeon*, April 10, 2018.

Siderits, Mark. *Personal Identity and Buddhist Philosophy: Empty Persons*. New York: Routledge, 2003.

Soames, Scott. *Philosophical Analysis in the Twentieth Century*. Vol. 1. Princeton, NJ: Princeton University Press, 2005.

Stoljar, Daniel. *Philosophical Progress: In Defence of a Reasonable Optimism*. New York: Oxford University Press, 2017.

Tanaka, Koji, Yasuo Deguchi, Jay L. Garfield, and Graham Priest, eds. *The Moon Points Back*. New York: Oxford University Press, 2015.

Van Inwagen, Peter. "Freedom to Break the Laws." *Midwest Studies in Philosophy* 28 (2004): 334–50.

1

HOW SHOULD WE LIVE?

Happiness, Human Flourishing, and the Good Human Life

STEPHEN J. LAUMAKIS

The purpose of this chapter is to compare and contrast the dominant Western philosophical accounts of "happiness," "human flourishing," or more generally, "the good human life" with Buddhist accounts of the same in order to consider their common ground. This is useful to do not only as an exercise in comparative philosophy, but also for the wisdom one can gain by reexamining one's own understanding of the elements of a morally praiseworthy human life.

Before going any further, however, it is important to say something about the precise subject matter of the chapter, especially given the recent proliferation of books and articles—from across a spectrum of disciplines—dedicated to the nature, origin, and pursuit of "happiness."[1] What many of these works are concerned with when they talk about happiness is something like "subjective well-being," which includes both global intellectual assessments of one's life with respect to how things are going overall and local emotional reports about how happy, content, or satisfied one feels right now. While these are certainly important and interesting subjects to investigate—even scientifically—they are not directly concerned with one of the most enduring philosophical questions: how to live the good human life. In other words, they are not concerned with "the good human life," understood philosophically as living a morally appropriate human life. It is precisely this conception of "the good human life" that Western philosophers, including Socrates, Plato, Aristotle, Kant, and Mill (to name just a few), as well as Eastern thinkers, including Confucius, Laozi, the Buddha and his numerous followers, were interested in examining and explaining.

Other than the proverbial question "Why?" (as in, "Why am I here?" "Why is there something rather than nothing at all?" and "Why do things happen as they do?"), one of the most fundamental and perennial questions that all philosophies—whether Eastern or Western—try to answer is: "How should I live my life?" Other near-neighbor versions of this question include "What is the best kind of life for humans?" and "What kinds of actions are good and bad, or right and wrong?" In fact, among all of the various questions that philosophers have raised and tried to answer, perhaps the most important and interesting, or at least the most practical, is the cluster concerned with how we ought to live our lives, which includes "How can I be happy?" "How can I live a fulfilling life?" "How can I find my purpose?" and "How exactly can I achieve my ultimate end or goal?"

In fact, if we ignore the cosmological speculations of the pre-Socratic philosophers and their search for the fundamental nature of reality, one might reasonably maintain that the real roots of Western philosophy begin with Socrates and his attempt to live the examined life. The same can also be said with respect to Eastern thinkers such as Confucius, Laozi, and the Buddha because even the most cursory survey of their various teachings reveals that one of the most enduring subjects of investigation and speculation concerns questions related to what I am calling "the good human life." Moreover, it is not entirely inappropriate to suggest that both Eastern and Western philosophical traditions are fundamentally concerned with questions about how to live a good, meaningful, and "happy" human life. It's just that their philosophical conceptions of "happiness" are not really concerned with "happiness" in the sense of subjective well-being that is all the rage today.

Given these precisions with respect to its subject matter, the chapter begins with a rough sketch of the three main Western views[2] of "the good human life." After considering the virtue theory of Aristotle, the deontological theory of Kant, and the consequentialism of Mill, the discussion then turns to a consideration of the classical teachings of the Buddha as they are found in the Theravāda tradition, and then their subsequent development in the Mahāyāna tradition. It ends with a consideration of the common ground of these different conceptions of "the good human life."

THE HISTORICAL ROOTS OF WESTERN ACCOUNTS OF HAPPINESS, HUMAN FLOURISHING, AND THE GOOD HUMAN LIFE

One of the easiest ways to understand Western philosophy is to think of it as a series of transitions in an extended conversation about how we have tried to make sense of the world and our place in it. Using this conceptual framework, the first Western attempts to understand the world are typically associated with the religious predecessors to the pre-Socratic philosophers—Homer and Hesiod. They were among the first Western thinkers who tried to understand and explain the natural events of the world by appealing to supernatural causes. In other words, they tried to explain the everyday world of life, growth, nourishment, reproduction, and death by appealing to a supernatural realm filled with gods who were ultimately responsible for the outcomes of events in the natural world. According to this religious way of viewing the natural world, our relationships with the gods causally determine how things are going to go for us in this world. In short, if we have the right kinds of relationships with the gods, then things will go better than they would otherwise. The justification for this "religious" worldview is found in classical Greek mythology and the stories of the gods found in the works of Homer[3] and Hesiod.[4]

It was to this way of understanding the world and our place in it that the pre-Socratic philosophers responded. According to their alternative way of trying to make sense of the world, natural events are better and more correctly understood by appealing to natural rather than supernatural causes. For example, Thales (c.620 BCE), who is typically recognized as the first philosopher, tried to explain ordinary events by appealing to a natural cause—water. It does not take a great deal of imagination to see why it would be obvious for people living on islands and peninsulas in and around the Mediterranean to think that water was a better vehicle for understanding and explaining the world and its events than invisible gods. Not only does water come in three forms—solid (ice), liquid, and gas (fog/breath)—but it is clearly essential for most of the ordinary events of daily life. We need it to live, to grow, and as nourishment, and clearly, too much or too little of it can lead to death.

Other pre-Socratic philosophers[5] proposed alternative explanations of the fundamental nature of reality. These included Anaximander, Anaximenes, Heraclitus, Parmenides, Zeno, Anaxagoras, Pythagoras, Democritus, and Leucippus. The Greeks soon discovered, however, that there was little agreement among the pre-Socratic philosophers, so eventually a new group of thinkers, the Sophists, proposed that there were in fact no ultimate answers to the pre-Socratic questions, and instead they turned their philosophical attention toward questions about how to live a "successful" life.

According to the Sophists, who were traveling teachers of rhetoric who charged a fee for their pedagogical services, not only were there no answers to the pre-Socratics' search (i.e., they were skeptics), but they also advocated for a kind of relativism with respect to moral matters, precisely because, as they knew from firsthand experience, people in different places tend to believe different things about what a good and successful life involves. In fact, their focus was on teaching their students the rhetorical skills necessary to achieve what they took to be a "successful" life—a life of money, power, fame, influence, and material possessions—via politics.

In direct response to the Sophists and their skepticism and relativism, however, Socrates pursued a life of philosophy dedicated to making conceptual clarifications, drawing distinctions, and providing justifications for what one believes, thinks, and knows. Clearly this was a different conception of philosophy, or "love of wisdom," from what his predecessors pursued. In fact, it was his life and his ideas about the kind of life worth examining and living that had such a profound and moving effect not only on his most famous student, Plato, but also on the entire Western philosophical tradition. If it is true, as Whitehead maintained, that "the safest general characterization of the European philosophical tradition is that it consists of a series of footnotes to Plato,"[6] it is also just as true that the basic outline and features of Plato's thought, as well as that of his student, Aristotle, can be traced to ideas and lessons they learned from Socrates. Moreover, it is even safer to suggest that together, Socrates, Plato, and Aristotle introduced the world to the way of life and thinking that we still call "philosophy" today. And even though their answers to various philosophical questions differ from one another, it is nevertheless true that they share a common understanding of philosophy, or "love of wisdom," as the pursuit of the best kind of life, or better, the search for a life that is most worth living—"the good human life."

The historical roots of this conception and practice of philosophy can, as previously noted, be traced through this series of transitions in the ongoing conversation about how philosophers have tried to make sense of the world and our place in it. They may also be seen in the distinct but related ways that philosophers have of distinguishing the main divisions of philosophy into metaphysical, epistemological, and ethical considerations. For the purposes of this chapter, however, I will focus exclusively[7] on ethical considerations and how these concerns were subsequently investigated during the history of Western philosophy. In particular, I want to focus on what I have been referring to as the philosophical pursuit of "the good human life."

THREE DOMINANT WESTERN VIEWS OF THE "GOOD HUMAN LIFE"

For the sake of clarity, one of the simplest ways to think about the major Western theories of the good human life is to see them as focusing on one of the three elements of this diagram:

1. Human person → 2. Human actions → 3. Consequences

According to this representation, the goal of any moral philosophy, ethical theory, or ethics[8] is to explain how the various elements of the process of a human person engaging in human actions will lead that human person to achieve whatever goals they are pursuing, such as a good human life.

In the history of Western philosophy, there have been three dominant accounts of the process: (1) virtue theories; (2) deontological theories; and (3) consequentialist theories. Each theory tends to focus on just one element of the diagram.

According to the virtue theory, as explained and defended by Aristotle (384–322 BCE), the way to realize "the good human life" is to have a person realize their end as a rational agent by acquiring a set of intellectual and moral virtues that will enable them to make the transition from a potentially good person to an actually good person via the inculcation of a series of habits that will help them learn how to know and to do the right thing, at the right time, in the right way, and in the right circumstances, or more generally, help them become a morally praiseworthy human who realizes their appropriate end, or *telos*, as a rational agent by acting with prudence or moral excellence. In other words, the virtue theory of happiness, human flourishing, and the good human life (*eudaimonia* for Aristotle) claims that if we can somehow craft a person as a certain kind of human being— as the achievement of what they are supposed to be as the kind of thing that they are, one with all the requisite intellectual and moral virtues or character—we know that such a human person will do morally appropriate human actions in all circumstances, and hence produce the best kinds of consequences in a fully realized human life.

According to the deontological theory, on the other hand, as explained and defended by Immanuel Kant (1724–1804), the aim or goal of moral philosophy or ethical theory is to provide an account of the conditions for the possibility of free moral actions. In fact, it is no exaggeration to claim that Kant hoped to do for the field of moral philosophy what Newton had done in physics—increase our knowledge by specifying the laws of matter and motion—because, as he famously claimed in his *Critique of Practical Reason*, "Two things fill the mind with ever new and increasing admiration and awe, the more often and steadily we reflect upon them: the starry heavens above me and the moral law within me."[9]

Without going into the details of Kant's metaphysics and epistemology, it is clear that he thinks that the moral quality of an action does not depend on the habits or virtues of the agent who does it (as virtue theorists, like Aristotle, claim), or the utility and benefits, in terms of pleasure or "happiness," that follow the action (as consequentialists like Bentham and Mill will claim), but rather on whether the agent's will was freely acting out of duty and respect for the moral law. In other words, the moral qualities of human actions, and consequently human lives, depend upon a human person acting not from self-interest or passion, but out of respect for the moral law that is not only legislated by human reason generating categorical imperatives or rules of action that prescind from self-interest, but also are recognized as laws that demand the respect of all rational agents, regardless of their particular circumstances, including the passions, wants, and desires of the individual agent. More succinctly, for Kant, the good human life consists in following the Categorical Imperative, which in its simplest form asserts that one act only on that maxim or rule whereby one can at the same time will that it should become a universal law.

For Kant, "it is impossible to conceive anything at all in the world, or even out of it, which can be taken as good without limitation, except a good will."[10] What this means for him is that what makes human actions, and by extension human lives, morally praiseworthy is the fact that they are done precisely because they are the kinds of actions that rational agents ought to do by acting according to their duty as moral agents, who do what they do neither from inclination or self-interest, but from respect for the moral law that is generated by their own rational powers. To act from any motive other than the duty of respecting the moral law is, for Kant, to engage in morally wrong actions.

So, unlike Aristotle and the virtue theorists, Kant believes that the moral quality of "the good human life" is determined by whether one's actions have been done in accord with the principles of a good will—a will that acts on a duty out of respect for the moral law. For Kant, "the good human life" is about not the character and virtues of the human agent who lives it, but rather the actions that the rational human agent wills in conformity with the moral law. Consequentialists like Mill will offer a third and decidedly different account of "the good human life."

According to the consequentialist theory, as explained and defended by John Stuart Mill (1806–1873), the goal of ethics or moral philosophy is to explain why and how human actions are good insofar as they tend to produce the greatest amount of pleasure and happiness for the greatest number of people, and bad insofar as they tend to do the opposite. Mill, like Kant, thinks that the virtue theory account of morality anchored in the psychology of the character and habits of the human person is not only inaccurate, but also contrary to the common experience of people choosing courses of action based on a cost-benefit analysis of their potential pleasure and pain outcomes. However, at the same time, he also thinks that Kant's deontological theory, when put into practice in the real world, is actually consequentialist.[11] In fact, Mill maintains that every major moral and religious theory[12] of good human action is ultimately consequentialist in its thinking. He thinks that even God, whose teachings are revealed through Jesus, is a good utilitarian/consequentialist. As a result, for Mill, "the good human life" is not about the moral qualities of the person who lives it (*pace* Aristotle) or the actions that constitute it (*pace* Kant), but rather the qualities of pleasure and pain or happiness and unhappiness that result from what we do in life.

THE HISTORICAL ROOTS OF THE EARLY BUDDHIST ACCOUNT OF HAPPINESS, HUMAN FLOURISHING, AND THE GOOD HUMAN LIFE

To discuss the Buddhist accounts of "the good human life," it is necessary to distinguish the early Buddhist tradition from its later development as Mahāyāna Buddhism. For the sake of clarity, it is also necessary to treat each of these rather complex plural traditions in a simplified form. So, for the purposes of this discussion, we shall distinguish Theravāda Buddhism—the "Way of the Elders"—from Mahāyāna Buddhism—the "Greater Vehicle" of Buddhism—and we shall also treat them as monolithic representations of early and later Buddhism.

While a detailed account of the religious and philosophical context in and from which the thought and teachings of the Buddha emerged is beyond the scope of this chapter, I have argued elsewhere[13] that one of the easiest ways of understanding the basic elements of classical Indian thought—and the Buddha's reaction to it—is to think of them as a collection of intellectual insights in a series of transitions in what we might call the "Indian Way"[14] of seeing and understanding reality. Conceived of in this way, it is helpful to think of the ancient Indians as offering us at least three distinct conceptual frameworks or views of reality in the same way that the predecessors to the pre-Socratics, the pre-Socratics, the Sophists, and Socrates had their own views of the world and our place in it.

The first view, what we might call the "pre-Vedic" view of things, seems to have countenanced belief in many gods (as Homer and Hesiod did), nature worship, fertility rituals, concerns about purification, and some basic ideas about both an afterlife and the possibilities of reincarnation. According to some scholars, the last two points in particular appear to be anchored in simple observations about the cycle of birth–life–death in nature, the phases of the moon, the seasons of the year, and obvious family resemblances. Recent archeological evidence also supports the claim that followers of this view appear to have been vegetarians who engaged in ascetic practices and yogic meditation.

The second Indian view, the vision of the *Vedas*, builds upon this early view of things and seems to have formalized it with ritual sacrifices and celebrations, the production of sacred texts concerned with the wisdom of poet-seers and hearers to whom it was revealed (like the prophets in the Hebrew Scriptures), and liturgical formulas and chants about what had been seen and heard. This second view also contains the philosophical (or merely human) reflections and speculations of the *Upanishads* (like the pre-Socratics and Socrates).

The third and final view, what we might call the "post-Vedic" understanding of reality, is actually a more sustained, careful, and detailed working out of the individual elements of the pre-Vedic and Vedic views of things. This rather complex understanding of reality includes a clarification and specification of the roles of the gods (or a denial of their existence) and their relation to the ultimate, single source of all things (i.e., Brahman), a delineation of the details of the *varṇa*/color and caste systems, as well as an account of the stages of life (i.e., studying under a teacher or being a student; returning home to marry and raise a family as a householder; relinquishing daily affairs to one's son by retiring and beginning meditative practices; and finally, leaving home to live and die in the forest as an ascetic) and the various aims of life (i.e., dharma, virtue or moral righteousness; *artha*/wealth and success, *kāma*/pleasure and fulfilling material desires, and *mokṣa*/liberation or achieving salvation). It also contains more serious reflection on samsara, the cyclical nature of birth–life–death, and the notions of rebirth and the prospects of release or liberation from this cosmic cycle. At a more fine-grained level of consideration, this third view includes what scholars have identified as the nine *darśanas* ("schools" or "viewpoints") of classical Indian thought (i.e., Sāṃkhya, Yoga, Mīmāṃsā, Vedānta, Nyāya, Vaiśeṣika, Jain, Cārvāka, and Buddhist views).[15]

So, if for space constraints we skip the remote origins of the Buddha's thought in the basic elements of the pre-Vedic view, as well as the basic elements of the Vedic view, and instead focus on the elements of the post-Vedic view and its nine schools as supplying the immediate context of the Buddha's own philosophical concerns and thinking, we discover a rather complex view that included a clarification and specification of the roles of the various deities of the pre-Vedic and Vedic views (or their nonexistence) and their relations to the ultimate, single source of all things (i.e., Brahman of the *Upanishads*), a delineation of the details of the *varna*/color and social caste systems, and the enumeration of the stages of life, as well as the various possible aims of individual lives. It also contained more serious and sustained philosophical reflection, and in fact vigorous disagreement—in which the Buddha himself participated—over the possible outcomes of the cyclical nature of birth–life–death, as well as the notions of rebirth and the prospects of release or liberation from this cosmic cycle. Finally, it involved more sustained philosophical debate about the notions and relations of the "self" and society (i.e., metaphysical and epistemological thinking) and social regulation (i.e., ethical thinking) through the increasingly complex ideas of norms, duties, obligations, virtues, karma, and dharma.

The Buddha, as we know, had his own views of each of these matters. Yet it was within the context of these competing views and their ongoing debates and disagreements that he worked out his own unique philosophical views and eventually became the Awakened One. It is to the basic elements of his view, as captured in the Theravāda tradition, that we now turn our attention.

THE THERAVĀDA BUDDHIST ACCOUNT OF THE GOOD HUMAN LIFE

For the purposes of this chapter, I shall refer to the earliest version of the teachings of the Buddha as Theravāda Buddhism. This version of Buddhism centers on the "original" teachings of the Buddha as presented in the "Three Baskets," or *Tipiṭaka*. The Three Baskets contain the *Sutta Piṭaka*, or the basket of sayings or discourses of the Buddha gathered into five "collections," known as *Nikāyas*, and grouped according to length; the *Vinaya Piṭaka*, or the basket of monastic rules and discipline that cover the day-to-day activities of the monastic community; and the *Abhidhamma Piṭaka*, or the basket of higher teachings, which includes philosophical and psychological explanations, clarifications, and commentaries on the teachings of the Buddha contained in the *Suttas*. For simplicity's sake, I shall focus on the most basic teachings of the Buddha contained in the *Suttas*.[16]

It should not be surprising that the Buddha's ideas about "the good human life" were worked out within the context of the competing views of the nine *darśanas* of classical Indian thought and their ongoing debates and disagreements. It also should not be surprising that his views were formulated in response to the particular features and events of his own life. Without going into questions about what we actually know about his life or the received view of the details of that life, which would take us far beyond the subject matter of this chapter, let it suffice to say that the Buddha's teachings are recognized for both continuing the line of classical Indian thought and their originality. In broad strokes, he accepts the Indian notions of karma, samsara, rebirth, and *mokṣa*, but he also extends them and makes his own unique contributions to Indian thought.

Like most people of India, the Buddha accepted the idea of karma—that actions have consequences and effects—and believed that everyone undergoes a series of lives (i.e., samsara) whose current qualities are determined by the morality of past actions, including those in previous lives. In short, morally good actions tend to produce good consequences, or "happiness," and morally bad actions tend to produce bad effects, or "unhappiness." However, the Buddha extended the idea of karma by insisting that not only actions, but also thoughts and intentions have and produce consequences and effects. In fact, the Buddha claims that both appropriate and inappropriate tendencies or habits, and even one's ways of thinking about things, ultimately produce fruits or consequences—in this life as well as in subsequent lives.

The Buddha also accepted the idea that release or liberation from the suffering of samsara—*mokṣa*—was possible, but not by way of ritual practices; release comes only by means of a kind of wisdom that follows from both insight into the truth about reality and a life of compassionate actions based on that insight. According to the Buddha, the ultimate realization of this release from samsara, known as "nirvana," is achieved by extinguishing the fires of greed, hatred, and delusion, as well as by reorienting one's habits of thinking and acting.

All these teachings are true, according to the Theravāda tradition, because they were not only experienced by the Buddha himself but also taught by him to his earliest followers. These early followers in turn transmitted his teachings orally until they were finally committed to writing as the *Sutta Piṭaka* of the "Three Baskets." According to this tradition, Siddhārtha Gautama—the man who would eventually become the Buddha, or the Awakened One—was living the life of a wealthy prince, with all of the pleasures, powers, and material goods commonly desired by human beings. After marrying and producing a son, he had a kind of profound existential experience (commonly referred to as the "Four Sights") involving an old man, a sick person, a corpse, and an ascetic wanderer whose lives were extremely different from his own. The vision of these sights and their world-shattering effect on him led Siddhattha not only to question his original understanding of the world, but also to seek a solution to the suffering and dissatisfaction that are part of the human condition. So, after leaving his family, renouncing his former life, and consulting various religious and meditative authorities, he became a homeless wanderer himself. Finally, after six years of rigorous ascetic practices, he sat under the bodhi tree to reflect quietly on the human condition. After an extended period of reflection, he apparently came to a realization of the ultimate truths about the human condition and solved the problem of human suffering.

According to the Theravāda tradition, on the night of his enlightenment, the Buddha realized three kinds of knowledge: (1) knowledge of his own and others' past lives; (2) knowledge of the laws of karma and rebirth; and (3) knowledge of his own liberation through his understanding of the Four Noble Truths. Having realized these and other truths (i.e., the Middle Way, the Three Marks, and the Eightfold Path) as a result of his own meditative and intellectual experiences, the Buddha then decided to offer the fruits of his efforts to anyone who was interested. He did, however, also insist that his followers "not go by oral tradition, by lineage of teaching, by hearsay, by scripture . . . by the seeming competence of a speaker, or because you think 'The ascetic is our teacher.' But when you know for yourselves . . . then you should do or do not."[17] His teachings cover almost every problem associated with how one ought to live one's life, or what I have been calling "the good human life." He taught for forty-five years, founded an order of monks and later nuns, and eventually died. According to the Theravāda tradition, he also realized nirvana and hence was not reborn. It is to a more detailed account of his basic teachings that we now turn our attention.

According to his earliest followers, the Buddha's awakening consisted essentially of a new way of seeing the world and understanding how we are to live in it. This new way of re-visioning life and his understanding of it is captured in the three most basic teachings of the Buddha: the Middle Way; the Four Noble Truths, which include the Eightfold Path; and the teaching on the Three Marks.

First, the Buddha teaches the Middle Way between the extremes of the sensual pleasure of self-indulgence and the rigors of ascetic self-mortification. Having lived and experienced both the excesses and deficiencies of these extremes, he was painfully aware of their debilitating consequences. On the one hand, the excesses of his princely life were not satisfying for at least two reasons. While enjoying them, he was poignantly aware of their imminent passing; and while not enjoying them, he found himself longing for what he knew could not truly satisfy him because of their inherent transience. On the other hand, his experiments with ascetic practices left him physically emaciated and mentally unfulfilled. Moreover, these practices failed to produce their advertised and promised ends; in fact, they left him both mentally distracted and physically enfeebled. So his followers insisted that one of the most basic teachings of the

Awakened One was his insistence on the Middle Way between these two extremes.

A second basic teaching of the Buddha involves a new philosophical outlook or truth—a new way of seeing and understanding the world and its metaphysical structure. This way of knowing and being in the world is set forth in what is traditionally referred to as his First Sermon and is succinctly summarized in what is commonly referred to as the Four Noble Truths. According to the Buddha:

> Now this, bhikkhus,[18] is the noble truth of suffering: Birth is suffering; aging is suffering; illness is suffering; death is suffering; sorrow and lamentation, pain, grief and despair are suffering; union with what is displeasing is suffering; separation from what is pleasing is suffering; not to get what one wants is suffering; in brief, the five aggregates[19] subject to clinging are suffering.
>
> Now this, bhikkhus, is the noble truth of the origin of suffering: it is this craving which leads to renewed existence, accompanied by delight and lust, seeking delight here and there; that is, craving for sensual pleasures, craving for existence, craving for extermination.
>
> Now this, bhikkhus, is the noble truth of the cessation of suffering: it is the remainderless fading away and cessation of that same craving, the giving up and relinquishing of it, freedom from it, non-reliance on it.
>
> Now this, bhikkhus, is the noble truth of the way leading to the cessation of suffering: it is this Noble Eightfold Path that is, right view, right intention, right speech, right action, right livelihood, right effort, right mindfulness, right concentration.[20]

According to this passage, the path to liberation from the cycle of rebirth and karma begins with a reorientation in one's knowledge, understanding, and causal interaction with the world and the way things are in it. In short, it involves the realization that everything involves *dukkha* (i.e., suffering or dissatisfaction); *dukkha* has an origin or cause and condition; *dukkha* can be overcome or cured; and there is an Eightfold Path for reorienting one's practices and life.

According to the Buddha, the Eightfold Path itself is a practical method of thinking, living, and relating to the world that ultimately leads to the cessation of *dukkha*. Its basic elements are traditionally grouped into three categories: (1) wisdom/*paññā* (right view, right intention); (2) morality/*sīla* (right speech, right action, right livelihood); and (3) mental concentration or meditative cultivation/*samādhi* (right mindfulness, right concentration).

Third, two of the more famous versions of the teaching of the "Three Marks" are found in the *Aṅguttara Nikāya* and the *Dhammapada*. According to the latter, the Buddha claimed:

> "All conditioned things are impermanent"—when one sees this with wisdom, one turns away from suffering. This is the path to purification.
>
> "All conditioned things are unsatisfactory"—when one sees this with wisdom, one turns away from suffering. This is the path to purification.
>
> "All things are not-self"—when one sees this with wisdom, one turns away from suffering. This is the path to purification.[21]

In the former, the Buddha said:

> We are told that whether Tathagatas arise in the world or not, this fixed law remains: that all conditioned phenomena are impermanent; that all conditioned phenomena are suffering; and that all phenomena whatsoever are non-self.[22]

In addition to these claims, according to the *Mahāsudassana Sutta* of the *Dīgha Nikāya*, the Buddha tells his disciple Ananda that "conditioned states are impermanent, they are unstable, they can bring us no comfort, and such being the case, we should not rejoice in conditioned states, we should cease to take an interest in them, and be liberated from them."[23] In fact, shortly after informing Ananda that he will not be reborn, he adds, "Impermanent are compounded things, prone to rise and fall, having risen, they're destroyed, their passing truest bliss."[24]

These quotes clearly highlight the metaphysical relationship between "conditioned states" and "compounded things" (i.e., beings that arise interdependently or through the process of *paṭicca-samuppāda*) and impermanence. They also, however, go beyond the purely metaphysical nature of the relationship and offer practical moral advice about how one is to act in response to these kinds of beings. The Buddha clearly encourages and instructs Ananda in the appropriate attitude and courses of action toward conditioned, impermanent things. He is not to rejoice in them; he is not to be interested in them; and finally, he is to be liberated from them because that is precisely what the historical Buddha himself had done in realizing his version of "the good human life." And this same realization is available to any person who is willing to do the necessary work, as the Buddha had done, and achieve the *arahant*[25] ideal of Theravāda Buddhism—ideally as a monk.

THE MAHĀYĀNA ACCOUNT OF THE GOOD HUMAN LIFE

No single book,[26] let alone part of one chapter, could possibly do justice to the rich and complex Mahāyāna tradition of Buddhism.

As a result, I can only hope to indicate in rather broad strokes what the Mahāyāna account of "the good human life" looks like. Once again, it is important to keep in mind that for the sake of clarity, I am oversimplifying a rather complicated network of plural traditions that includes Tantra, Pure Land, Zen, and Nichiren Buddhism (among numerous others), practiced in locations throughout Asia and East Asia (as well as in the West), with a large number of authoritative texts from various teachers. As a result, I shall focus on a rather small set of common Mahāyāna teachings, including the Bodhisattva ideal, the Six Perfections, skillful means, *bodhicitta*, Buddha-nature, and emptiness. The first four ideas tend to focus principally on ethical themes, while the last two are more metaphysical in nature.

As we have seen, among the most basic teachings of the Buddha and Theravāda Buddhism is the claim that humans lack a fixed-essence or -self, such as an *ātman* or soul, and thus one of the marks of existence is that we are empty of an unchanging nature or fixed-self. In the Mahāyāna tradition, however, this concept of emptiness, or no-fixed-self, is extended from human beings to all things so that everything is said to be empty of fixed-self, or *śūnyatā*. At the same time, the Mahāyāna tradition claims that all beings possess a Buddha-nature or potential for enlightenment or realization of what all things ultimately are. While difficult to explain, the basic idea of Buddha-nature tries to express (and ultimately cannot express!) what the Buddha realized in his enlightenment—namely, that all beings have the potential for enlightenment and all things share this same fundamental nature.

As a consequence of these two metaphysical claims, the Mahāyāna tradition extends the basic ethical teachings of Theravāda Buddhism by proposing a new model of ethical excellence with its Bodhisattva ideal. Instead of each human focusing on their own liberation from suffering, as was the case with the *arahant* ideal of Theravāda Buddhism, the Mahāyāna tradition claims that the Bodhisattva, or "enlightenment being," whose actions are based on the activities of the Buddha prior to his ultimate enlightenment, forgoes his own final enlightenment or realization of nirvana until he has helped all other beings escape samsara. Such an ideal of ethical excellence, according to the Mahāyāna tradition, is not only superior to the *arahant*, who selfishly pursues his own individual enlightenment, but also describes a being of infinite wisdom and compassion who has made an extraordinary altruistic commitment.

The Mahāyāna focus on the undoubtedly long and difficult Bodhisattva path across numerous lifetimes includes not only the cultivation of both the thought of enlightenment known as *bodhicitta* and the Six Perfections, but also the practice of skillful and wholesome means, or *upāya*. *Bodhicitta* refers to the heartfelt aspiration to strive to realize one's Buddha-nature for its own sake and for the sake of helping all suffering beings, as a result of the wisdom and compassion for the suffering of all beings acquired through numerous lifetimes of thoughts and deeds. The Six Perfections, or *Pāramitās*, are the virtuous qualities cultivated and realized by the Bodhisattva in this life; they include generosity or giving, morality, patience or forbearance, zealous striving, focused mind, and wisdom or insight. Some forms of Mahāyāna Buddhism also have four additional moral perfections that are realized in the realm of heavenly beings when the Bodhisattva exercises skillful means in helping other beings, masters karma, perfects *upāya*, and achieves the perfect realization of Buddha-nature. In fact, each of these latter perfections can be usefully thought of as so many forms of skillful means in adapting and adopting the teachings of the Buddha to the particular context and situation of the beings involved.

Understood in this way, they represent a decidedly different ethical focus from the early Theravāda teachings. In that case, as we have seen, the focus was on specifying the Middle Way, the Four Noble Truths, and the Eightfold Path, as well as understanding the Three Marks as the means for helping individuals overcome *dukkha*, achieve liberation from samsara, and realize nirvana. Here, on the other hand, the focus is on cultivating wisdom and compassion, with a decidedly ethical focus on the practical means necessary to help all beings realize their Buddha-nature. It is, as Peter Harvey[27] claims, as if in the Mahāyāna tradition, the concept of ethics, or *śīla*, has become so broadened and highlighted as to be seen no longer as just one component of the Buddha's path (in addition to meditative cultivation, *samādhi*, and wisdom, *prajñā*), but to have encompassed the whole of it as the ultimate realization of "the good human life."

THE COMMON GROUND OF BUDDHIST AND WESTERN ACCOUNTS OF THE GOOD HUMAN LIFE

At the most abstract level of consideration and comparison, it is not obvious that there is a lot of common ground between Buddhist and Western philosophical accounts of happiness, human flourishing, and the good human life, for two obvious reasons: first, they are not addressing the same kinds of practical problems or questions; and second, they are not using the same kind of method to answer the questions or solve the problems.

While it is certainly true that Buddhists and Western philosophers alike are concerned with general questions about the nature of reality, how we know it, and how to live in the light of that knowledge, the historical circumstances in which the views of each were developed and formalized were entirely different. It is simply not the case, for example, that Aristotle and the Buddha were responding to the exact same kinds of practical problems and questions. And it is perfectly clear to anyone who reads the writings of Buddhists and Western philosophers that they are not using the same kind of philosophical method or modes of justification, even though they are trying to get at the heart of the same questions.

Western philosophers who work in the area of ethics or moral philosophy typically distinguish theoretical questions about the source and justification of moral claims and principles (metaethics) from practical questions about specific rules of morally appropriate conduct or standards of moral action (normative ethics). The former tends to focus on systematic ethical theorizing into the nature and meaning of moral terms and concepts, the justification of moral principles, and the ultimate foundations of moral philosophy, including matters of motivation as well. The latter tends to focus on rules of human conduct that help one know the difference between morally good and morally bad actions. In Western philosophy, questions about morality usually involve (1) theoretical metaethical considerations, (2) general normative advice, and (3) practical applications in particular circumstances and specific situations (i.e., where the tire of one's moral theory, so to speak, meets the road of practical everyday life).

Buddhist thinkers, on the other hand, especially those who focus primarily on ethics as opposed to metaphysics and epistemology, have tended to concentrate on normative and applied ethics, with less attention given to metaethics. Yet that should not be surprising, given the practical orientation of the Buddha's own teachings, especially when we think of these after the model of a doctor caring for a patient.[28]

As we have seen, the Buddha's enlightenment involved a realization of both the fundamental nature of reality and the human condition. In that sense, it involved a kind of metaphysical insight into the nature of the world and the human condition. Nevertheless, it is also important to keep in mind that the realization itself was the result of a serious and dedicated kind of practice, not unlike a patient who rigorously follows the advice of their doctor to achieve health goals. Understood in this way, the Buddha's teachings about the Four Noble Truths, and the Eightfold Path in particular, are usefully seen as a diagnosis, explanation, prescription, and action plan for overcoming a disease, which in this case is *dukkha*. In fact, the same tradition insists that the most basic teachings of the Buddha involve integrating, in a very practical way, the wisdom and insight of one who sees things as they really are, without ignorance or delusion and with the compassion of one who appreciates and responds to the needs of others as well as oneself. As a result, it is precisely accurate to insist that practical, moral concerns, rather than metaphysical and epistemological speculation, are at the heart of Buddhist theory and practice, and that every aspect of the Buddhist path is morally relevant.[29] In this respect, at least, the Buddhist approach to "the good human life" is fundamentally different from the Western philosophical tradition, especially as expressed and defended in the works of Aristotle, Kant, and Mill.

Nevertheless, despite these fundamental differences, there is some important common ground—both theoretical and practical—between Buddhist and Western philosophical approaches to our subject matter. We will consider the theoretical common ground first, and then the practical common ground.

First, both approaches specify particular goals or targets at which they are aiming. Second, both offer practical advice about how to go about achieving their goals, which includes things like virtues, character traits, or modes of thinking and acting that must be inculcated and practiced in order for practitioners to achieve their ultimate goals. Third, each offers some account of the ultimate outcomes or consequences—"the good human life"—that will be achieved by one who follows its advice and practices.

On the practical level, on the other hand, both offer specific directions about exactly what kind of mental and physical activities are called for if one wants to achieve one's goals and live the appropriate kind of good human life. For example, the Buddha tells us to cultivate wisdom or insight as well as moral and mental discipline. He also instructs us to cultivate compassion and to avoid killing, lying, stealing, inappropriate sexual conduct, and using alcohol. The Mahāyāna tradition encourages us to follow the path of the Bodhisattva by cultivating the perfections or virtuous qualities of generosity, moral discipline, patience, zealous striving, meditation, and wisdom or insight.

Aristotle tells us to cultivate both moral and intellectual virtues of character, including prudence, justice, temperance, courage, liberality, magnanimity, truthfulness, modesty, and friendliness. He also tells us to aim for the mean (virtue) between the extremes of excess (vice) and deficiency (vice), to imitate the morally virtuous, and to cultivate their friendship. And he quite prudently suggests that sometimes we need to go to extremes in order to help ourselves find the mean. Finally, he tells us to engage in philosophy or philosophical contemplation in order to exercise the highest and best power of our soul.

Kant tells us to put aside our passions, wants, and desires in any particular situation, and instead to focus on reason and its power to rationally recognize our duty with respect to the moral law, and to follow the Categorical Imperative.

And finally, Mill directs us to engage in a simple cost-benefit analysis of the pleasures and pains associated with different courses of action. On the one hand, he suggests that this strategy is good for any particular situation in which one finds oneself. On the other hand, he also recommends that we learn from the accumulated wealth of human experience, and relies on human law and common-sense advice to help us with the day-to-day activities that constitute an ordinary human life.

While it should be clear that the various kinds of practical advice are different for each thinker, I nevertheless think that it should also be clear that both traditions have something to learn from each other at both the theoretical and practical level when it comes to questions about what is involved in how one goes about living one's life in the pursuit of "happiness," "human flourishing," and "the good human life." Let me close this chapter with a brief reflection on what we can learn from a Buddhist approach to these pursuits.

THE REAL-WORLD AND PHILOSOPHICAL BENEFITS OF A BUDDHIST APPROACH

Aside from the similarities and differences between the main Western and Buddhist approaches to living the good human life, there is at least one fundamental philosophical insight that the Buddhist approach offers that has important real-world benefits—namely, the idea that any useful account of the good human life must respond, here and now, to the practical circumstances of the life that one is actually living. This point comes through clearly in the well-known "Parable of the Arrow," an early Buddhist story in which a man who has been wounded by a poisoned arrow will not allow the doctor to treat him until all his questions have been answered. There the Buddha explains that one must (1) recognize the urgency of the situation in which one finds oneself, and (2) respond in a suitably appropriate way to those unique circumstances. Here's what the story says:

> Suppose, Malunkyaputta, a man were wounded by an arrow thickly smeared with poison, and his friends and companions, his kinsmen and relatives, brought a surgeon to treat him. The man would say: "I will not let the surgeon pull out this arrow until I know whether the man who wounded me was a noble or a brahmin or a merchant or a worker." And he would say: "I will not let the surgeon pull out this arrow until I know the name and clan of the man who wounded me; . . . until I know whether the man who wounded me was tall or short or of middle height; . . . until I know whether the man who wounded me was dark or brown or golden-skinned; . . . until I know whether the man who wounded me lives in such a village or town or city; . . . until I know whether the bow that wounded me was a long bow or a crossbow; . . . until I know whether the bowstring that wounded me was fibre or reed or sinew or hemp or bark; . . . until I know whether the shaft that wounded me was wild or cultivated; . . . until I know with what kind of feathers the shaft that wounded me was fitted—whether those of a vulture or a heron or a hawk or a peacock or a stork; . . . until I know with what kind of sinew the shaft that wounded me was bound—whether that of an ox or a buffalo or a deer or a monkey; . . . until I know what kind of arrow it was that wounded me –whether it was hoof-tipped or curved or barbed or calf-toothed or oleander."
>
> All this would still not be known to that man and meanwhile he would die. So too, Malunkyaputta, if anyone should say thus: "I will not lead the holy life under the Blessed One until the Blessed One declares to me: 'the world is eternal' . . . or 'after death a Tathagata neither exists nor does not exist,' that would still remain undeclared by the Tathagata and meanwhile that person would die."[30]

Now whatever else one takes this story to be about, there can be little doubt that it signals the Buddha's reluctance to engage in metaphysical speculation—or abstract ethical theorizing—because he did not see this as useful, conducive to edification, or practically important in view of the urgency of the particular circumstances of a life characterized by *dukkha*.

While it is certainly true that ethical teachings lie at the heart of the Buddha's teachings, these are not put forward as dogmatic rules. Rather, the normative force of these teachings is grounded in a practice that involves the cultivation of wisdom, compassion, and mindfulness. This is a practice aimed at developing the qualities of mind that are conducive to ethical insight and promote true happiness and flourishing.

Consider, for instance, how the Buddha responds to the Kālāmas of Kesaputta when they ask him for help in sorting out the competing claims made by different religious teachers concerning the right way to live:

> Now, Kālāmas, don't go by reports, by legends, by traditions, by scripture, by logical conjecture, by inference, by analogies, by agreement through pondering views, by probability, or by the thought, "This contemplative is our teacher." When you know for yourselves that, "These qualities are skillful; these qualities are blameless; these qualities are praised by the observant; these qualities, when adopted & carried out, lead to welfare & to happiness"—then you should enter & remain in them.[31]

The message here is that the truth of an ethical teaching must ultimately be verified in our own personal experience. Later in the discourse, the Buddha explicitly exhorts the Kālāmas to cultivate within themselves the wisdom, as well as the concomitant feelings and dispositions (lovingkindness, compassion, empathetic joy, and equanimity), necessary for moral clarity—a mind free from greed, "undeluded, alert, and resolute," and "abundant, expansive, . . . free from hostility, free from ill will."[32] But as the Buddha also points out, the benefits that follow from cultivating these skillful qualities of mind do not depend on knowing whether there is "a world after death" or "the fruit of actions rightly & wrongly done," because the best possible outcome is already assured in either case.

Common to all the traditions of Buddhism is the idea that awakening is facilitated by a meditative practice aimed at cultivating insight into the metaphysical truth of nonself, together with the qualities of mind described previously. For the Mahāyānist, however, the fullest form of awakening involves the convergence of wisdom (*prajñā*) and compassion (*karuṇā*). As the eighth-century Indian Buddhist teacher Kamalaśīla explains in *The Stages of Meditation*, the realization of the radical emptiness (*śūnyatā*) of all things not only reveals the full reality of the suffering of the world, but also the realization of the deep interconnectedness of all who are entangled in the web of suffering. This profound insight that all sentient beings are one, both in their suffering and in their desire to be happy, gives rise to the "great compassion" (*mahākaruṇā*) of the bodhisattva, who vows to use the skillful means (*upāya-kauśalya*) necessary to liberate all beings from suffering.

The Buddhist idea that meditation provides the grounds for believing that we *ought* to live in a certain way not only contrasts sharply with the main Western ethical theories considered in this chapter, but also offers us a different way of understanding the relation between ethical thought and practice. Buddhism offers both a global vision of the meaning and purpose of life—a theory about the nature and causes of suffering and the path that leads to liberation—as well as a practice that helps one develop the insight and the motivation to respond appropriately to the suffering at hand. This mindful engagement with the real-world circumstances of our moral lives, with its eminently practical approach to addressing the problem of human suffering, supports a useful and compelling idea of philosophy as a way of life—not simply a life devoted to philosophical theorizing,[33] but a consciously reflective life of dedicated self-cultivation and inner transformation that shapes one's way of being in the world.[34] This is most clearly evident in the Mahāyāna understanding of ethics, in which the feelings and attitudes (lovingkindness, compassion, empathetic joy, and equanimity) cultivated through dedicated meditative practice are rooted in a deep insight into the nature of things, are constitutive of the bodhisattva's way of life.

The encounter with Buddhist thought thus offers both real-world and philosophical benefits to Western thinkers concerned with how we should live our lives. First, it offers practical advice that is suitably and flexibly fitted to the particular circumstances of one's *own* life. Second, it combines normative ethical teachings with a practice of mental and moral training that deepens our insight into the inner causes of suffering that prevent us from realizing true happiness or flourishing. This insight grounds our ethical understanding of how we should live and provides the proper motivation for moral action.

This unique philosophical approach to how we ought to live not only challenges our own Western conceptions of the answer to that question, but also offers us new ideas, insights, and methods that we may consider in reexamining our own understanding of the elements of a morally praiseworthy human life.

NOTES

1. These genres include philosophy, psychology, sociology, economics, history, theology, neuroscience, and business, to name just a few.
2. While there are obviously many ethical theories in the field of moral philosophy, space constraints demand that I limit my focus to the major

theories: virtue theory (Aristotle), deontology (Kant), and consequentialism (Bentham/Mill).
3. See, for example, his *Iliad* and *Odyssey*.
4. See, for example, his *Theogony* and *Works and Days*.
5. For a concise account of the pre-Socratics, see Catherine Osborn, *Presocratic Philosophy: A Very Short Introduction* (New York: Oxford University Press, 2004).
6. Alfred North Whitehead, *Process and Reality*, corrected edition, ed. David Ray Griffin and Donald W. Sherburne (New York: Free Press, 1978), 39.
7. It is important to keep in mind, however, that numerous philosophers would insist that ethical considerations always have implications for metaphysical and epistemological matters, and vice versa. In fact, another instructive way of thinking about the field of philosophy is to see it as an ongoing discussion about what kinds of questions—metaphysical (about what is), epistemological (about what can be known), and ethical (about how to live)—are more basic or fundamental.
8. It will be helpful to keep in mind that numerous Western philosophers distinguish moral philosophy, ethical theory, and ethics—as the rational systematic study of moral matters—found in university departments of philosophy, on the one hand, from more general ideas about how we ought to live our lives in the moral teachings of any particular person, school, or tradition on the other. This is not an unimportant or merely terminological matter to keep in mind because it marks an important and fundamental difference in approach between Western philosophy and Buddhism, and more generally, Eastern thinking, to questions about how we ought to live. Although the basic difference between Western and Eastern approaches to moral matters may appear to be merely methodological, the difference in method may actually have profound effects on what both "philosophies" hope to achieve.
9. Immanuel Kant, *Critique of Practical Reason* (New York: Hackett, 2002), 191.
10. Immanuel Kant, *Groundwork for the Metaphysics of Morals* (New York: HarperCollins, 2009), 61.
11. John Stuart Mill, *Utilitarianism* (New York: Hackett, 2002), 4.
12. Mill, *Utilitarianism*, 17, 21–22.
13. Stephen J. Laumakis, *An Introduction to Buddhist Philosophy* (New York: Cambridge University Press, 2008); Stephen J. Laumakis, "The

Philosophical Context of Gotama's Thought," in *A Companion to Buddhist Philosophy*, ed. Steven Emmanuel (West Sussex, UK: Wiley-Blackwell, 2013), 13–25.

14. This designation is inspired by John M. Koller, *The Indian Way: An Introduction to the Philosophies and Religions of India*, 2nd ed. (Upper Saddle River, NJ: Pearson Prentice Hall, 2006).

15. This follows J. N. Mohanty, *Classical Indian Philosophy* (Lanham, MD: Rowman & Littlefield, 2000), 153–58.

16. See, for example, Bhikkhu Bodhi, trans., *The Connected Discourses of the Buddha: A Translation of the Saṃyutta Nikāya* (Boston: Wisdom, 2000); Bhikkhu Bodhi, trans., *In the Buddha's Words: An Anthology of Discourses from the Pali Canon* (Boston: Wisdom, 2005); Maurice Walshe, trans., *The Long Discourses of the Buddha: A Translation of the Dīgha Nikāya* (Boston: Wisdom, 1995); Bhikkhu Nanamoli and Bhikkhu Bodhi, trans., *The Middle-Length Discourses of the Buddha: A Translation of the Majjhima Nikāya*, 2nd ed. (Boston: Wisdom, 2001); Nyanaponika Thera and Bhikkhu Bodhi, trans. and ed., *Numerical Discourses of the Buddha* (Walnut Creek, CA: Altamira, 1999).

17. *In the Buddha's Words*, trans. Bhikkhu Bodhi, 89–90.

18. Monks.

19. The Buddhist tradition has identified five aggregates or processes or bundles as constitutive of our true "selves": *Rupa*, material shape/form—the material or bodily form of being; *Vedana*, feeling/sensation—the basic sensory form of experience and being; *Sanna/Samjna*, cognition—the mental interpretation, ordering, and classification of experience and being; *Sankhara/Samskara*, dispositional attitudes—the character traits, habitual responses, and volitions of being; and *Vinnana/Vijnana*, consciousness—the ongoing process of awareness of being.

20. *Dhammacakkappavattana Sutta* (SN 56.11), trans. Bhikkhu Bodhi, Sutta Central, https://suttacentral.net/sn56.11/en/bodhi.

21. *Dhammapada* (vv. 277–279), trans. Acharya Buddharakkhita, Access to Insight, https://www.accesstoinsight.org/tipitaka/kn/dhp/dhp.20.budd.html.

22. *Numerical Discourses of the Buddha*, trans. Nyanaponika Thera and Bhikkhu Bodhi, p. 51.

23. *The Long Discourses of the Buddha*, trans. Maurice Walshe, 290.

24. *The Long Discourses of the Buddha*, trans. Maurice Walshe, 290.
25. *Arahant*, or "worthy one," designates an enlightened individual who has overcome the cognitive and spiritual impurities that cause rebirth and has attained nirvana as the result of following the teachings of the Buddha.
26. Paul Williams's book, *Mahāyāna Buddhism: The Doctrinal Foundations* (London: Routledge, 1989), is an accessible and useful introduction to the topic, though.
27. Peter Harvey, *An Introduction to Buddhist Ethics* (Cambridge: Cambridge University Press, 1990), 130.
28. A second, equally enlightening image is an athlete who, through discipline and hard work, is able to realize their sporting goals. In that case, the Buddha's teachings, like the instructions of a good coach, serve as practical advice or moral directives about what one ought to do if one hopes to achieve their ultimate athletic goals.
29. On this point, see William Edelglass, "Buddhist Ethics and Western Moral Philosophy," in *A Companion to Buddhist Philosophy*, ed. Steven M. Emmanuel (West Sussex, UK: Wiley-Blackwell, 2013), 476.
30. *Cūḷamāluṅkya Sutta* (MN 63), trans. Bhikkhu Bodhi, Sutta Central, https://suttacentral.net/mn63/en/bodhi.
31. *Kālāma Sutta* (AN 3.66), trans. Thanissaro Bhikkhu, Access to Insight, https://www.accesstoinsight.org/tipitaka/an/an03/an03.065.than.html.
32. In the Theravāda tradition, the classic manual of meditation is *The Path of Purification*, written by the fifth-century Buddhist commentator Buddhaghosa.
33. Such a view is put forward, for instance, by John Cooper in *Pursuits of Wisdom: Six Ways of Life in Ancient Philosophy from Socrates to Plotinus* (Princeton, NJ: Princeton University Press, 2013).
34. This idea is similar to that described by Pierre Hadot, *Philosophy as a Way of Life*, ed. Arnold I. Davidson, trans. Michael Chase (Oxford: Blackwell, 1995).

BIBLIOGRAPHY

Bodhi, Bhikkhu, trans. *The Connected Discourses of the Buddha: A Translation of the Saṃyutta Nikāya*. Boston: Wisdom, 2000.

Bodhi, Bhikkhu, trans. and ed. *In the Buddha's Words: An Anthology of Discourses from the Pali Canon*. Boston: Wisdom, 2005.

Cooper, John. *Pursuits of Wisdom: Six Ways of Life in Ancient Philosophy from Socrates to Plotinus*. Princeton, NJ: Princeton University Press, 2013.

Edelglass, William. "Buddhist Ethics and Western Moral Philosophy." In *A Companion to Buddhist Philosophy*, ed. Steven M. Emmanuel, 476–90. West Sussex, UK: Wiley-Blackwell, 2013.

Emmanuel, Steven, ed. *A Companion to Buddhist Philosophy*. West Sussex, UK: Wiley-Blackwell, 2013.

Hadot, Pierre. *Philosophy as a Way of Life*. Ed. Arnold I. Davidson. Trans. Michael Chase. Oxford: Blackwell, 1995.

Harvey, Peter. *An Introduction to Buddhist Ethics*. Cambridge: Cambridge University Press, 1990.

Kant, Immanuel. *Critique of Practical Reason*. New York: Hackett, 2002.

Kant, Immanuel. *Groundwork for the Metaphysics of Morals*. New York: HarperCollins, 2009.

Koller, John M. *The Indian Way: An Introduction to the Philosophies and Religions of India*. 2nd ed. Upper Saddle River, NJ: Pearson Prentice Hall, 2006.

Laumakis, Stephen J. *An Introduction to Buddhist Philosophy*. New York: Cambridge University Press, 2008.

Laumakis, Stephen J. "The Philosophical Context of Gotama's Thought." In *A Companion to Buddhist Philosophy*, ed. Steven M. Emmanuel, 13–25. West Sussex, UK: Wiley-Blackwell, 2013.

Mill, John Stuart. *Utilitarianism*. New York: Hackett, 2002.

Mohanty, J. N. *Classical Indian Philosophy*. Lanham, MD: Rowman & Littlefield, 2000.

Nanamoli, Bhikkhu, and Bhikkhu Bodhi, trans. *The Middle Length Discourses of the Buddha: A Translation of the Majjhima Nikāya*. 2nd ed. Boston: Wisdom, 2001.

Osborn, Catherine. *Presocratic Philosophy: A Very Short Introduction*. New York: Oxford University Press, 2004.

Thanissaro, Bhikkhu, trans. *Dhammapada: A Translation*. Barre, MA: Dhamma Dana, 1998.

Thera, Nyanaponika, and Bhikkhu Bodhi, trans. and eds. *Numerical Discourses of the Buddha*. Walnut Creek, CA: Altamira, 1999.

Walshe, Maurice, trans. *The Long Discourses of the Buddha: A Translation of the Dīgha Nikāya*. Boston: Wisdom, 1995.

Whitehead, Alfred North. *Process and Reality*. Corrected ed. Ed. David Ray Griffin and Donald W. Sherburne. New York: Free Press, 1978.

Williams, Paul. *Mahāyāna Buddhism: The Doctrinal Foundations*. London: Routledge, 1989.

2

WHAT IS KNOWLEDGE?

Knowledge in the Context of Buddhist Thought

DOUGLAS DUCKWORTH

This chapter raises some questions concerning the topic of knowledge, and in particular a deceptively simple one: what is knowledge? These questions will be raised in the context of some ways that Buddhists have framed the notion. Knowledge is a slippery subject, and I will not so much offer any new answers to the big questions of knowledge as bring to light some issues for consideration when outlining its status in a cross-cultural context. In doing so, I take a cue from Bertrand Russell, who stated, "No definition can be satisfactory which introduces the word 'knowledge', both because this word is highly ambiguous, and because every one of its possible meanings can only be made clear after much epistemological discussion."[1] In this discussion, I hope to bring some clarity to the question of knowledge by exploring it through the lens of Buddhism in a cross-cultural light.

Three main issues concerning knowledge will be discussed here in separate sections: (1) conceptual versus perceptual knowledge; (2) knowledge of things versus self-knowledge, which also relates to a difference between knowledge *about something* versus knowledge *by acquaintance;* and (3) propositional knowledge, as opposed to knowledge of a skill—that is, knowledge *that* versus knowledge *how*. Although the topics of these sections are interrelated, approaching them separately can help elucidate the nature of knowledge. To begin to address these issues, we will first discuss the notion of knowledge in Buddhism.

BUDDHISM AND EPISTEMOLOGY

An important characteristic of knowledge in classical Indian thought is that knowledge, like awareness, is temporally structured; it is episodic. A Sanskrit root that can mean "knowledge" is *jñā*, which is cognate with the English term "know" (and the Greek *gnosis*). Deriving from *jñā*, *prajñā*—meaning "higher knowledge," "discernment," or "insight"—has a broad semantic range. In a Buddhist context, this important notion is divided into three types based on the source from which it derives: knowledge through studying, knowledge through contemplation, and knowledge through meditation.[2] Each of these types reflects a different level of knowledge. For instance, simply hearing about a topic like impermanence and death is one kind of knowledge, whereas contemplating it results in another, and integrating this understanding through meditating on it brings forth an even further assimilation of its meaning.

An important topic in Mahāyāna Buddhism (and around which a distinct genre of literature is framed) is the "perfection of knowledge" (*prajñā-pāramitā*). The perfection of knowledge (or insight) in Mahāyāna Buddhism is liberating knowledge, and it guides other Buddhist practices, such as generosity, discipline, and patience. This knowledge is integral to the path of awakening; it is likened to vision, and the other practices to method. With only knowledge and no method, one is said to be like a sighted person without legs, and with only method without knowledge, one is like a blind person with legs. It is through the cooperation of the two wings of knowledge (vision) and method (legs) that the path to awakening is traveled upon.

The perfection of knowledge is insight into the ultimate truth—"no-self" and the emptiness of things. For Buddhist traditions, knowledge of the ultimate truth is the most important type of knowledge because it enables liberation from false concepts—like the concept of a singular, unitary self—that distort the experience of the world and thereby bring suffering. In Buddhist contemplative traditions, knowledge of the ultimate can also work as a purgative, whereby the view of emptiness (along with all other views) is expelled along with the ignorance that it subverts.

Further, the ultimate truth of emptiness is at times described as a positive truth to be known, and at times as an absence that is known only *via negativa*—that is to say, by knowing what is not. The difference between contentless and contentful knowledge of emptiness can be likened to the ways of knowing silence: as knowing the *presence* of silence as opposed to the *absence* of sound. In the former sense, knowledge of emptiness is knowledge of an ineffable reality. In the latter, the "content" of knowledge is simply an absence. In both cases, ultimate knowledge is not directly describable; yet paradoxically, it is through this knowledge that liberation is presumed a possibility for Buddhists.

Skepticism about the possibility of knowledge lingers close to Buddhist claims of emptiness. Nāgārjuna, an influential second-century Buddhist philosopher, famously argued in his *Dispelling Disputes* that the means of knowledge depend upon the objects of that knowledge, while the validity of those objects are in turn confirmed by the validity of the means:

> If for you the establishment of warranted objects is by means of a reliable source of knowledge and the establishment of a reliable source of knowledge is by means of warranted objects, neither is established for you.[3]

Nāgārjuna points out here that the status of knowledge (as valid or not) is determined by the status of the object known, and vice versa. For instance, the validity of a perception of smoke is confirmed by clear eyesight, and yet clear eyesight in turn is confirmed by smoke being seen; they are mutually confirming. The statuses of both the knower and the known mutually rise and fall. Other than an appeal to consensus (or to another source of knowledge, and to yet another to validate that), there is no way out of the circularity without affirming a foundational knowledge, a God's-eye view (outside the relational structure), and/or a self-validating cognition (which is independent and foundational).

In the twentieth century, an iconoclastic Tibetan philosopher, Gendün Chöpel, elaborated on the implications of Nāgārjuna's view in terms of the relationship between inference and perception:

> The object of inferential cognition comes from a mind of perception, and
> Perception is discerned by inference as veridical or defective.
> This makes the son the father's witness . . .
> I am uncomfortable with asserting conventional reality as validly established.[4]

Gendün Chöpel here reiterates the circularity of the warrants of knowledge and the contents of knowledge. He does so in terms of a dichotomy of knowledge, inferential and perceptual, made famous by the sixth-century Indian scholar Dignāga, who was a primary architect of an influential system of Buddhist epistemology (*pramāṇa*), or means of knowledge. Epistemology has an important role to play in the way that knowledge (*pramā*) has been framed within philosophical traditions across India.

The spectrum of views in Buddhist epistemology span on the one hand from a species of coherentism, in which things are held to hang together in a radically relational way (without foundations), and on the other a kind of foundationalism that appeals to a special kind of perception (in meditative experience and yogic perception in particular), which serves as the final arbitrator of truth and thus a ground for knowledge. Thus, in Buddhist philosophy, the knowledge of reality, the truth of "how things are," can be seen to oscillate between a denial of any final nature of reality—where there is no "how things are anyway"—to an experiential ground of reality that enfolds the domains of epistemology and ontology (or rather reveals that an ontological-epistemological divide is a false construction) and culminates in a unified experience of the truth (e.g., the Buddha's awakening) as to how things are.[5] I will map this spectrum of views here by considering questions about knowledge in the light of Buddhist epistemology in three sections, beginning with a purportedly clear-cut distinction between conceptual knowledge and perceptual knowledge.

CONCEPTUAL KNOWLEDGE AND PERCEPTUAL KNOWLEDGE

In formulating a Buddhist theory of knowledge, Dignāga described a dichotomy of conception and perception: inference conceives unreal universals, and perception perceives real particulars. Particulars are the objects of perception rather than linguistic entities or objects of thought that are the domain of inference. In contrast to the particulars that constitute perceptual content, inferences apprehend universals because when we use concepts and language, we necessarily think and speak in terms of general, universal properties.

A "universal" is a concept of a distributed entity, like "fire," "cup," or "self"; it is a class of things that is held to be the same (distributed) across space (e.g., one table) and time (e.g., yesterday's table is today's table). In this tradition, all such notions of enduring singular things are conceptual, and hence distortions of reality. Because Buddhists like Dignāga claim that all conditioned things are impermanent, they do not impute a reality to static entities above and beyond their status as conceptual constructions. For instance, we use the word "fire" to convey the meaning of a common property of something that is hot and burns. But such a universal property, distributed across all particular instances of what we call "fire," does not exist out in the world. We use the word "fire" to refer to something that is extended in time and space (yesterday's "fire," a forest "fire," and a kitchen "fire" are all "fire"), but no such singular object really exists outside our imputation. A concept, or universal, exists only in our thoughts and language, not in the real world. That is, we don't get burned by the singular "fire" that we impute with our thoughts and words; we get burned by particular instances of fire that are hot and burn.

We can see in this Buddhist epistemology a dichotomy of unmistaken, nonconceptual perception and mistaken, conceptual thought. Yet the reality of unique particulars, being nonconceptual, cannot be expressed, and this creates a problem: if we cannot talk about them, how can we know them? Yet isn't there more to knowledge than expressibility? And if so, how can we really *know* it? While nonconceptual cognition has a privileged place in Dignāga's epistemology, its status is dubious because an implication of being nonconceptual is a lack of communicability and determinacy.

Two ways of addressing the problem of reconciling conception and perception reflect two broad tendencies in philosophical thought: rationalism and empiricism. A rationalist seeks logical coherence and sees the logical processes of reason and rationality as arbitrators of true knowledge. For the rationalist, to count as knowledge is to be communicable and rationally justified. An empiricist, in contrast, believes that experience is primary and that what is known through the senses is the baseline for knowledge, rather than logical coherence. That is, empiricists hold knowledge to be accountable to experience, regardless of whether we can fit experiences neatly into our logical categories. The debate between rationalism and empiricism (in their various guises) has continued to animate a philosophical conversation in ancient and modern philosophies across the globe.

Wilfred Sellars, a twentieth-century American philosopher, showed his rationalist legacy (inflected by Kant) when he denied that experience has any cash value until it is conceptualized; or, in his words, that an experience does not count as knowledge until it is brought into the logical space of reasons:

> The essential point is that in characterizing an episode or a state as that of *knowing*, we are not giving an empirical description of that episode or state; we are placing it in the logical space of reasons, of justifying and being able to justify what one says.[6]

Thus, for Sellars, an experience alone cannot count as knowledge; it only becomes knowledge when we can rationally justify it.[7]

In contrast, an empiricist gives pride of place to perception and distinguishes experiential knowledge from the abstract intellectualism of the rationalist. While Buddhist epistemology shares an affinity with an empiricist stance, empiricism as developed in Europe and North America has primarily appealed to sensory perceptions. In Buddhist epistemology, however, sources of knowledge go beyond the five senses to include mental perception, as well as a distinctively meditative knowledge that results from contemplative training.

Dharmakīrti, one of Dignāga's commentators, outlined four means of valid perception. Sense perception—from the eyes, ears, nose, tongue, and rest of the body—is just one of these means of empirical knowledge. He additionally designated mental perception, self-awareness, and yogic perception as types of perception. These last three types have an important place to play in a Buddhist theory of knowledge, so we will discuss each in turn next.

To begin to consider the role of these other types of perception, we can ask the following questions about sensory knowledge: Is seeing believing? That is, the eyes register blue, but does that constitute *knowing* blue? If so, then when the lens of a camera registers blue, does that constitute knowledge of blue too? This leads to further questions—namely: What is perceived when we perceive "blue"? How can conception relate to perception? If it is true that conceptual knowledge knows only universals (concepts), and that sense perceptions interact only with inexpressible particulars, then what joins these two?

One attempt to address the problem of joining percepts to concepts, familiar to twentieth-century sense-data theorists, is to assert a temporal gap between perception and conception, such that a second instance of conceptual knowledge forms a judgment following the first moment of a bare (nonconceptual) perceptual encounter with the *raw feels* or ineffable sense data. In fact, Buddhists have described "mental perception" as what serves to join the perceptual to the conceptual in this way. It acts as a kind of filter for the stimuli that surround us.

The distinction between knowledge from the five sense perceptions and from mental perception (known as the "sixth sense") can be expressed as the difference between, for instance, knowing blue versus knowing that "it is blue."[8] This difference between *seeing* and *seeing as*, as in knowing blue and knowing that "it is blue," is linked to the role of mental perception, which has been posited as that which interprets the raw data of particulars and converts it into a conceptual knowledge or judgment. Commenting on Dharmakīrti, Prajñākaragupta characterized mental perception as "a cognition that apprehends its object as 'this.'"[9] The category of mental perception is thus one that Buddhists have drawn upon to reconcile conception and perception.

Another attempt to relate perception and conception is found in the role of self-awareness, another category of perception. In thirteenth-century Tibet, Sapaṇ attributed to self-awareness the role of bridging the gap between content-free perception and conceptual cognition, with the analogy of an interlocutor introducing a blind speaker (conception) to a mute seer (perception).[10] Self-awareness, as a type of immediate perception, serves as a bridge between conceptually mediated knowledge and nonconceptual (immediate) cognition. In every instant of cognition, there is an immediate self-acquaintance (self-awareness); thus, even an instance of mistaken conceptual knowledge has an aspect that is nonconceptual and indubitable.

Before we discuss yogic perception, the last of Dharmakīrti's four types of perception, we will explore some implications of the notion of self-awareness to further consider the boundaries of knowledge. While considering self-awareness, we will extend our discussion of nonconceptual versus conceptual knowledge into another distinction relevant to the question of knowledge—*knowledge that* versus *knowledge by acquaintance*. We will see how the notion of self-awareness as knowledge by acquaintance challenges a narrowly construed definition of knowledge as solely what is conceptually or linguistically circumscribed.

KNOWLEDGE BY ACQUAINTANCE AND SELF-AWARENESS

Despite denying the existence of a self, some Buddhists hold that self-awareness is an intrinsic property of awareness, as primary and foundational, and claim that it serves as a ground for undeniable knowledge, or "acquaintance." Dan Zahavi, a contemporary phenomenologist, has also characterized self-awareness as the "acquaintance [that] consciousness has with *itself* and *not* as an awareness of an experiencing *self*."[11]

To understand this distinction, it can be helpful to consider the following questions: Are you aware of seeing blue when you see it? Or is a higher-order perception or thought necessary for you to know that you know? When considering self-knowledge or self-awareness, we can distinguish between (1) knowledge of objects, or object-directed knowledge; and (2) knowledge of awareness, or the sense of subjectivity. Unlike the former, which is a representational or propositional knowledge, knowledge of awareness (a.k.a. subjectivity) must be known from within.

The following two ways of relating to the mind help clarify these two distinctive ways of knowing: relating to the mind as an object and as a subject. Treated as an object, the mind is known just like everything else; the mind as an object does not have a privileged status among entities. In contrast, knowing the mind as a subject (i.e., by acquaintance) ascribes a unique status to it.

The distinction between *knowledge of objects* versus *knowledge of/as subjects* made by phenomenologists reflects in significant ways another distinction, between *knowledge about* something and knowledge *by acquaintance*, which was popularized by the philosophers Bertrand Russell and William James.[12] William James pointed out the phenomenological difference between "the immediate *feltness* of a feeling, and its perception by a subsequent reflective act."[13] Conscious experience that is known by acquaintance (or identity)[14] is not an internal space as opposed to external objects, but is a nonthetic presence (i.e., not representable by proposition). Moreover, this experience is arguably the condition for the possibility of subjects and objects and thus is not something that can be fully represented by description.

Phenomenologists have argued that subjectivity—as an experiential, lived reality—is irreducibly constitutive of the world and defies representation. As a nonobject or nonthing, it constitutes the phenomenal character or qualitative perspective that is distinct to subjects of experience. Thus, knowledge of subjectivity is unique, and not unique among things because it is not taken as a thing. Subjectivity is not a *thing* because it is precisely the opposite of an objectified thing, and arguably, it cannot be reduced to a thing because it is integral to the structure by which things are known. This kind of appeal is taken up by some Buddhist contemplative traditions in order to grant a privileged status to knowledge derived from special kinds of meditative experience.

Yet some Buddhist arguments target this kind of entity, a conscious principle that takes on a unique (independent) status, as well as any notion of an independent reality. For instance, Tsongkhapa (1357–1419), an influential Tibetan philosopher, rejected the idea of self-awareness as a metaphysical posit and another false conception of self.[15] Others, like Sellars, have argued that this kind of knowledge does not constitute knowledge at all; it does not qualify as knowledge because it is not *about* anything, for it cannot be expressed. Yet the constriction of the import of knowledge to explicability has been challenged recently by the analytic philosopher Galen Strawson, who stated that self-awareness—by acquaintance—is a condition for the possibility of knowledge:

> There's a narrow, philosophically popular, independent-justification-stressing conception of knowledge that makes it hard for

some to see this [self-knowledge by acquaintance] is really knowledge, but the claim doesn't really need defence. Rather the reverse: this particular case of knowledge, self-knowledge in non-thetic self-awareness, shows the inadequacy of the narrow conception of knowledge. This general point is backed up, most formidably, by the fact that knowledge of this kind must lie behind all knowledge of the narrower justification-involving sort, as a condition of its possibility. This is because it's a necessary truth that all justification of knowledge claims is relative to something already taken as given.[16]

Contending that nonthetic (nonpropositional) self-awareness is a condition for the possibility of knowledge, Strawson claims that knowledge is not limited to justification. He argues that there is a domain of knowledge that is more primary and fundamental than a narrowly construed and propositional "space of reasons."[17]

It is notoriously difficult to define knowledge, and a popular definition of knowledge as "justified true belief" is challenged by the notion of knowledge by acquaintance in the case of self-awareness. Edmund Gettier famously raised another challenge to the conception of knowledge as "justified true belief," with examples where this definition seems to fail.[18] For instance, consider the following case: Jenny is in the desert and sees a mirage by a sand dune. She goes toward the dune and finds water there (there was water in the vicinity of the dune, but she did not see it until she was there; she had only seen a mirage before she reached the water).[19] Does seeing a mirage justify Jenny's (true) belief that there was water in this spot? According to a definition of knowledge as simply justified true belief, it would (she based the quenching of her thirst on the sight of a mirage).

Cases like these raise questions about the role of justification in knowledge, and they also lead us to the arena of pragmatic truth, another important aspect to consider when thinking about knowledge. In the next section, we will see how pragmatic truth and knowledge of skill both push the boundaries of what constitutes knowledge beyond the confines of a propositional definition.

KNOWING-HOW AND YOGIC PERCEPTION

Gilbert Ryle famously made a distinction between *knowing that* and *knowing how*. He described "knowing how" as follows:

> When a person knows how to do things of a certain sort (e.g., make good jokes, conduct battles or behave at funerals), his knowledge is actualised or exercised in what he does. It is not exercised (save *per accidens*) in the propounding of propositions.[20]

Knowing how to do something, such as knowing how to play the piano, is not simply theoretical. Unlike knowing a fact or a proposition, knowing how is a matter of embodying a skill.

Knowledge as skill relates to the fourth means of perception for Dharmakīrti, yogic perception (*yogipratyakṣa*), in addition to knowledge through sense perception, mental perception, and self-awareness. Yogic perception is an instrument of *transformative* knowledge aimed at liberation. Dharmakīrti depicted yogic perception as the internalization of good inference,[21] as a way to cultivate knowledge, such an insight into impermanence, to heightened clarity. This kind of perception is developed through habit and practice, similar to the way that deeper levels of knowledge are cultivated through the consistent practices of study, contemplation, and meditation. Yogic perception is a distinctly meditative means of knowledge that is held to be inaccessible to untrained, ordinary perception.

By considering knowledge as a developed skill as well as knowledge by inherent acquaintance, we can see how the four noble truths in Buddhism are known in different ways. For instance, for the first truth, that of suffering, one has to suffer—to feel—in order to know it. This involves subjective knowledge by acquaintance. The second noble truth, the origin of suffering, concerns what is to be eliminated. To eliminate the causes of suffering, not only must one *know what* the causes of suffering are (i.e., ignorance, attachment, hatred), but one must *know how* to counteract these afflictions. The third noble truth, the cessation of suffering (nirvana), is to be actualized. For a Buddhist, nirvana is not just theory; it is a lived truth. Thus, the actualization of nirvana, like the first truth of suffering, is knowledge by acquaintance (or identity)—one has to experience it to know it. The fourth truth, the path to nirvana, involves know-how, knowledge of a skill. Like the second truth, about the cause of suffering, the fourth truth involves *knowing that* and *knowing how*. That is, not only must one *know that* nirvana is brought about by following the right path, but one must *know how* to follow that path. Thus we can see many forms of knowledge at play in these fundamental Buddhist truths.

The concept of truth is integrally linked with that of knowledge. For a Buddhist, the four noble truths (suffering, the cause of suffering, the cessation of suffering, and the path to that cessation) are truths because they are seen to lead to liberation, not because they correspond to a mind-independent reality. The Buddha likened his teachings to a raft. Once you have reached the other shore, you do not need to carry the raft with you. The metaphor of the raft shows how the truth of the Buddha's teaching is not absolute (context independent). Like a raft that serves its purpose (getting you across a body of water), the truth of Buddhist truths is found in its efficacy. That is, once you have reached the dry land on the other shore (of nirvana), there is no need to carry the raft of dogma on your head. In this light, Buddhist truths are pragmatic; they make sense as truths in their efficacy.

A classic example of the roles of pragmatic truth and skill is found in the parable of the burning house in the *Lotus Sūtra*. A father looks upon his burning house (a metaphor of life in suffering) that is about to be consumed by flames. His teenage boys are in the house, but he does not have enough time to go in the house and rescue them, as the house is about to collapse. So he devises a scheme to get them out, to get them to leave the games in which they are absorbed upstairs in their rooms (a task that is not so easily accomplished by a simple command, especially with teenagers!). He does this by calling out to them, telling each of his sons that he has a gift of a cart for him, with each cart pulled by the respective son's favorite animal: a goat cart for one son, a deer cart for another, and an ox cart for the third. When the boys come running outside to get their carts, they are saved, and he gives them *all* ox carts.[22]

This parable is a metaphor for Buddhist teachings. The father succeeds in getting all his sons to come out of the house—he saves their lives—by promising to give them what they want. Yet when they are outside, he gives them all ox carts—not what they all *thought* they wanted, but what they *really* wanted (because goats and deer won't pull carts, he gave them ox carts, the cart that works best). Although this story has a particular context of meaning for Mahāyāna Buddhism (e.g., many paths and one goal), for our purposes, this story illustrates skillful means (the knowledge of skill) and pragmatic truths (truths are contextual and depend upon their effects). The father has knowledge—or skill—of an effective way to save his sons and care for them. The truth of this knowledge, its content, is not found in its correspondence to a fact or proposition, but rather in its ability to produce effects.

We can see how Buddhists place a primary value upon the soteriological effects brought about by knowledge. Knowledge of mind-independent truths, in contrast, are irrelevant to the way we experience the world, so only truths that affect our experience of the world count as knowledge. In particular, pragmatic truths that bring an end to suffering—as we see in the doctrine of skillful means, where a skilled teacher like the Buddha leads the way out of suffering by pointing the way to its end—are the content of transformative knowledge. Thus, the skill of knowing how to eliminate suffering, along with the ability to teach others how to do so, are an integral part of the pragmatic logic that underpins a distinctively Buddhist theory of knowledge.

CONCLUSION

Considering questions of epistemology brings to light a number of challenges for any simple definition of knowledge. Knowledge of the ultimate truth of emptiness in Buddhism raises one kind of challenge: it is not limited to propositional knowledge because knowledge of emptiness is without content. A further challenge is raised by the status of content-free knowledge: if it cannot be conceived or expressed, then how can it be knowledge? This is not a problem simply in the case of emptiness, but in the case of nonconceptual perception in Dharmakīrti's theory of knowledge. Furthermore, if perception is nonconceptual, how can perception and conception communicate?

Self-awareness—as knowledge by acquaintance—marks a difference between the subjective knowledge of an experience and the content of that experience. It has been offered as a foundation for knowledge, as well as a means to bridge conceptual and nonconceptual knowledge. Another kind of knowledge and means to account for the connection between the conceptual and nonconceptual is found in yogic perception, the assimilation of knowledge through the development of a skill. This kind of knowledge that is a skill—knowing *how*, as opposed to knowing *that*—is another type of knowledge that does not fit neatly into a simple model of propositional knowledge, such as justified true belief.

As knowledge is tied to truth, pragmatic truth expands the domain of what constitutes knowledge as well. A pragmatic criterion of truth extends what constitutes knowledge beyond the domain of mental representations of objective facts. As with the notion of "truth," knowledge is not always simple. Also like truth, knowledge is not always what it seems.

Considering philosophical questions in a cross-cultural way can be an effective means of casting light on some of the presuppositions tacitly embedded in an inquiry that may otherwise go unnoticed. The dialogical process of a cross-cultural conversation also can reveal different metaphysical pictures of the world that accompany specific kinds of epistemologies. Taking stock of the Buddhist approach to knowledge in particular can expose a tightly knit relationship between the domains of ontology and epistemology—what there is and how we know it—as well as the close ties between the theory and practice of philosophy. Through engaging in this kind of philosophical inquiry, we may thus come to know a bit more about ourselves, others, and what lies in between.

NOTES

The author would like to acknowledge helpful feedback on this chapter from Professor Philip Atkins, Professor Han-Kyul Kim, and Professor Jay Garfield.

1. Bertrand Russell, *Theory of Knowledge* (New York: Routledge, 1992), 46.

2. See Vasubandhu, *Abhidharmakośa* under 6.5; English trans. in Leo Pruden, *Abhidharmakośa Bhāṣyam*, from French trans. by Louis de la Vallée Poussin (Berkeley, CA: Asian Humanities Press, 1990), vol. 3, 912–13.
3. Nāgārjuna, *Vigrahavyāvartanī*, v. 46.
4. Gendün Chöpel, *Ornament of Nāgārjuna's View* (Chengdu, China: Nationalities Press, 1989), 163; English trans. in Donald Lopez, *The Madman's Middle Way: Reflections on Reality of the Tibetan Monk Gendun Chopel* (Chicago: Chicago University Press, 2006), 62.
5. For an elaborate discussion of this spectrum in Tibetan Buddhist philosophy, see Douglas Duckworth, *Tibetan Buddhist Philosophy of Mind and Nature* (New York: Oxford University Press, 2019).
6. Wilfred Sellars, *Empiricism and the Philosophy of Mind*, 2nd ed. (Cambridge, MA: Harvard University Press, 1997 [1956]), 76.
7. See Jay L. Garfield, ed., *Sellars and Buddhist Philosophy: Freedom from Foundations* (New York: Routledge, 2019).
8. Dignāga, *Pramāṇasamuccaya* under v. 4; English trans. in Hattori, *Dignāga on Perception* (Cambridge, MA: Harvard University Press, 1968), 26.
9. Prajñākaragupta, *Pramāṇavartikkālaṃkāra*, 308, 14–15; cited in Hisayasu Kobayashi, "Self-Awareness and Mental Perception," *Journal of Indian Philosophy* 38 (2010): 242–40.
10. Sapaṇ, *Treasury of Epistemology*, 10. Compare Kant's famous dictum: "Without sensibility, no object would be given to us, without understanding, no object would be thought. Thoughts without content are empty, intuitions without concepts are blind." Immanuel Kant, *Critique of Pure Reason*, trans. Norman Kemp Smith (London: Macmillan, 1929), B75. The role of self-awareness here is structurally similar to the one played by the transcendental unity of apperception in Kant. On this parallel, see Georges Dreyfus, *Recognizing Reality: Dharmakirti's Philosophy and Its Tibetan Interpretations* (Albany: State University of New York Press, 1997), 397–99.
11. Dan Zahavi, *Selfhood and Subjectivity: Investigating the First-Person Perspective* (Cambridge, MA: MIT Press, 2005), 100, italics in original.
12. See William James, *The Principles of Psychology*, vol. 1 (New York: Henry Holt and Co., 1890), 221. We find this language of acquaintance in Bertrand Russell as well, who said, "All of knowledge, both knowledge

of things and knowledge of truths, rests upon acquaintance as its foundation." Bertrand Russell, *The Problems of Philosophy* (New York: Oxford University Press, 1997 [1912]), 48.
13. James, *The Principles of Psychology*, 189, italics in original.
14. On this distinction, see, for instance, Robert Forman, "Mystical Knowledge by Identity," *Journal of the American Academy of Religion* 61, no. 4 (1993): 705–38.
15. See Tsongkhapa, *Middling Stages of the Path*, 300; English trans. in Jeffrey Hopkins, *Tsong-Kha-Pa's Final Exposition of Wisdom* (Ithaca, NY: Snow Lion, 2008), 46.
16. Galen Strawson, "Radical Self-Awareness," in *Self, No Self? Perspectives from Analytical, Phenomenological, and Indian Traditions*, ed. Mark Siderits, Evan Thompson, and Dan Zahavi (Oxford: Oxford University Press, 2011), 288.
17. Sellars, *Empiricism and the Philosophy of Mind*, 76.
18. See Edmund Gettier, "Is Justified True Belief Knowledge?," *Analysis* 6 (1963): 121–23.
19. For more on this example, see Dreyfus, *Recognizing Reality*, 292–93.
20. Gilbert Ryle, "Knowing How and Knowing That: The Presidential Address," in *Proceedings of the Aristotelian Society* 46 (1945): 8.
21. Dharmakīrti, *Nyāyabindu*, I.11.
22. See Burton Watson, trans., *The Lotus Sutra* (New York: Columbia University Press, 1993), 56–62.

BIBLIOGRAPHY

Dharmakīrti. *Nyāyabindu with Dharmottara's Nyāyabinduṭīkā and Durvekamiśra's Dharmottarapradīpa*. Ed. Dalsukh Malvania. Tibetan Sanskrit Works Series 2. Patna, India: Kashi Prasad Jayaswal Research Institute, 1955.

Dignāga. *Compendium of Epistemology* (*Pramāṇasamuccaya, tshad ma kun btus*). In *The Tibetan Tripitika, Peking Edition*, ed. D. T. Suzuki. (P. 5700). Tokyo: Tibetan Tripitika Research Institute, 1957.

Dreyfus, Georges. *Recognizing Reality*. Albany: State University of New York Press, 1997.

Duckworth, Douglas. *Tibetan Buddhist Philosophy of Mind and Nature*. New York: Oxford University Press, 2019.

Forman, Robert. "Mystical Knowledge by Identity." *Journal of the American Academy of Religion* 61, no. 4 (1993): 705–38.

Garfield, Jay, ed. *Sellars and Buddhist Philosophy: Freedom from Foundations*. New York: Routledge, 2019.

Gendün Chöpel. *Ornament of Nāgārjuna's View (dbu ma'i zab gnad snying por dril ba'i legs bshad klu sgrub dgongs rgyan)*. In *mkhas dbang dge' dun chos 'phel gyi gsung rtsom phyogs sgrig*, 133–249. Chengdu, China: Nationalities Press, 1989; English translation in Donald Lopez, *The Madman's Middle Way: Reflections on Reality of the Tibetan Monk Gendun Chopel*. Chicago: Chicago University Press, 2006.

Gettier, Edmund. "Is Justified True Belief Knowledge?" *Analysis* 6 (1963): 121–23.

Hattori, Masaaki. *Dignāga on Perception*. Cambridge, MA: Harvard University Press, 1968.

Hopkins, Jeffrey. *Tsong-kha-pa's Final Exposition of Wisdom*. Ithaca, NY: Snow Lion, 2008.

James, William. *The Principles of Psychology*. Vol. 1. New York: Henry Holt and Co, 1890.

Kant, Immanuel. *Critique of Pure Reason*. Trans. Norman Kemp Smith. London: Macmillan, 1929.

Kobayashi, Hisayasu. "Self-Awareness and Mental Perception." *Journal of Indian Philosophy* 38, no. 3 (2010): 233–45.

Nāgārjuna. *Dispelling Disputes (Vigrahavyāvartanī, rtsod zlog)*. In *The Tibetan Tripitika, Peking Edition*, ed. D. T. Suzuki (P.5228). Tokyo: Tibetan Tripitika Research Institute, 1957.

Russell, Bertrand. *The Problems of Philosophy*. Oxford: Oxford University Press, 1997 [1912].

Russell, Bertrand. *Theory of Knowledge*. New York: Routledge, 1992.

Ryle, Gilbert. "Knowing How and Knowing That: The Presidential Address." In *Proceedings of the Aristotelian Society* 46 (1945): 1–16.

Sapaṇ. *Treasury of Epistemology (tshad ma'i rigs gter)*. Beijing: Nationalities Press, 1989.

Sellars, Wilfred. *Empiricism and the Philosophy of Mind*. Cambridge, MA: Harvard University, 1997 [1956].

Strawson, Galen. "Radical Self-Awareness." In *Self, No Self? Perspectives from Analytical, Phenomenological, and Indian Traditions*, ed. Mark Siderits, Evan Thompson, and Dan Zahavi. Oxford: Oxford University Press, 2011.

Tsongkhapa. *Middling Stages of the Path* (*Hyang chub lam rim 'bring ba'i sa bcad kha skong dan bcas pa*). Mysore, India: Sera Je Library, 2005.

Vasubandhu. *Treasury of Abhidharma* (*Abhidharmakośa, chos mngon pa'i mdzod*). In *The Tibetan Tripitika, Peking Edition*, ed. D. T. Suzuki. (P. 5509). Tokyo: Tibetan Tripitika Research Institute, 1957; English translation in Leo Pruden, trans. *Abhidharmakośa Bhāṣyam*, from French trans. by Louis de la Vallée Poussin. Vols. 1–4. Berkeley, CA: Asian Humanities Press, 1990.

Watson, Burton, trans. *The Lotus Sutra*. New York: Columbia University Press, 1993.

Zahavi, Dan. 2005. *Selfhood and Subjectivity: Investigating the First-Person Perspective*. Cambridge, MA: MIT Press.

3

DOES REALITY HAVE A GROUND?

Madhyamaka and Nonfoundationalism

JAN WESTERHOFF

The question of what the foundation of reality is has a long history in Western philosophy, going all the way back to the pre-Socratic philosophers. It is, after all, a natural question to ask. Once we have discovered the hidden nature of certain objects (e.g., the kernel in the fruit, the bones underneath the skin, the soporific effect of poppies), it is easy to take the step toward extending this inquiry in both breadth and depth: what do we end up with if we proceed with our discovery further and further down and include more and more objects? Western philosophy, and Indian philosophy as well, of course, have come up with a variety of answers as to what the real kernels inside all the appearing fruit, and what the fundamental categories underlying the reality of the world we observe every day, really are.

The contribution of Madhyamaka philosophy to this question is unique. Madhyamaka is one of the main schools of Mahāyāna Buddhism, going back to the works of the Indian philosopher Nāgārjuna (first to second centuries CE). It continued to play a prominent position in the Indian philosophical debate until the disappearance of scholastic Buddhism from the Indian subcontinent by the end of the twelfth century. Since then, the

Madhyamaka tradition has been developed primarily in Tibetan Buddhism, where it continues as the dominant philosophical school up to the present day.

Madhyamaka argues that there is nothing that could possibly act as a foundation underlying reality. Within the Western philosophical tradition, we find a few attempts that move in this direction by asserting versions of nonfoundationalism. One example is constituted by the various forms of structuralism in the philosophy of mathematics, theories that do not endorse the claim that there is a basic level of mathematical objects on which all mathematical truths are grounded.[1] Another is the ontic structural realism developed by James Ladyman and Don Ross,[2] an account that rejects the idea of an ultimate foundational level of physical individuals, arguing instead that the nature of the material world should be understood as "patterns all the way down."

However, apart from their sometimes limited scope, these nonfoundationalist theories are also usually realist about whatever underlying entities they postulate (i.e., they understand the nonfoundationalist scenario as itself providing a foundation).[3] Madhyamaka nonfoundationalism is both global and applies to itself. The purpose of this chapter is to describe how the Mādhyamakas arrived at this startling philosophical picture, whether it can be defended, and its further ramifications.

NONFOUNDATIONALISM AND THE THEORY OF EMPTINESS

The Buddha famously described all existence as characterized by three marks: all things are suffering, they are intrinsically unsatisfactory; all things are impermanent, they do not last; and all things are without self. It is helpful to understand the Madhyamaka theory of emptiness and the comprehensive nonfoundationalism that it entails as an elaboration of the third of these characteristics. Underlying the view that all things are without self is the concept that all persons lack a self, which is based in turn on a form of mereological reductionism. If we consider how a material object and its parts are related to one another, we are faced with four possibilities. The most natural assumption is that for some partite object such as a chariot, there is both the chariot as a whole and the various parts (wheels, spokes, axles, etc.) put together in the right way. Yet this raises the immediate question of how these two kinds of objects are related. We can never find the whole of the chariot separately from its parts put together in the right way, so if the whole is a separate object, *where* is it located? The best way of answering this question is to assume that it is exactly where the parts are—that is, the two objects spatiotemporally coincide. Of course, the whole is a spatially extended object, so it has parts, and (obviously) so do all the parts put together. But these former parts cannot be the same as the latter, since *ex hypothesi*, the wholes of which they form a part are not identical. So we have everything twice over—the normal wheels, spokes, and other parts of the chariot, and also the wheels, spokes, and other parts that are part of the whole (call these wheels*, spokes*, etc.). But once we have gone that far, we have come full circle, now we have to face the question of how the wheels*, spokes*, and other parts, put together in the right way, relate to the whole. Consistency seems to demand that we regard these as separate objects as well, and then we are well on our way to an infinite regress of more and more parts and wholes that are empirically undifferentiable. At this stage, things get sufficiently messy that we might well abandon this approach and look for a more satisfactory theory of parts and wholes.

There are two other possibilities to consider: to restrict ourselves to asserting the existence of the whole and denying the existence of the parts, or to deny the existence of both. The first results in monism, which considers the parts as existent only as abstractions from the whole, while the second results in nihilism, the denial that there is anything that either has a part or is a part of anything else. While there is a certain attraction to treating a whole, such as a chariot, as ontologically primary and its parts only as the result of breaking it apart mentally, we need to be aware that such wholes are generally parts of other, larger wholes, which means that in the end, we are left with only one whole, the Big One, comprising everything there is. This raises the challenge of having to account for the various causal powers of the parts of the Big One that our mind carves out. Drinking milk and drinking poison have very different effects, but in the monist picture, we would not be able to attribute these to fundamentally different properties of these substances because there is only one thing.

Nihilism, on the other hand, denies that there is anything to which part-talk could be applied at all, which might not leave the world entirely bereft of everything (abstract objects might still exist if we accept that they do not really have parts), but as it needs to rule out the existence of most of what we interact with on a daily basis, it is also somewhat unlikely that this is the theory of parthood that we really want to choose. This leaves us, then, with the final, fourth possibility, which the Buddhist thinkers adopted—namely, the parts exist but the whole does not. As the monist believed that parts exist only through mental analysis, this view claims that wholes exist only by mental synthesis (i.e., by a form of conceptual superimposition that decides to treat a bunch of objects as *one* object).

This view amounts to mereological reductionism. Wholes are to be accepted as existent in a manner of speaking, as a useful shorthand, but talk of wholes does not refer to anything that exists at the level of ontology. At the level of fundamental reality, there are the parts but no wholes.

The chief application of this reductionist position is in the analysis of personal identity. The Buddha characterized the person as having five parts, five physico-psychological constituents (the five *skandha*s), and if we accept this analysis (or indeed any other one, according to which persons are partite entities), we can immediately infer that there is no unified whole that these person-parts jointly constitute. This is the key Buddhist argument to establish the nonsubstantiality or emptiness of persons.

In the further development of Buddhist philosophy, additional emphasis was put on elaborating a comprehensive understanding of emptiness—one that did not incorporate just the emptiness of persons (*pudgalanairātmya*), but also the emptiness of entities more generally (*dharmanairātmya*). It is this more comprehensive understanding of emptiness that we will focus on during the remainder of this chapter.

Emptiness in this sense is not simply the absence of a person (*pudgala*), but the absence of a substantial core (*svabhāva*) in things. A key characteristic of this "own-being" (*sva-bhāva*) is its intrinsicality. Things have a substantial core to the extent to which they could be what they are in the absence of other things. If some object can have a property in a lonely state, without anything else around, then this will be a good candidate for a property that the object has by *svabhāva*. How do the Mādhyamikas argue for the claim that everything is empty and that nothing has *svabhāva*? A first attempt can obviously be the extension of the mereological reductionist point. Wholes of all kinds cannot exist substantially because they could not exist without their parts. And if we also deny the existence of atoms (as various Buddhist authors, such as Vasubandhu in his *Vimśatikā*, have tried to do by means of independent arguments) so that everything is considered to have parts, then everything is a whole and nothing can exist substantially.

This argument is fine as far as it goes, although it is able to serve as a general argument for emptiness only if everything is considered to be material. This is a position that we might not want to share (if we want to include abstract objects into our ontology, for example) and that the Buddhist philosophers did not share, with many of them accepting a form of interactionist dualism based on the theory of the five *skandha*s, where the mental and the physical belong to distinct categories. The person is an example of an object where these categories come together; the first of the *skandha*s is the physical body, while the other four belong to the realm of the mental.

This is one of the reasons why Buddhists have set out to develop an argument for emptiness that is based directly on targeting plausible candidates of a comprehensive ontological theory. If emptiness could be demonstrated for this ontology, it would be possible to mount a stronger case for the claim that *everything* is empty. For the Buddhist metaphysicians, the theory of dharmas provided an example of such an ontology. Everything is fundamentally composed of dharmas, entities that in the framework of Western metaphysics are best conceptualized as momentary property-particulars. These are properties such as the particular shade of white of this chrysanthemum right now (and thereby distinct from the whiteness of any other chrysanthemum at a different place in space or time), with the additional qualification that they exist only for an extremely brief period of time, and that what appears to us as a persistent whiteness of the chrysanthemum is in fact a rapid succession of momentary whiteness-particulars, with each one causing the next. Ordinary individuals are therefore to be understood as complexes of such dharmas; the white chrysanthemum is thus a complex of a whiteness property-particular, a shape property-particular, and so on.

What we need to determine in this context, however, is how the various property-particulars are to be individuated. The obvious answer is that this is done by referring to space and time: this whiteness property-particular is different from that whiteness property-particular because it is here now and that was there then. But the difficulty that arises in this context is that if the theory of dharmas is a comprehensive account of ontology, space and time are dharmas, so we have not solved the problem after all. The best solution, it appears, is to differentiate the dharmas by way of the other dharmas with which they co-occur in complexes. In this way, the two whiteness property-particulars would be distinct because one co-occurs with a particular shape property-particular, and the other with another one. Yet this move is also an immediate argument for the claim that none of the dharmas can exist by *svabhāva*. If we cannot even individuate a dharma without referring to other dharmas, this means that none can be what it is in a lonely state, but the nature of each essentially requires reference to objects distinct from it. For this reason, the best way to understand the ontology of tropes is to let them appear as entities that are all empty.

A second argument sets out to show that all causally produced entities are empty. This can serve as the basis for a fairly comprehensive proof of emptiness, given the fact that acausal entities do not play a great role in Buddhist metaphysical thinking (i.e., the ontology of abstract objects does not feature prominently in ancient Indian philosophical discourse). Its key premise is the theory of momentariness—that is, the idea that all phenomena last for only an instant and immediately pass out of existence once they have arisen. What appears to us as phenomena persisting through time is merely a succession of staccato moments, each one quickly following another.[4] If we now combine the theory of momentariness with a causal account of the world, we end up with a curious consequence. Because causation takes time and because cause and effect are not simultaneous, when the cause exists, the effect does not yet exist, and when the effect has arisen, the cause, being momentary, has already passed out of existence.[5] Yet that means that the causal relation connecting cause and effect is always short of one relatum. But we cannot have a relationship where only one of the two relata actually exists.

Rather than deny that, contrary to appearances, there is no causation at all, we should solve the problem by arguing that the missing relatum is to be supplied either by memory (if the cause is in the past) or by anticipation (if the effect is in the future). In this case, causation can still obtain, although it could no longer connect two entities "out there"; rather, it will always include reference to a mental entity. What this means is that it makes no sense to conceive of a causal sequence that obtains objectively in a world untouched by mental activity. Causality is inexplicably bound up with the mental through conceptualization, and as such, objects that we consider to be essentially causally produced (the majority of objects that surround us) also essentially involve reference to the mental. As the entire sequence of causation cannot be self-standing, and as it could not exist in the lonely state in the absence of minds, it, and all its constituents, must be empty.

The final argument for emptiness that we will consider here combines ideas from the Yogācāra and the Madhyamaka schools. Yogācāra is a branch of Mahāyāna Buddhist thought that denies the existence of external objects and postulates mental objects as the only reality.[6] It comes up with a variety of arguments for this position of "mere mind" (*cittamātra*), and unfortunately we do not have enough space in this chapter for explaining them in detail, let alone for discussing their validity.[7] We will, for the sake of argument, assume that the Yogācāra theory stands up to scrutiny and we are therefore justified to confine all existence assumptions to the mental.

Having reduced the basis of our ontology in this way, we can then proceed to question the fundamentality of the mental. Mental phenomena, and in particular mind-moments, which are the chief objects of the Buddhist's concern when they consider the ontology of the mental, are entities that do not cohere well with the loneliness criterion for existence by *svabhāva*. It is hard to conceive, for any particular mind-moment, how just *it* could exist, even though none of the other mind-moments would. These moments depend on one another causally, and more important in the Yogācāra context, they are about one another. When I perceive any object that in a nonidealist framework would be considered as external (a teacup, say), the Yogācārin has to argue that this is merely the mental in disguise. We misconstrue certain mental phenomena by considering them as external, material objects, but in fact there is simply a collection of some mental moments directed at other mental moments. Noting this intricate mutual dependence between mind-moments, we can then conclude that all of them are empty because none exist by *svabhāva*, and this entails that everything is empty because we have just shown that everything is mental.[8]

IS NONFOUNDATIONALISM A CONSISTENT POSITION?

A question that immediately arises when considering the Mādhyamika's view that everything is empty is whether such a thorough nonfoundationalism is actually consistent. Do we not need at least *some* kind of foundation? This worry was already raised by various Indian critics of Madhyamaka. What they were particularly concerned with was the question of whether, given the infinite regress that nonfoundationalism seemed to entail, we would not end up with a theory according to which *nothing* exists, such that Madhyamaka would reduce to nihilism. If existence is infinitely deferred and if every object is unmasked as a conceptual construction of the basis of something else, would existence not simply dissipate altogether? At this point, only two equally unattractive choices would remain open to the nonfoundationalist: maintain the nonexistence of the world in the face of our everyday experience or modify the universal claim of emptiness to allow a basis somewhere that could stop the regress.

The Madhyamaka philosophers managed to find a way out of this dilemma, and the theory that they defend in consequence is noteworthy both for its radical nature and for being practically unprecedented in the history of philosophy, Eastern and Western. Their solution is based on the theory of the two truths, according to which we must distinguish between two kinds of truth: the conventional truth, according to which we all live our lives; and the ultimate truth, which corresponds to the enlightened view of the world, the way that the world appears to a Buddha who has completed the path to enlightenment. Accordingly, the Mādhyamika does not need to deny the appearance of the world at the level of conventional reality, although matters are quite different when we come to the level of ultimate truth. But is *this* actually a consistent position? Is the Mādhyamika not like one who postulates the existence of the upper floors of a skyscraper but refuses to admit that there is a ground floor and foundations that hold the whole structure in place? As a matter of fact, such a position is perfectly consistent, although modern developments in logic and mathematics have made this easier to appreciate.

Variants of set theory have been developed that do not presuppose that at the bottom of every set, there are either individuals or there is the empty set. Instead, sets can contain sets that contain further sets, all the way down, or the descending chain of set membership can loop back on itself, thereby creating a circular structure.⁹ Of course, the existence of such structures does not prove anything about whether the Madhyamaka conception of the world is right. It does, however, remove the underlying worry that nonfoundationalist projects such as Madhyamaka would somehow give rise to a contradiction when thoroughly analyzed. As unintuitive as the idea of an infinitely descending ontological skyscraper may be, it is perfectly consistent.

However, another worry might arise at this point. Suppose that the Madhyamaka view of ontology has been sufficiently worked out and we have settled on a suitable structure, whether it is an infinite regress of dependence relations, a circular structure, or a combination of both. This, the product of our ultimate analysis, is what the world looks like at the level of ultimate reality. Are we not now committed to accepting that at least *this* truth holds no matter what, and are we then not forced to admit that there is at least one nonempty thing—namely, the product of our ultimate analysis? There appears to be an exception to the Madhyamaka claim that everything is empty.[10]

FOUNDATIONS OF BEING, FOUNDATIONS OF TRUTH

The way that Madhyamaka can respond to this criticism is by going yet another step further, extending the theory of universal emptiness to the set of *truths* as well. When saying that all things lack *svabhāva*, the Mādhyamika would want to be understood as speaking about truth as well. What would it mean to say that all truths are empty? As we have seen, one good criterion for something being not empty is that it could exist in a lonely state, independent of other things around it. And this is precisely the way in which a realist about truth is going to understand it. Even if everything depends on everything else, the *fact* that everything depends on everything else does not itself depend on anything else—it is just how the world is. His Madhyamaka opponent, therefore, defends a global antirealism about truth, which is global because it does not simply withhold the "true no matter what"-ness from local varieties of truth (e.g., because they reduce to some other kinds of truth), but rather withholds it across the board. Global antirealism about truth has not found many defenders in the Western philosophical tradition; the Madhyamaka philosophers of ancient India and their later successors across Asia worked out its implications in the greatest detail.

Before discussing this further, however, let us first consider what reasons one could give for global antirealism about truth, independent of the fact that it seems to be necessary to prevent the reintroduction of entities with *svabhāva* through the back door when "the structure of the universe" is being appealed to. One promising route (recently explored by Mark Siderits in a presently unpublished work) proceeds via the notion of semantic contextualism. The fundamental idea is that any kind of truth-apt talk can be interpreted only against a substantial collection of background assumptions.[11] Thus, in order to determine the truth of some statements, we have to accept the truth of some background conditions that we hold fixed. How do we determine *their* truth? We need to consider other statements as background conditions and determine their truth relative to them. This does not necessarily mean that we need an infinite number of propositions. One set of propositions may form a background in some cases but not others. But this then entails that no theory can be true "no matter what," simply because it is underwritten by the world, independent of all other statements.

An alternative way of reaching the same conclusion can come from worries concerning the consistency of "absolute generality" (universal quantification about absolutely anything) and the idea of a complete collection of all there is in the universe. The view that "whenever there are things of a certain kind, there are all of those things," together with the belief that we can quantify over all of them, requires close scrutiny. If our ontology is a theory of all there is, it will require us to speak about everything. To do so, we need a language, and for this, we need semantics, and if this is constructed in the familiar set-theoretic way, we need a domain, some set or collection that subsumes everything that we are talking about. Yet if this set or collection is something on top of the members, our theory does not speak about everything because this set is not included in the domain. So we would have to conclude that our ontological theories always must be incomplete.[12]

Whichever route we take to substantiate the Mādhyamika's global antirealism about truth enshrined in its theory of the emptiness of emptiness, it becomes clear that it has peculiar metaphilosophical implications. Our attempt to come up with a theory of how things are at the most fundamental level appears to imply that there is no way that things are at the most fundamental level.

There are two conclusions we could draw from this. First, we could regard it as an argument that metaphysics as a philosophical enterprise is impossible. If our search for foundations leads us to the conclusion that there are no foundations, we should abandon the search. Second, we may consider the Madhyamaka position as a criticism of metaphysical theorizing as it is commonly understood. The Mādhyamika will agree that *if* we demand that metaphysics comes up with an ultimately true theory of the world, we will draw a blank. But this in itself does not entail that there could not be other ways of construing what the enterprise is about.

What could such an alternative conception be? In answering this question, it is useful to think of theories (metaphysical or otherwise) as ranked according to some kind of bestness ordering. In the Buddhist context, bestness is assessed in fundamentally ethical terms: a theory is better than another if it reduces grasping, and thereby reduces the suffering that results from that grasping being frustrated. For this reason, Yogācāra idealism is considered a better theory than, say, the Abhidharma theory of dharmas because the Yogācāra system is supposed to eliminate the distinction between subject and object, internal and external, which is still present in the Abhidharma distinction between matter (the *rūpa-skandha*) and the remaining four of the five physico-psychological elements, the *skandha*s, thereby providing an object for a subtle form of clinging. According to this understanding, one metaphysical theory can rank higher than another because it provides fewer instances of items to which one might become emotionally attached in a more or less subtle way. But no theory needs to come out as the top in this bestness ranking, as doing so would contravene the ethical consideration that motivates the ranking in the first place. If one theory were better than any other (by reducing clinging more than any other), this very property could act as a new entity to be clung to.

What is particularly interesting about the Mādhyamika's global antirealism about truth is that it provides an example of a philosophical perspective that is rarely discussed in the Western philosophical context. If we consider the main positions that dominate the discussion in contemporary metaphysics, we appear to have a choice between versions of naturalist realism and versions of Kantian idealism. According to the former, our best sciences provide the most reliable account of what the world is really like, and our best scientific theories are true because they correspond to the structure of the world at more fundamental levels than that of our everyday experience. The latter denies that such correspondence could actually be established because our view of the world is so heavily dependent on our conceptual scheme that any conception of the world as it "really is," untouched by human mental activity, is impossible to achieve. We can accept that there is some kind of reality underlying all of our conceptual practices—the raw material that gets shaped by our conceptual activities—but this is where our certainties must end. When talking about the world, we talk first and foremost about a construction based on a foundation about which we can say nothing at all.

The Mādhyamika would be willing to take the Kantian criticism of the naturalist realist on board, but they would not remain content with the picture that the Kantian presents as the final position—that is, with the view that there is an unknowable basis and a known set of constructs (which we regard as our world) that our mind superimposes on this. As the Mādhyamika holds that such a theory must be as empty as everything else, neither the unknowable basis nor the ontological dichotomy between it and the constructs can ultimately be real. We can only regard these as further products of our conceptualizing activity, so the unknowable basis must turn out to be a construct itself.

The resulting theory is obviously nonfoundationalist. Analyzing the world of appearances, we arrive at their source, the unknowable basis, which turns out to be another appearance, which can be further analyzed, and so on. At no point do we escape from the circle of conventions and encounter an entity that could be regarded as existing substantially, in its own right, by its intrinsic nature. It is not even clear what an escape from the circle of conventions might mean because this presupposes that there is a fundamentally real level behind the level of appearances that imprisons us. But in the same way in which the Buddhist theory of the self is not a theory that there is a real self hidden behind the various entities that we mistakenly identify with a self, the Madhyamaka does not postulate a ground behind the appearances of the world either. The terminology of imprisonment and escape from the structure of conventions is inapplicable because without these conventions, there is nowhere to escape to and no one to escape in the first place.

It has now become clear that Madhyamaka not only defends the vision of a thoroughgoing, nonfoundationalist picture in great detail, and with considerable sophistication, but it also entails a reassessment of what the metaphysical enterprise is supposed to be for. Arriving at an ultimately true theory of the world obviously cannot be the aim. It must rather be the insight that no such ultimate theory can be had, but without concluding that the entire enterprise was a waste of time in the first place. What is important is the effect that the realization of the absence of any ultimately true theory, of the emptiness of emptiness, has on us, on our lives, and on our relation to the world. The claim that this insight has transformative power provides the soteriological dimension of Madhyamaka—a dimension that is essential when assessing Madhyamaka as a philosophical project.

NOTES

1. See, for example, Stewart Shapiro, *Philosophy of Mathematics: Structure and Ontology* (Oxford: Oxford University Press, 1997).
2. James Ladyman and Don Ross, *Everything Must Go: Metaphysics Naturalized* (Oxford: Oxford University Press, 2007).
3. For further examples of nonfoundationalist theories in contemporary Western philosophy, see Randall R. Dipert, "The Mathematical Structure of the World: The World as Graph," *Journal of Philosophy* 94, no. 7 (1997):

329–58; Alexander Bird, "A Regress of Pure Powers," *Philosophical Quarterly* 57 (2007): 513–34; and, more generally, Graham Priest, *One: Being an Investigation into the Unity of Reality and of Its Parts, Including the Singular Object Which Is Nothingness* (Oxford: Oxford University Press, 2014).

4. Buddhist authors provide various arguments for this extraordinary idea, but reasons of space do not allow us to go into them further here. The interested reader may want to consult Mark Siderits, *Buddhism as Philosophy: An Introduction* (Aldershot, UK: Ashgate, 2007), 119–23; and Joel Feldman and Stephen Phillips, trans., *Ratnakīrti's Proof of Momentariness by Positive Correlation* (New York: American Institute of Buddhist Studies, 2011).

5. Note that the underlying view of time here is a presentist one, in which only the current moment exists. The argument would not work with a block-universe account in which past, present, and future moments are all considered to exist in some transtemporal sense.

6. In contemporary Buddhist studies, we find some accounts that characterize Yogācāra as a form of phenomenology that does not deny the existence of external, material objects; see Dan Lusthaus, *Buddhist Phenomenology: A Philosophical Investigation of Yogacara Buddhism and the Ch'eng Wei-shih lun* (London: RoutledgeCurzon, 2002). Nevertheless, the majority of Buddhist and non-Buddhist authors interacting with Yogācāra texts appear to have understood it precisely as a form of idealism. Compare Lambert Schmithausen, *On the Problem of the External World in the Ch'eng wei shih lun* (Tokyo: International Institute for Buddhist Studies, 2005), 49, and Birgit Kellner and John Taber, "Studies in Yogācāra-Vijñānavāda Idealism I: The Interpretation of Vasubandhu's Vimśatikā," *Asia* 68, no. 3 (2014): 709–56.

7. A *locus classicus* for such arguments is Vasubandhu's discussion in his *Vimśatikā*, in which he sets out to dispel some of the most important objections to an idealist theory, such as the observation that objects display spatiotemporal determinacy (despite the nonexistence of either space or time as mind-independent objects), or that the same world appears to different beings, although there is no set of external objects they could all be epistemologically related to.

8. This combination of Yogācāra and Madhyamaka concepts reflects the idea of Indian philosophers such as Śāntarakṣita and Kamalaśīla to form a synthesis of the two systems. Their fundamental idea was that

Yogācāra is to be considered the best theory of conventional truth, while Madhyamaka and its theory of universal emptiness constitute the best analysis of ultimate truth. See Jim Blumenthal, "Two Topics Concerning Consciousness in Śāntarakṣita's Yogācāra-Madhyamaka Syncretism," in *Madhyamaka and Yogācāra: Allies or Rivals?*, ed. Jay Garfield and Jan Westerhoff (New York: Oxford University Press, 2015), 242–51.

9. Peter Aczel, *Non-Well-Founded Sets*, CSLI lecture notes no. 14, Center for the Study of Language and Information (CLSI), Stanford University, Stanford, CA, 1988.

10. In fact, in at least one of the ways of spelling out the ontology (namely, conceiving of it as a circular structure in which everything is existentially dependent on everything else), we find more of a correspondence with the Huayan school of Chinese Buddhism, a school based on the Avataṃsakasūtra, than with Madhyamaka.

11. A considerable amount of evidence in the contemporary linguistic literature supports this hypothesis. For example, see Francois Recanati, "Literalism and Contextualism: Some Varieties," in *Contextualism in Philosophy*, ed. Gerhard Preyer and Georg Peter (Oxford: Oxford University Press, 2005), 171–96.

12. For further development of this idea, see Patrick Grim, *The Incomplete Universe: Totality, Knowledge, and Truth* (Cambridge, MA: MIT Press, 1991); and Augustín Rayo, Gabriel Uzquiano, eds., *Absolute Generality* (Oxford: Clarendon Press, 2006).

BIBLIOGRAPHY

Garfield, Jay L. *Engaging Buddhism*. New York: Oxford University Press, 2015.

Garfield, Jay L., and Jan Westerhoff, eds. *Madhyamaka and Yogācāra: Allies or Rivals?* New York: Oxford University Press, 2015.

Ruegg, David Seyfort. *The Literature of the Madhyamaka School of Philosophy in India*. Wiesbaden, Germany: Harrassowitz, 1985.

Siderits, Mark. *Buddhism as Philosophy: An Introduction*. Aldershot, UK: Ashgate, 2007.

Westerhoff, Jan. *Nāgārjuna's Madhyamaka*. New York: Oxford University Press, 2010.

4

CAN CONSCIOUSNESS BE EXPLAINED?

Buddhist Idealism and the "Hard Problem" in Philosophy of Mind

DAN ARNOLD

Arguing that the Buddha's ultimately true teachings are best understood in terms of philosophical idealism, the Indian Buddhist philosopher Vasubandhu (fl. 360 CE) could exploit central Buddhist commitments of long standing, for he recognized that some of the Buddhist tradition's main commitments may already entail idealist conclusions. This makes it unsurprising that perhaps the most influential philosophers in the history of Indian Buddhism—Dignāga (c. 480–540 CE) and his successor, Dharmakīrti (c. 600–660 CE), who are read to this day by traditionally trained Tibetan Buddhists—advanced cases for kinds of idealism.

The fact that many if not most Indian Buddhist philosophers were idealists makes it especially interesting that so many contemporary philosophers and scientists should think of Buddhists as philosophical allies. These contemporary exponents rightly recognize Buddhist thinkers as typically arguing (like themselves) for reductionist accounts of the person. However, many if not most of the contemporary thinkers who claim Buddhists as allies are physicalists (i.e., they think everything about the mind must be explicable in terms of brain events and the like because only *physical* things are ultimately real); but the Buddhist Dharmakīrti, an idealist, argued at length that mental states cannot be reducible to physical events. This is, in fact, the thrust of Dharmakīrti's celebrated proof of rebirth, which many in the Buddhist tradition take to be the definitive such argument.

With some perennially debated issues in philosophy of mind, then, Buddhist philosophers thus stand at odd angles vis-à-vis contemporary debates. While many contemporary thinkers suppose that some sort of physicalism virtually follows from reductionism, among classical Indian Buddhists, we find reductionists who argued for idealism. There is an opportunity, then, to uncover some unappreciated features of the various positions if we put them in play together. In that spirit, I will enlist some arguments from Dignāga and Dharmakīrti as a different way to characterize one of the most vexed issues in philosophy of mind—the one, indeed, that philosopher David Chalmers aptly and influentially christened the *hard problem*. Engaging these Buddhist arguments can help us see that the hard problem is not a problem just for physicalists, after all; the hard problem may look different if we appreciate that something of the same problem arises in some of the Buddhist tradition's arguments *for idealism*.

As typically presented, the "hard problem" concerns why and how certain physical events—paradigmatically, those of a body's sensory and neurophysiological systems—should happen to be accompanied by subjectivity. Why are certain neurophysiological events (i.e., objective events involving an environment's impinging upon the sense faculties of an organism) also *conscious* events? How can it be that for the subjects of such events, there is "something it is like" for them to occur, some way in which these events are *for the subject*? As Chalmers puts it, "The hard problem of consciousness is the problem of experience. Human beings have subjective experience: there is something it is like to be them. We can say that a being is conscious in this sense—or is phenomenally conscious, as it is sometimes put—when there is something it is like to be that being. A mental state is conscious when there is something it is like to be in that state."[1] The problem is that no matter how great the advances in scientific understanding of such neurophysiological goings-on as *cause* conscious mental events, no wholly third-personal understanding of these can capture what is for their subjects their most salient feature: that occurrences of consciousness are *about* something (i.e., they have *content*); and that there is some way that it feels to encounter that. Insofar as this feature—call it *subjectivity*[2]—would go missing on any wholly impersonal analysis of experience, it would seem to be irreducible to any interactions among *objects*; but how, in that case, could subjectivity be part of the natural world? How could any physical occurrences produce or entail there being (from the inside, as it were) "something it is like" for them to occur? A hard problem, indeed.

Contemporary discussion of this problem, however, may mislead in suggesting that the real difficulty centers on what kind of *stuff* existents are made of—that the hard problem has particularly to do with how *physical* things or events could ever constitute or produce subjectivity. Chalmers, for example, characterizes the hard problem in the course of considering "consciousness and its place in nature," where the problem is phrased thus: "On the most common conception of nature, the natural world is the physical world. But on the most common conception of consciousness, it is not easy to see how it could be part of the physical world."[3] Once we have engaged some arguments from Dignāga and Dharmakīrti, though, we may see that there is in the vicinity of Chalmer's "hard problem" a more conceptually basic problem—one quite independent of whether or how consciousness can emerge from physical existents.

BUDDHIST DUALISM AND DHARMAKĪRTI'S PROOF OF REBIRTH

Indian Buddhist philosophers were emphatically *not* physicalists; they tended, rather, to be committed dualists of a sort, and if there was pressure toward any kind of monism in their thought, it was clearly in the direction of idealism. We can, then, appreciate that the issue of physicalism may not be central to the hard problem if we consider how the same problem arises *in one of the Buddhist tradition's arguments for idealism*. The fact that a variation on the hard problem should bedevil Buddhist philosophers, despite their strenuous rejection of physicalism, surely tells us something interesting about what's going on.

Now, some will be surprised to hear it said that any Buddhist philosophers were dualists; surely some will have heard it said that Buddhist thought (perhaps even "Eastern philosophy" more generally) is nondualist. (This preconception informs the classic joke about the Zen Buddhist's request of a hot dog vendor: "Make me one with everything.") What makes it particularly tempting to accept that Buddhists were nondualists is that they commonly affirmed, as a cardinal doctrine of the tradition, that persons are "without self" (*anātma*)—that we are not (or do not have) enduring and unitary selves. Perhaps especially because dualism is for modern readers most familiarly epitomized by Descartes—whose famous "I think, therefore I am" argued that *I* must denote a really existent self, a thinking *thing* (*res cogitans*)—it can seem that nothing could be more nondualist than to affirm, with Indian Buddhists, that there are no real "selves" or "souls," and that persons ultimately consist just in causally continuous series of momentary events. Isn't the denial that there is any *self* over and above one's fleeting experiences precisely a denial of dualism?

Many Buddhist philosophers indeed exemplify a *reductionist* approach to persons, reducing apparently enduring wholes to the momentary events that alone really exist, for they hold that there is no enduring *identity* of "persons," that the causal continuity of momentary events of experiencing sufficiently explains the illusion that there is. It is perhaps especially their reductionism that makes Buddhist philosophers look to some modern enthusiasts like veritable "mind scientists." Are not Buddhists much like contemporary cognitive scientists, in showing that experience consists entirely in causal interactions among innumerable subpersonal events?[4] While it's perhaps tempting to think so, it matters that many Buddhists in fact affirmed a kind of dualism. It's important to appreciate that a Buddhist's *event-based ontology*—a view, that is, on which the ultimately real existents are not substances, but *events*—does not, after all, rule out there being essentially different *kinds* of events. It's possible to affirm, as most Buddhists do, that no enduring substances really exist (that every candidate for the status of "substance" turns out, like the "self," to be reducible to innumerable momentary events)—and at the same time to urge, without contradiction, that *mental* events are essentially different in kind from *physical* ones.

Indian Buddhists had a strong stake in arguing just that; for it is because mental events are independent of physical ones that, even in the absence of enduring selves, something worthy of the name "rebirth" can occur. Of course, the English word (with its prefix *re-*) misleadingly suggests that there must be some one thing that is repeatedly undergoing the same experience.

Buddhists can, however, coherently affirm simply that a causally continuous series of mental events continues even after the manifest demise of the body. Indeed, if mental events do not essentially depend on a body, series of them can continue indefinitely.

This is just what Dharmakīrti's celebrated proof of rebirth aims to show. The proof consists in a series of arguments showing that mental states cannot coherently be thought to depend on physical things because any view on which they do depend entails numerous absurd consequences.[5] Together with some other widely shared Buddhist views—such as that every mental event must have among its causes a previous mental event—these arguments are taken to show that a mental series cannot begin at birth; rather, what we take as the first mental activity occurring in this life must really be the effect of a previous such moment from another life. This is evident, Dharmakīrti's commentators note, in the purposeful behavior exhibited by newborn infants; an infant's "knowing" how to suckle is due precisely to this mental continuity.

Of course, this picture raises (among other things) all the problems that familiarly bedevil dualists. If, for example, mental events are really independent of bodily events, why are they only ever experienced *as embodied*? How could a mental series that is independent of a body work in such precise coordination with one? At the end of the day, though, Dharmakīrti may not much care about reconciling mental and physical; the chief point of his proof of rebirth is really to show that mental continuity is ineliminably basic—*mental* phenomena, not physical, are all that ultimately exist. Insofar as he is finally an idealist, it bothers him little if his arguments for this make it hard to understand how physical stuff fits in—indeed, it's so much the better for his final view if that's the case.

In advancing, then, what the Buddhist tradition considered the best argument for the reality of rebirth, Dharmakīrti furthered a larger case for some kind of idealism—a family of views toward which there was strong pressure in the Buddhist tradition. The tradition's tendency toward idealism is a function not only of the commitment to the reality of rebirth, but indeed of the tradition's basic diagnosis of the human situation; integral to the possibility of Buddhist transformation is the extent to which *minds* create the kind of world we experience. Through appropriate cultivation of the mind, then, one can change what kind of world is experienced; this is what it is to become a Buddha. This idea is reflected in a traditional view of long standing—the view that it is the "actions" (karma) of sentient beings that produce the world, and karma ultimately consists in *thought*. Taking this idea to its perhaps inevitable conclusion, the philosopher Vasubandhu argued that idealism is positively entailed by these cardinal Buddhist commitments; his arguments are different enough from those of Dignāga and Dharmakīrti that the latter may come more sharply into focus if we first briefly consider Vasubandhu's argument.

INTERLUDE: VASUBANDHU'S METAPHYSICAL ARGUMENT FOR IDEALISM

Vasubandhu's influential body of writings attests the working out, over the course of his whole career, of conclusions that he takes to be entailed by basic Buddhist commitments—chief among them the view that it is the karma of sentient beings that creates our experience of the world.[6] In his *Treasury of Abhidharma* (*Abhidharmakośa*)—a massive text representing his engagement with the Abhidharma traditions of Buddhist philosophy that prevailed in his day—Vasubandhu expresses this idea in the course of arguing against theism, which he says is (among other things) unnecessary because there is a ready explanation for everything that theism would explain: "This whole manifold world is produced by the karma of sentient beings." Significantly, he immediately adds that karma essentially consists in thought (*cetanā*); it is thought that finally impels action, so it is thought that must be changed if we are to desist from producing worlds of suffering.[7]

If, however, karma creates worlds, and if karma is finally something mental, might it not make the most sense that *the world itself* is somehow mental? This would be a more ontologically parsimonious view; otherwise one has the difficult task of explaining how thought could produce (say) essentially physical existents—eggplants and tables and rivers and whatnot. Vasubandhu presses this point in one of his late works, a short treatise of twenty-two verses (the number is rounded so that the text can be entitled *Twenty Verses*), which together argue that the best way to understand the definitive teaching of the Buddha is in terms of idealism—that, as he baldly puts it at the outset of the text, "All this is nothing but mental representations."[8] A pivotal move in the text comes early on, in a discussion of the hells so vividly imagined by Buddhists. Having argued that the beings who populate hells share experiences of suffering just on account of their shared karma (and not on account of their sharing any physical space), Vasubandhu entertains the possibility that perhaps their karma produces really existent beings (real guardians of hells) that inflict their torment. Why, that is, couldn't the torturers in hell, for all that they are karmically produced, nevertheless be physically real beings?

The problem with this picture, Vasubandhu argues, is that it is much more complicated than the view that naturally follows from embracing the mental character of karma. As he says in verse 6, "If you admit that it is material elements that arise in hells (and transform as they do) due to the karma of the beings there, why not allow that this pertains only to consciousness?" Why, that is, additionally posit material elements? The problem with doing so, he then says in verse 7, is that it saddles karma theory with too much to explain: "You imagine that the traces of karma are in one place, their result in another; why not just accept that the results occur in the very same place where the traces are?" Why not, that is, accept the more elegant view that the results of our actions occur (that *what we experience* occurs) in the same place where the causes occur? On the view that the causes in question are traces of past actions (i.e., karmically habituated mental dispositions to act), why not accept that the effects, too, occur "in" the same series of mental events in which these traces first emerged?

Now, this is not itself Vasubandhu's *argument* for idealism; he is at this point in his text just disarming obvious objections to his thesis, thereby showing that his counterintuitive claim is not, after all, implausible. The real argument for the claim comes in verses 11–15, which advance an essentially *metaphysical* argument. By this, I mean that the argument does not involve a posteriori analysis of conscious experience; rather, it involves a priori analysis of the adequacy of our concepts—in particular, the concept of "atoms," which are (as Vasubandhu argues) necessarily presupposed by anyone who would affirm the reality of physical entities. His argument against them is that no coherent account of atomism can be given. This is because atoms which had spatial extension—atoms which, able to join with other atoms on all sides, could combine to form macro-objects—would, ipso facto, be reducible because they would have, for instance, left and right sides.[9] (This can be expressed as the point that anything with spatial extension would be infinitely divisible, and hence "reducible.") On the other hand, nothing without spatial extension could constitute things *having* spatial extension; if really extensionless atoms combined, the combinations would be no larger than the atoms themselves and thus could not add up to the macro-objects of ordinary experience.

Vasubandhu thus argues that realism about external objects is fundamentally incoherent: the realist both *must* and *cannot* give a coherent account of atoms. This is, as I said, a *metaphysical* argument. As such, it distinctively consists in not just showing (as Dignāga and Dharmakīrti will) that only mental items are directly encountered in experience; rather, it also aims to demonstrate the stronger conclusion that nonmental existents *cannot* coherently be conceived. The distinctive force that Vasubandhu took the argument to have is evident in the question to which the argument gives an answer. As noted, his text begins by scouting obvious objections to idealism, showing them not, after all, to be disabling. Following the previously noted discussion of hell beings comes a line of basically hermeneutic interrogation: how, given Vasubandhu's thesis, can we make sense of the countless places in Buddhist scripture where the Buddha is represented as referring to various things of the material world? Vasubandhu answers that such texts, like all scriptures, must be interpreted and that his interpretation is preferable. According to that interpretation, the Buddha invariably said such things with a specific *intention*—that of introducing the doctrine to people not yet prepared for its full force.

It is just this hermeneutical claim that occasions Vasubandhu's argument for idealism, as he anticipates that one might now ask: "But how can it be known that the Buddha taught the existence of things like form with just this intention, but that those things which individually become the objects of mental events representing things like form do not really exist?"[10]

Even granting, that is, that scriptures naturally require interpretation, how can we be sure that they should be interpreted in just such a way as to come out consistent with idealism? Why should *Vasubandhu's* claim be thought to provide the interpretive key to all the Buddha's teachings? The distinctive force of the argument from atomism is clear if we appreciate why that argument counts as answering this question; the answer, we are clearly to understand, is that idealism *must* be what the Buddha ultimately taught because *that is the only coherent view to hold*. It is clear, then, that Vasubandhu's is a peculiarly strong argument to the effect that the reality of a physical world *cannot* be coherently conceived; and, writing as a Buddhist philosopher, he takes it as axiomatic that of course, all the views attributed to the Buddha must be coherent, and the Buddha therefore must have intended that his teachings be interpreted in terms of idealism.

DHARMAKĪRTI'S EPISTEMIC ARGUMENTS FOR IDEALISM

The distinctiveness of Vasubandhu's argument was recognized by one of Dharmakīrti's commentators (a certain Manorathanandin), who alludes to Vasubandhu's argument in the course of clarifying what Dharmakīrti can and cannot reasonably claim to have shown. Dharmakīrti (as we will see) aims to show that every act of cognition turns out to be immediately acquainted only with other mental items of some sort (e.g., mental representations or sense data); it is only an inference that an external world is represented by them. However, showing that we are not immediately *aware* of an external world is not the same as showing that no such thing *exists*. Clarifying how Dharmakīrti's arguments work, Manorathanandin concedes as much; Dharmakīrti's arguments, he says, can show only that what is present to us is just "appearing" to consciousness, and that these appearings are not themselves external—regardless of what really *exists*, things show up for us only in mental states. Manorathanandin allows, though, that if you want to argue for the strong claim that there *cannot* be physical entities—if, as he puts it, your desire to refute realism is "heavier" than can be borne by Dharmakīrti's arguments—in that case, "the arguments of the teacher should be considered." Which teacher is that? The one, Manorathanandin clarifies, whose arguments concern "the refutation of atoms (by considering whether or not they have parts)."[11]

Dharmakīrti's commentator thus distinguishes Vasubandhu's a priori analysis of the concept of atoms from the conceptually different kind of case made by Dharmakīrti, who followed his predecessor, Dignāga, in advancing essentially *epistemic* arguments for idealism—arguments, that is, based on analysis of what is (and what is not) immediately present to awareness. For the purposes of this sort of argument, one can set aside the question of whether what is present to awareness represents anything outside that; the point that we are immediately aware only of mental items entails no commitments about the status of the world beyond. The approach of Dignāga and Dharmakīrti thus represents a route to idealism that follows from particularly privileging perception as the most exemplary way of knowing—which is to say that this route to idealism runs through *empiricism*.

This is an appealing route for philosophers like Dignāga and Dharmakīrti, who greatly advanced the cause of cross-traditional debate in Indian philosophy by first venturing epistemological arguments for commitments not unlike Vasubandhu's.[12] Before Dignāga and Dharmakīrti, Buddhist philosophical thought had been advanced predominantly in the discourse stemming from Abhidharma literature; this was largely intramural in character, always finally driven by such hermeneutical considerations as we saw in Vasubandhu's celebrated argument for idealism. Arguing, instead, in ways meant to be (at least in principle) persuasive across party lines—which means, among other things, not framing one's arguments as interpreting scriptures whose authoritativeness others deny—Dignāga and Dharmakīrti exploited the fact that an epistemic case for idealism starts from ideas that are much more intuitively plausible (and therefore much more likely to be admitted by their interlocutors) than Vasubandhu's stronger claim that only mental events really exist. Indeed, their epistemic argument for idealism gets going from the seemingly innocuous thought that perception, uniquely among the ways in which we know things, will admit of a wholly causal description.

Consider, then, that perceiving consists, in John McDowell's felicitous phrase, in "impingements by the world on a possessor of sensory capacities"[13]—in the world's *causing* us to have certain experiences (as when rays of light strike the retinas of our eyes). This is what Kant had in mind in characterizing our perceptual capacities as a faculty of *receptivity*; according to an intuitively plausible causal picture of experience, perceiving is distinguished from other ways of knowing chiefly by its being, uniquely, *caused* by its object. The idea that we are, according to this picture, *acted on* by something in the world is precisely the appeal of the empiricist thought that perception is the paradigmatic way of knowing; what could better warrant the objectivity of knowledge than those cognitive moments in which we come up against the world as we do in perceiving? Perceptual cognitions alone, as Dharmakīrti emphasizes, are actually *caused* by what they are about.

Now, though, the proponent of idealism can exploit the fact that once this picture seems natural, it can come to seem clearly right that the world, as J. J. Valberg puts it, is "possibly irrelevant."[14] It seems right that what is immediately *caused* by our perceptual encounters with the world is just *mental representations* (e.g., the empiricist's "sense data")—that what is really present to the mind's eye is just "pictures" inside the head. However, once it is granted that we are immediately acquainted only with mental representations of whatever sort, the status of the world outside us becomes essentially doubtful; our grasp on the world becomes only as sure as the inference that it must be a world of physical objects that causes the mental representations we experience—and Dharmakīrti's wager is that there are other, preferable inferences to be drawn.

Such is the slippery slope toward which Dharmakīrti aims to push his interlocutor when, in elaborating just such a causal account of perception, he introduces the idea of mental representations. Here, then, is what he says in characterizing *perceptible* objects as against the kinds of things we can know only inferentially:

> There are only two kinds of things, perceptible and imperceptible. Among these, the perceptible is what causes the content of cognition to track its own presence and absence. That—unique, having the nature of a thing—is a unique particular. But the imperceptible, lacking the capacity for projecting its nature directly into thought, is something with which immediate acquaintance is impossible.[15]

A real existent's capacity thus to *cause* the content of cognition—evident in cognition's varying depending on whether that existent is present—is here contrasted with everything that lacks the capacity thus to "project" its own form "directly into thought." A really existent object—a particular ruminant, say, located at an appropriate distance from an observer—can actually impinge upon our sensory capacities, producing mental representations whose content is uniquely vivid; in contrast, abstract items like the concept "cow" do not directly "produce" representations in anything at all like the same way. An empiricist will say that that is just why perceptual awareness is foundational.

To similar effect, Dharmakīrti says elsewhere that "there is nothing at all worth the name 'being apprehendable' apart from being a cause." That is, to be the kind of thing that can be perceptually "apprehended" is just to be the kind of thing that can *cause* mental representations. Dharmakīrti recognized, however, that this raises a problem; he anticipates someone objecting that the sense faculties themselves are surely among the causes of awareness—why, then, are *the sense faculties* not also "apprehended" in experience? Indeed, many of the things that cause any moment of experience (e.g., firings of the optic nerve) are not themselves what the experience is *of* or *about*; only some of the causes—the scene outside my window, for example, reflected light from which is striking my eyes—correspond to the content of the awareness. How, then, can we distinguish among the different kinds of things that can be causes of cognition, or specify exactly how that one among the causes that is also what the cognition is *of* differs from all the other kinds of causes? Is there any principled reason why some causes must remain phenomenologically inaccessible to a subject (why we will never *see* our own neural activity), while others are precisely *what we are experiencing*?

Simple, Dharmakīrti answers; it is just that cause *whose image* the awareness bears that counts as the one in which we are interested: "Among the various causes of awareness, the one in whose image a thought arises is the one that is said to be 'apprehended' by the thought." Having seen, though, that we may be talking about essentially different *kinds* of causes—the scene outside my window does not, it seems, *cause* my experience in just the same way that neurophysiological events in my body do—we may wonder whether Dharmakīrti's answer is sufficient. We can press that question by turning now to Dignāga, who closely considers the two conditions that, as we have seen, must be met by the objects of perceptual awareness: they must make sense both as *causing* perception and as *what is showing up* therein.

DIGNĀGA AND THE REAL ROOT OF THE HARD PROBLEM

Dharmakīrti's apparent confidence that we can pick out just that cause "in whose image thought arises" may be premature; it is actually hard to say how or whether anything can really be identified at the same time as the *content* of cognition and as a *cause* thereof. Among the problems, Dharmakīrti recognized, is that reference to the *causes* of cognition brings into play all manner of subpersonal events (various neurological goings-on, in a contemporary idiom)—and while there is something intuitively plausible about his response to this problem (duh—the cause whose image appears to us is the one we're aware of!), there is a more conceptually basic problem here that still eludes us. The thing is, it's hard to see that we are even talking about the same kinds of things when we include the phenomenal content of awareness along with subpersonal sensory events as likewise being *causes* of awareness. Is it right to say the kinds of things that we're typically aware of—common-sense objects of all sorts (furniture, vegetables, overhead lighting, pets, or whatever) really are *causes* of cognitions in anything like the same way that, say, such things as neural synapses are? Suppose we acknowledge, then, that essentially different kinds of causation are occurring—one kind involves interactions among whatever basic entities are acknowledged as ultimately real (synaptic discharges, perhaps, for a scientific realist, or the momentary mental states acknowledged by Dharmakīrti); the other kind involves all the common-sense entities of ordinary experience. Now the problem is that, just insofar as these are acknowledged as irreducibly distinct sorts of causation, it seems only one of them can be *real*; the objects of ordinary experience must "really" consist in altogether different kinds of things, and it is only as so described that these are *causing* anything. Could either sort of causation, however, make sense as explaining the other if the two accounts cannot even be understood as alternative descriptions *of the same things*?

These are among the questions engaged in a concise text by Dharmakīrti's predecessor, Dignāga, and with this, we arrive at an argument I am proposing as illuminating the "hard problem." The text, which consists in just eight verses along with Dignāga's own commentary thereon, is called "Critical Analysis of the *Ālambana*" (*Ālambanaparīkṣā*), where the Buddhist technical term in the title denotes a concept that has to do with precisely the foregoing questions. Of the many basic taxonomies of impersonal events and factors posited by Buddhist philosophers, the one implicated in Dignāga's text lists the distinct kinds of "causal conditions" (*pratyaya*) that figure in the occurrence of moments of consciousness. Authors of the Abhidharma literature generally agreed that there are four such conditions: a moment of (say) *seeing some autumn trees* thus has as its causes, (1) a properly functioning ocular sense faculty (this is the *adhipati-pratyaya*, or "predominant condition"); (2) a previous moment of ocular experience (the *samanantara-pratyaya*, or "immediately preceding condition"—a category that explains how a series of fleeting moments of experience can seem, phenomenologically, to be a continuous flow; we don't experience each new moment of seeing as having just popped into being because it is just in the nature of such events to occur in continuous series); (3) a collection of other causes (the *hetupratyaya*, or "causal conditions which are causes," where *hetu* refers to another list of causes);[16] and (4) *the autumn trees themselves*, insofar as they are among the causes of my seeing them. The latter is the *ālambana-pratyaya*, which we might translate as the "percept."[17]

Dignāga's concise text analyzes this last category, which was defined by Buddhist philosophers as meeting just the two conditions of being an object of perceptual awareness; thus, "percept" denotes that one among the causes of a cognition that, uniquely, is at the same time what the cognition is *of*. Incisively characterizing the basic problems with the idea that what *causes* a cognition could also be the *content* thereof, Dignāga's analysis provides the occasion for an argument for idealism; he particularly aims to show that *physical* objects could not satisfy both these conditions and thus could never be present to awareness. As we will see, though, it is not entirely clear that Dignāga's proposed alternative—that perceptual content is produced only by previous moments of awareness—fares any better. His idealist alternative, I suggest, remains stuck with something like the hard problem—a problem, we can appreciate by considering its arising for an idealist, that has less to do with what kind of *stuff* experience is made of than with the more basic problem of reconciling *first-person* and *third-person* perspectives on mental content.

Dignāga argues, then, that the kinds of things we typically take cognitions to be *of* cannot, in principle, be among the causes of cognitions. That "in principle" may make this argument more akin to Vasubandhu's metaphysical argument than meets the eye; Dignāga, too, argues from analysis of a concept, and the problem he identifies is closely related to the problem demonstrated by Vasubandhu's analysis of atomism. The argument is simple, and presupposes these premises: To be *real*, for most Buddhists as for most empiricists, is just to be capable of causally interacting with other existents; anything without this capacity doesn't ultimately exist.

(Consider the thought that because you can stub your toe on a *brick* but not on the concept "brick," the former really exists in a way the latter doesn't.) But on a Buddhist account, only *irreducible* things could count as ultimately real—and if that's right, then for someone who affirms the reality of physical objects, it can really be only spatiotemporal atoms that are doing any "causing." Dignāga's opponent would thus have to allow, we can say, that *that chair over there* isn't causing my cognition of a chair; it's only that chair *under a completely different description* that is really "causing" anything—as described, for example, in terms of the structural properties of its parts, or their material composition, or whatever (their molecular or even subatomic makeup? it's not clear how we would know just how fine-grained to make our identification of a chair's ultimately existent parts).[18]

All that could be thought to *cause* any cognition, then, is atomic-sensible particulars (fleeting occurrences of shape and color and solidity and whatnot) because only these are ultimately real. The problem, though, is that what is present to us in experience is not irreducibly fleeting sensory atoms (we do not experience ourselves as seeing merely momentary occurrences of shape and color); rather, our experience typically concerns what J. L. Austin memorably referred to as "medium-sized dry goods"—school buses and carpets and dogs and all the other stuff of everyday experience. In terms, then, of the Buddhist category that Dignāga is analyzing, the problem is that the kinds of things that can meet the causal condition (e.g., atoms, momentary sensa) do not meet the content condition; experience is manifestly not *of* such things. Conversely, the kinds of things that do meet the content condition (temporally enduring wholes that mostly are readily identifiable as instances of famililar kinds of things) do not, on a Buddhist view, ultimately *exist*—and that just is to say they cannot cause anything.

Let us here recall Dharmakīrti's confidence that we can specify that one among the causes of any thought "in whose image the thought arises." Dignāga, we can now see, gives us reason to think that there is a basic conceptual problem with this: The things present to us in consciousness *cannot* be the same kinds of things that figure in the causation of consciousness; mental content (we might most generally say) typically involves wholes (relations, continuities, types)—causation, for these Buddhists, on the other hand really occurs only among irreducibly basic existents. Dignāga concludes that it therefore cannot be anything *reducible* – it cannot, in particular, be really existent external objects, since these ultimately consist in the atoms to which they are reducible—that is present to awareness. Does that leave any way, though, to salvage the idea that perceptual content can be characterized in terms of its causes?

Dignāga proposes that an idealist account can circumvent the problems scouted here. Thus, he takes the foregoing considerations to recommend the conclusion that only something *intrinsic to cognition*, only something that is itself "mental," could be at once a cause and the content of any moment of consciousness. Dignāga laconically says as much in verse 6 of his brief text: "What appears as though it is external is something whose nature is to be known internally; only this satisfies the criteria of the percept, since this has the nature of cognition itself, and since it is also a causal condition thereof." This needs some unpacking.

This verse gives two reasons why only something *intrinsic to cognition*—something itself of the type "mental"—could meet both relevant conditions. The first reason ("since it has the nature of cognition itself") is that as something that is itself mental, Dignāga's "something whose nature is to be known internally"— he has in mind such things as "mental representations" or "sense data" (*ākāra*), but also the mental artifacts of one's own deep psychological past (e.g., the "traces" of karma, the latent dispositions habituated by past actions)—makes sense as developing "in" one's mental continuum. Among the ideas here is that the content of cognition has to make sense as something that is somehow "in" cognition; there is no problem in explaining how mental *content* is related to mental *events* if the former turns out to be ontologically of the same kind as the latter.

Dignāga thus contends that *mental* items can make sense as the content of awareness insofar as they are "in" awareness; at the same time, he contends, the mental items intends can also meet the other criterion of a percept—as the above verse laconically says, "since it is also a causal condition thereof." This is where things get tricky. To make good on his claim that the posited mental items make sense also as *causing* the very cognitions whose content they explain, Dignāga ends up having to concede that there are a couple of different senses of "being a cause" in play. The first way of being a cause is one that makes sense if we adopt an objective, third-person perspective on the occurrence of mental events. From this perspective—which need not make any reference to what the subject of a cognition themself takes the content to be—Dignāga's "something whose nature is to be known internally" is temporally prior to the mental event it causes. (Indeed, temporal priority would seem to be a sine qua non for *being a cause*; effects never come before their causes.) On this view, what *causes* the mental content we experience is things like mental "seeds" (*bīja*) or "latent dispositions" (*vāsanā*)—beginninglessly habituated capacities and tendencies to experience the world in certain ways. (Consider, as comparable, the kinds of psychological causes that moderns might say figure in "the unconscious"; the kinds of things unearthed in psychoanalysis, we might thus say, similarly figure as causing the kind of experience we have.)

I say that causes like these are identified from a *third*-person perspective because even though there is indeed a sense in which the nature of these is "to be known internally"—specifically, they are carried forward within a mental continuum, passed down until they "ripen" within the same series—they are nevertheless *phenomenologically inaccessible.* That is, the envisioned process of long-term mental development is not transparent to the subjects thereof, and the kinds of things Dignāga has in mind—long-transmitted dispositions to act this way or that—are not available to introspection. From the subject's perspective on any moment of experience, it is not *seen* that his or her experience represents the fruition of unconscious mental processes. (That's why it takes practices such as psychoanalysis or Buddhist meditation to discover these kinds of things.)

Of course, this is to say that moments of experience are typically not *of* things like "habituated dispositions" or other past mental events; but wouldn't that mean that Dignāga's appeal to these various psychological artifacts cannot, after all, satisfy the content condition? Dignāga will answer that the artifacts of past mental events that he has in mind are not, so long as their capacities are dormant, part of experiential content; they *become* contentful only when they "ripen," at which point they show up as part of this or that experience. The Buddhist image of *seeds* is supposed to make sense of this. Just as a seed's capacity remains dormant until it is no longer a seed but a sprout, subconscious processes likewise can continuously transmit latent dispositions until some moment when they somehow burst into consciousness.[19] Insofar, however, as moments of experience are thus shaped mostly by all the "seeds" of past action, it turns out we are misled by experience; while our present moments of awareness, seem chiefly to be about a contemporaneous world, in fact they are most significantly shaped by the weight of our own psychological pasts.

Suppose that we grant that it makes sense for there to occur moments of experiencing that just intrinsically seem to their subjects to be about something, even though they are really produced only by the series that precedes them. Even if we agree, however, that a real world then becomes (as Valberg says) "possibly irrelevant" to any experience's seeming as it does, there is still a problem; now, the mental item that figures as the content of experience—a latent disposition or "seed," let's say, at just the moment that it "ripens" so as to become an occurrent sense datum—has to be understood, it seems, as *part* of (as "in") that experience. But if the phenomenal content of any cognition must be understood as a *part* thereof, it becomes hard to see how that could still make sense as *causing* the cognition. In particular, it doesn't make sense that a presently integral part of something could yet *cause* the whole that comprises it; given the temporal priority of causes, that would mean something presently *comprised* by an effect could yet precede that effect as its cause.

It seems, then, that when mental content is identified from a *first-person* perspective—that is, when we attend not to an experience's psychogenesis, but to what is most salient for the subject thereof (namely, its seeming to be an experience *of* something)—it is hard to retain the same notion of causation that figures in the account that involves "seeds," "habituated dispositions," and the like. Thus, to salvage his claim that "something whose nature is to be known internally" can make sense as both *content* and *cause* of awareness, Dignāga has to allow that when considered from a first-person perspective, experiential content meets the causal condition—it counts, that is, as also a *cause* of the cognition whose content it is—*only on a different understanding of what "being a cause" consists in*. He appeals, in particular, to an alternative understanding of "cause" according to which anything *co-occurrent* with some event—for example, anything's *defining characteristic* is, ipso facto, occurrent along with the thing itself—can be called one of that event's "causes."[20]

Thus, the phenomenologically accessible content of any cognition—what the cognition seems to its subject to be about—can be reckoned as one of the causes of the cognition only in the limited sense that whenever a cognition occurs, it is in the nature of the case for its content to be occurrent, too. Clearly, though, that is a very different sense of "cause" than when we entertain the idea that moments of experience are caused by a long and complex psychological past. Indeed, I suggest that Dignāga's difficulties here show that when we try to reconcile *first-person* accounts of the occurrence of contentful mental events with *third-person* accounts thereof, there's an important sense in which we are just not referring to the same things.

CONCLUSION: BACK TO THE HARD PROBLEM

I suggest that this argument clarifies something at the root of the "hard problem"; the conceptually basic question that now comes into view is how or whether *first-person* perspectives of cognitive events can ever be reconciled with *third-person* perspectives of the same events. Perhaps what's really intractable about the problem of getting subjectivity out of objectivity isn't whether or how one kind of *stuff* can emerge from another kind; rather, the real problem may be in reconciling two essentially different *perspectives*, each of which involves a distinct temporality.

Recall, then, the observation with which we began: much discussion of the "hard problem" has centered on questions like whether physicalism leaves any room for consciousness at all. The foregoing line of argument from the Buddhist philosopher

Dignāga, in contrast, argues for *idealism*—despite which there arises for Dignāga, as acutely as for physicalists, what I take to be a conceptually more basic form of the "hard problem." The more basic problem, I have suggested, is that in setting out to reconcile first-person perspectives on cognitive events with what can be identified from a third-person perspective on what is putatively the same event, it's hard to see how we could know that we are identifying the same events. In one contemporary idiom, this is a problem that bedevils the project of identifying the supposed "neural correlates" of experience; how could we possibly know that when we observe this or that objective occurrence (say, heightened neural activity in some brain region), we have identified the "outsides" (as it were) of the very same events whose "insides" are conscious experiences?[21]

Our consideration of Dignāga's argument gives us reason to think that we could never be sure of this. He argues that there can be no relating *physical* objects even to those mental states that are supposedly about them, because the causal efficacy of physical objects could only be the causal efficacy of their atomic constituents—and there's no explaining how fleeting atoms could cause the images of unitary wholes that are present to experience. But Dignāga has, as we have seen, some difficulty getting clear on his own, idealist alternative; he, too, is at pains to explain why it makes sense for such mental items as "habituated dispositions" to explain—as composite physical objects, he has shown, cannot—both the *occurrence* and the *content* of cognitions. This alternative works, he has to allow, only insofar as we admit two totally different senses in which anything can be a "cause" of cognition: The sense that's relevant for a third-person perspective (from which we can identify complex psychological factors as causing present moments of experience) and the sense that's relevant for a first-person perspective (the perspective from which what is most salient about any moment of experience is not its psychogenesis, but its *content*). Being itself a *part* of the experience, however, mental content cannot at the same time *cause* the very event that contains it—so, the features of experience that show up for a first-person perspective can count as "causes" only in a fundamentally different sense than do things like the functioning of sensory capacities.

Whether one is an idealist or physicalist, then, may not finally matter for getting clear on what is so elusive about consciousness.[22] The really hard problem, I suggest, is not how or whether subjectivity can be gotten out of objects; rather, it is how or whether we could ever be sure that third-personally identified cognitions are in any sense the same things that are first-personally experienced by the subjects thereof—a problem that can, as engagement with an argument by the Buddhist philosopher Dignāga shows, arise just as intractably for an idealist as for a physicalist. To see this as the more conceptually basic version of the hard problem is to see how really intractable the problem is; before we address the question of how subjectivity can be instantiated in objects, we have to get clear on what subjectivity *is*—and Dignāga's argument affords one perspective on why there may be nothing that makes sense as explaining that.

NOTES

1. David J. Chalmers, "Consciousness and Its Place in Nature," in *Blackwell Guide to the Philosophy of Mind*, ed. S. Stich and F. Warfield (Malden, MA: Blackwell, 2003), 103. A *locus classicus* for the "something it is like" criterion is Thomas Nagel, "What Is It Like to Be a Bat?," *Philosophical Review* 83, no. 4 (1974): 435–50. See, as well, Joseph Levine, "Materialism and Qualia: The Explanatory Gap," *Pacific Philosophical Quarterly* 64 (1983): 354–61.

2. I beg the reader's indulgence for my inconsistent alternation among the terms "consciousness," "experience," "subjectivity," and the like. All such terms are here intended in a minimal sense as commonly involving *qualia* ("felt" phenomenal qualities) and intentionality (the fact that they are *about* something).
3. Chalmers, "Consciousness and Its Place in Nature," 102.
4. The literature on Buddhist thought vis-à-vis the cognitive sciences is vast; one can begin to see this by perusing the website of the Mind and Life Institute (https://www.mindandlife.org/). For an accessible and appropriately critical account of the "Buddhism and science" meme more generally, see Donald Lopez, *The Scientific Buddha: His Short and Happy Life* (New Haven, CT: Yale University Press, 2012).
5. For example, if everything about being a person were reducible to facts about the body, there would be no way to distinguish a living body from a dead one; after all, the latter still consists in precisely the same physical stuff as the former. Further, there is the fact that mental activity can continue even when some or all of the sense faculties are damaged; however, the sense faculties are useless if no mental activity occurs, which shows that the latter is clearly basic. For more on Dharmakīrti's proof of rebirth, see Richard Hayes, "Dharmakīrti on Rebirth," in *Studies in Original Buddhism and Mahāyāna Buddhism*, vol. 1, ed. Egaku Mayeda (Kyoto, Japan: Nagata Bunshodo), 111–29; Roger Jackson, *Is Enlightenment Possible? Dharmakīrti and rGyal tshab rje on Knowledge, Rebirth, No-Self, and Liberation* (Ithaca, NY: Snow Lion, 1993); and John Taber, "Dharmakīrti against Physicalism," *Journal of Indian Philosophy* 31 (2003): 479–502.
6. Note the shift that makes a move toward idealism seem natural: The intuitively plausible soteriological intuition here is that *how we think* shapes *what experience is like*; when that intuition is made the basis of a complete worldview, it also can become an explanation of what there is to be experienced (which is a logically distinct matter). On Vasubandhu's project, see Jonathan Gold, *Paving the Great Way: Vasubandhu's Unifying Buddhist Philosophy* (New York: Columbia University Press, 2014).
7. These passages from Vasubandhu center on *Abhidharmakośa* 4.1; for a translation, see Gelong Lodro Sangpo (based on the French translation by Louis de La Vallée Poussin), *Abhidharmakośa-Bhāṣya of Vasubandhu* (4 vols.; Delhi: Motilal Banarsidass, 2012). The equation of karma with thought (*cetanā*) should not be taken to imply that our

actions are impelled particularly by *deliberative* thought, for thoughts, on this account, are themselves *effects* of habituated patterns and include all manner of unconscious dispositions. For more on *cetanā*, see Karin Meyers, "Freedom and Self-Control: Free Will in South Asian Buddhism" (PhD dissertation, University of Chicago, 2010). See, too, Maria Heim, *The Forerunner of All Things: Buddhaghosa on Mind, Intention, and Agency* (New York: Oxford University Press, 2013).

8. The text of Vasubandhu that I have in mind here is the *Viṃśatikā*; translations from this text are my own (and are fairly liberal) and are done from the 1925 edition of Sylvain Lévi in *Vijñaptimātratāsiddhi: Deux traités de Vasubandhu* (Paris: H. Champion, 1925). For another widely available translation, see Stefan Anacker, *Seven Works of Vasubandhu* (New Dehli: Motilal Banarsidass, several editions), 161–75. See also, and especially, Birgit Kellner and John Taber, "Studies in Yogācāra-Vijñānavāda Idealism I: The Interpretation of Vasubandhu's *Viṃśikā*," *Asia* 68, no. 3 (2014): 709–56.

9. It's a fair question whether this sense of being reducible is the same as the sense in which persons, for example, are at least plausibly reducible to more basic parts. On the argument of this particular part of Vasubandhu's text, see Matthew Kapstein, *Reason's Traces: Identity and Interpretation in Indian and Tibetan Buddhist Thought* (Boston: Wisdom, 2001), 181–204.

10. This is the sentence of Vasubandhu's commentary that immediately introduces verse 11.

11. I have discussed this passage from Manorathanandin, and also more generally Dharmakīrti's epistemic arguments for idealism, in "Buddhist Idealism, Epistemic and Otherwise," *Sophia* 27 (2008): 3–28.

12. For further references on Dignāga and Dharmakīrti, see my "Philosophical Works and Influence of Dignāga and Dharmakīrti," *Oxford Bibliographies Online* (http://oxfordbibliographiesonline.com/obo/page/buddhism).

13. John McDowell, *Mind and World* (Cambridge, MA: Harvard University Press, 1996), xv.

14. J. J. Valberg, *The Puzzle of Experience* (Oxford: Clarendon Press, 1992), 11. Valberg's discussion of the philosophical havoc wrought by the intuitively plausible "causal picture of experience" is uncommonly good.

15. This passage and the following quotes from Dharmakīrti in this chapter appear in my *Brains, Buddhas, and Believing* (New York: Columbia University Press, 2012), 25–26.
16. The relatively indeterminate character of the category *hetu-pratyaya* made that available when Yogācāra philosophers introduced the "storehouse consciousness" (discussed below, in note 19); thus, in Yogācāra appropriations of Abhidharma (e.g., Asaṅga's *Abhidharmasamuccaya*), it was claimed that *hetu-pratyaya* refers precisely to this unconscious repository of "seeds."
17. "Percept" is the translation of *ālambana* that is favored in a very helpful volume on Dignāga's surprisingly rich text: Douglas Duckworth, Malcolm David Eckel, Jay L. Garland, John Powers, Yeshes Thabkhas, and Sonam Thackchoe, *Dignāga's Investigation of the Percept: A Philosophical Legacy in India and Tibet* (New York: Oxford University Press, 2016). I have also benefited from the translation given in Fernando Tola and Carmen Dragonetti, "Dignāga's Ālambanaparīkṣāvṛtti," *Journal of Indian Philosophy* 10 (1982): 105–34. Translations from this text (again fairly liberal) are my own, from the edition given by Tola and Dragonetti.
18. The fact that the scale at which an "ultimately true" description is to be given is not self-evident reflects the kind of problem that we are stalking here.
19. The relevant subconscious processes are called by Buddhists "store-house consciousness" (*ālayavijñāna*), about which see William Waldron, *The Buddhist Unconscious: The Ālayavijñāna in the Context of Indian Buddhist Thought* (London: RoutledgeCurzon, 2003); and Paul Griffiths, *On Being Mindless: Buddhist Meditation and the Mind-Body Problem* (LaSalle, IL: Open Court, 1986).
20. Dignāga can appeal here to the Abhidharma category of *sahabhūhetu*, which denotes the kind of "cause" (*hetu*), which simply goes "with [something's] being" (*sahabhū*); see *Abhidharmakośa* 2.50c-d (see note 7 in this chapter), in which Vasubandhu gives the relation between "characteristic" and "characterized" as among the examples of this.
21. As Ned Block argues to similar effect, "What we lack is an objective neuroscientific concept that would allow us to see how it could pick out the same phenomenon as our subjective concept of [any experience]." He says as much in the course of here arguing for a naturalistic account of consciousness proposed as mitigating the problem of the

"explanatory gap" that ostensibly figures in the hard problem; he allows, though, that the line of reasoning that we are characterizing here "*does not do away with the explanatory gap* but rather reconceives it as a failure to understand how a subjective and an objective concept can pick out the same thing" (emphasis in the original). See Ned Block, "Comparing the Major Theories of Consciousness," in *The Cognitive Neurosciences*, 4th ed., ed. M. S. Gazzaniga et al (Cambridge, MA: MIT Press, 2009), 1111–22; both of the passages here quoted are on page 1115.

22. Consider, in this regard, Tim Crane and D. H. Mellor, "There Is No Question of Physicalism," *Mind*, New Series, 99, no. 394 (1990): 185–206. Against the kind of physicalism that supposedly makes the "hard problem" so intractable, Crane and Mellor argue that we do not in fact possess an understanding of the *physical* that is anywhere near sufficient to entitle us to suppose that we understand that better than we understand conscious subjectivity. In particular, they say, "In order for the issue of physicalism to be a serious one, there has to be a principled distinction between the mental and the physical which explains why non-mental sciences have an ontological authority which psychology lacks" ("There Is No Question of Physicalism," 196). *Causation* is among the criteria proposed as explaining that, and the considerations developed in this chapter can be added to those adduced by Crane and Mellor ("There Is No Question of Physicalism," 191–96) in support of their overall conclusion that "there is no divide between the mental and the non-mental sufficient even to set physicalism up as a serious question, let alone as a serious answer to it" (206).

BIBLIOGRAPHY

Anacker, Stefan. *Seven Works of Vasubandhu: The Buddhist Psychological Doctor*. Delhi: Motilal Banarsidass, 1984.

Arnold, Dan. *Brains, Buddhas, and Believing: The Problem of Intentionality in Classical Buddhist and Cognitive-Scientific Philosophy of Mind*. New York: Columbia University Press, 2012.

Arnold, Dan. "Buddhist Idealism, Epistemic and Otherwise." *Sophia* 27 (2008): 3–28.

Arnold, Dan. "Dharmakīrti and Dharmottara on the Intentionality of Perception: Selections from *Nyāyabindu* (*An Epitome of Philosophy*)." In *Buddhist Philosophy: Essential Readings*, ed. William Edelglass and Jay L. Garfield, 186–96. Oxford: Oxford University Press, 2009.

Block, Ned. "Comparing the Major Theories of Consciousness." In *The Cognitive Neurosciences*, 4th ed., ed. M. S. Gazzaniga et al, 1111–22. Cambridge, MA: MIT Press, 2009.

Chalmers, David. *The Conscious Mind: In Search of a Fundamental Theory*. New York: Oxford University Press, 1996.

Chalmers, David. "Consciousness and Its Place in Nature." In *Blackwell Guide to the Philosophy of Mind*, ed. Stephen Stich and Ted Warfield, 102–42. Malden, MA: Blackwell, 2003.

Chalmers, David. "Facing up to the Problem of Consciousness." *Journal of Consciousness Studies* 2, no. 3 (1995): 200–19.

Crane, Tim, and D. H. Mellor. "There Is No Question of Physicalism." *Mind*, New Series, 99, no. 394 (1990): 185–206.

Dennett, Daniel. *Consciousness Explained*. Boston: Little, Brown, 1991.

Dreyfus, Georges. *Recognizing Reality: Dharmakīrti's Philosophy and Its Tibetan Interpreters*. Albany: State University of New York Press, 1997.

Dunne, John. *Foundations of Dharmakīrti's Philosophy*. Boston: Wisdom Publications, 2004.

Eltschinger, Vincent. "Dharmakīrti." *Revue internationale de philosophie* 64, no. 253 (2010): 397–440.

Franco, Eli. *Dharmakīrti on Compassion and Rebirth*. Vienna: Arbeitskreis für tibetische und buddhistische Studien Universität Wien, 1997.

Gelong Lodrö Sangpo. *Abhidharmakośa-Bhāṣya of Vasubandhu*. Translation based on the French translation by Louis de La Vallée Poussin. 4 vols. Delhi: Motilal Banarsidass, 2012.

Gold, Jonathan. *Paving the Great Way: Vasubandhu's Unifying Buddhist Philosophy*. New York: Columbia University Press, 2014.

Griffiths, Paul. *On Being Mindless: Buddhist Meditation and the Mind-Body Problem*. LaSalle, IL: Open Court, 1986.

Hattori, Masaaki. *Dignāga, on Perception, Being the Pratyakṣapariccheda of Dignāga's Pramāṇasamuccaya (from the Sanskrit Fragments and the Tibetan Versions)*. Cambridge, MA: Harvard University Press, 1968.

Hayes, Richard. *Dignāga on the Interpretation of Signs*. Dordrecht, Netherlands: Kluwer, 1988.

Jackson, Roger. *Is Enlightenment Possible? Dharmakīrti and rGyal tshab rje on Knowledge, Rebirth, No-Self, and Liberation.* Ithaca, NY: Snow Lion, 1993.

Kellner, Birgit, and John Taber. "Studies in Yogācāra-Vijñānavāda Idealism I: The Interpretation of Vasubandhu's *Viṃśikā*." *Asia* 68, no. 3: 709–56.

Kapstein, Matthew. *Reason's Traces: Identity and Interpretation in Indian and Tibetan Buddhist Thought.* Boston: Wisdom, 2001.

Levine, Joseph. *Purple Haze: The Puzzle of Consciousness.* New York: Oxford University Press, 2001.

Lopez, Donald. *Buddhism and Science: A Guide for the Perplexed.* Chicago: University of Chicago Press, 2008

Lopez, Donald. *The Scientific Buddha: His Short and Happy Life.* New Haven, CT: Yale University Press, 2012.

McDowell, John. *Mind and World, with a New Introduction.* Cambridge, MA: Harvard University Press, 1996.

McMahan, David L. "Modernity and the Early Discourse of Scientific Buddhism." *Journal of the American Academy of Religion* 72, no. 4 (2004): 897–33.

Nagel, Thomas. *The View from Nowhere.* New York: Oxford University Press, 1986.

Nagel, Thomas. "What Is It Like to Be a Bat?" *Philosophical Review* 83, no. 4 (1974): 435–50.

Schmithausen, Lambert. *On the Problem of the External World in the* Ch'eng wei shih lun. Tokyo: International Institute for Buddhist Studies, 2005.

Siderits, Mark. "Is Reductionism Expressible?" In *Pointing at the Moon: Buddhism, Logic, Analytic Philosophy*, ed. Mario D'Amato, J. L. Garfield, and Tom J. F. Tillemans, 57–69. New York: Oxford University Press, 2009.

Taber, John. "Dharmakīrti against Physicalism." *Journal of Indian Philosophy* 31 (2003): 479–502.

Tola, Fernando, and Carmen Dragonetti. "Dignāga's Ālambanaparīkṣāvṛtti." *Journal of Indian Philosophy* 10 (1982): 105–34.

Valberg, J. J. *The Puzzle of Experience.* Oxford: Clarendon Press, 1992.

Waldron, William. *The Buddhist Unconscious: The Ālayavijñāna in the Context of Indian Buddhist Thought.* London: RoutledgeCurzon, 2003.

Williams, Paul. "On the Abhidharma Ontology." *Journal of Indian Philosophy* 9 (1981): 227–57.

5

IS ANYTHING WE DO EVER REALLY UP TO US?

Western and Buddhist Philosophical Perspectives

on Free Will

RICK REPETTI

This chapter brings together Western and Buddhist perspectives on free will. In the first section, "The Free Will Problem in Western Philosophy," I explain the free will problem and identify the strongest arguments that challenge the belief in free will. In Western philosophy, the free will skeptic poses a dilemma to the optimist about free will (the Optimist's Dilemma), uniting two arguments that I will sketch here: If choices are lawfully determined consequences of prior conditions (determinism), then choices are not up to us (the Consequence Argument); but if choices are random (indeterminism), then they are not under our control and thus are not up to us (the Mind Argument). Either way, choices are not up to us.

Another argument asserts that if our choices were sufficiently manipulated without our knowledge, they would be unfree—that there is no principled difference between determinism and manipulation, and thus if determinism was true, we would be unfree (the Manipulation Argument). Another argument says that regardless of whether determinism or indeterminism is true, choices are necessarily a function of the mental state that one is in at the moment of choice, but our mental states are always influenced by prior conditions (the first of which we could not have brought about without having created ourselves ex nihilo, which is logically impossible), so we can never be ultimately responsible for our choices, and thus free will is impossible (the Impossibility Argument).

In the second section of the chapter, "Free Will from the Buddhist Perspective," I discuss the problem from various Buddhist perspectives, I explain the various positions that have been taken by different types of Buddhists, and I offer powerful Buddhist counterarguments that may be leveled against all the Western skeptical arguments described earlier—interestingly, despite the nearly pan-Buddhist denial of the reality of an agent/self.

THE FREE WILL PROBLEM IN WESTERN PHILOSOPHY

We tend to think that we have free will, but what do we think it means to have free will? I think our prephilosophical or folk-psychological understanding of it involves something like what is described next. Unless we are suffering from some sort of loss of, or limitation on, our usual capacities, as might be the case with certain forms of pathology, under the influence of psychoactive substances, coercion, hypnosis, or other unusual conditions, we believe the following:

- We can *do* as we please spontaneously, *choose* to do as we please (when a choice seems required), or *deliberate* (when choosing seems complicated) to figure out what we wish to do, and we *can do so*, accordingly.

- Our choices and actions originate in our minds in ways that are *voluntary,* or up to us.
- What we choose to do and what we actually do are things that *we* are ultimately responsible for bringing about.
- We can deliberate about two or more alternatives that are actually *accessible* to us.
- Going through the decision-making process, coming to a decision or making a choice, and acting on that choice are all related to each other in the right kind of way, such that it was our deliberating, deciding, and making an intentional effort to bring about the action that *explain the occurrence* of our action.
- These sorts of mental activities are *causally effective* in bringing about our actions in the way that we imagine they do.
- Even though we chose one of the two or more alternatives we considered, we *could have* chosen one of the other alternatives we considered, or simply decided not to act at all, had we somehow been back in time at that same choice moment under the exact same circumstances (i.e., we *could have done other* than what we did).
- Even if our desires to do *x* are strong, we are able to *not* do *x*.

There may be other intuitions that inform our sense of having free will, but these will do for our present purposes. Are they true? How did we come to suspect they might not be?

The Historical Origins of the Western Problem

Traditionally, the ancient Greeks rarely and only indirectly discussed free will. One instance was that the early atomists thought that otherwise mechanical atoms would sometimes have to move randomly—veer off course—if anything genuinely novel (such as free action) were possible. Another instance was that Aristotle considered the idea that all meaningful statements are either true or false in some timeless sense, such that it is either true or false that there will be a sea battle tomorrow: the statement is either true or false, independent of time and our knowledge of its truth value (which suggests that we are unable to alter the truth value of such statements, which suggests that there are no real alternatives, and thus no free will). Aristotle also thought that an action would be praiseworthy or blameworthy only if it were performed *voluntarily*. But none of these considerations historically influenced the development of the version of the free will problem that has gripped the imagination of modern and contemporary philosophers, so I will not elaborate on them here.

According to Flanagan,[1] Garfield,[2] and others, the modern and contemporary free will problem began several centuries later, with early Catholic theodicy (the attempt to explain how an all-loving, all-powerful God could allow apparent evil in the world to occur) when St. Augustine first claimed that we possess a "faculty of will" that is free (i.e., free will) in order to take the blame for evil off God and place it onto us: God gave us free will, which is good, but we misuse it, causing evil. This seems to be the first explicit mention of free will in Western philosophy; whether it is the origin of the belief remains to be seen.[3] Two free will problems immediately arise: how can we have free will if God is omniscient, and how can God be omnipotent if our wills freely bring about states of affairs in God's world?

If God foreknows everything and cannot be wrong, then we cannot falsify what God foreknows about our choices; so, if God foreknows that I will choose *x*, then choosing not-*x* is not a real alternative. However, if we have genuine free will, then God cannot foreknow what we will freely choose. And if God has limitless power, will, and intentions for how every detail in the universe should turn out but has given us free will, then what happens is up to *us*, not God. Thus, if we are free to make the world turn out differently, that contradicts God's limitless ability to will the world's unfolding. Therefore, either God is omnipotent and we lack free will or we have free will and God is not omnipotent.

There are interesting ways that these problems overlap, as well as interesting possible solutions to them, but space considerations prevent further discussion of them here.[4] Rather, most modern and contemporary interest in free will stems from considerations arising from our emerging scientific understanding.

The Optimist's Dilemma

The scientific revolution brought Galilean, Newtonian, and related ideas about the mechanistic, lawful operations of nature front and center in the Western philosophical community. Modern science suggests that all macro-level natural phenomena (from subatomic to intergalactic levels) are deterministic—causally necessitated by law and prior conditions; this posed the first modern philosophical problem for free will because it suggests that choices are necessitated and lack genuine alternatives and thus they are unfree. However, more recently, quantum science suggests that micro-level (quantum) phenomena are indeterministic—not just epistemically (meaning that we just cannot know what determines them), but metaphysically (meaning that there really is nothing that determines quantum phenomena); this posed the more recent problem for free will because it suggests that if choices could even be amenable to quantum influences, they would be purely random, in which case they cannot be controlled and thus are unfree.

Perhaps the strongest skeptical challenge facing the person who is *optimistic* about free will is the "Optimist's Dilemma," which consists of equally negative implications from either option, determinism or indeterminism. In short, that argument goes something like this:

1. Either determinism is true or indeterminism is true.
2. If determinism is true, then there are no alternatives, in which case we cannot do other than what we are determined to do, and thus there is no free will.
3. If indeterminism is true (of choices), then choices are utterly random, in which case they are not really under our control or up to us, and thus there is no free will.
4. Thus, either way, there is no free will.

Let us grant that premise 1 is true in the exclusive sense of "or," which rules out both determinism and indeterminism being true together (say, determinism at the macro-level and indeterminism at the micro-level), and which insists that if indeterminism is true at all, even for one quantum event, then determinism is false, even if it is true for everything else. This understanding follows from the universal scope of the word "Every" in the claim "Every event is determined."[5] Let us turn next to premise 2, which asserts that determinism precludes the possibility of free will.

THE DETERMINISM AND FREE WILL PROBLEM

According to the thesis of determinism, all events are causally necessitated by previous conditions and events in accordance with universal laws of nature: whatever happens is determined in such a way that it is the only physically possible outcome of all the causal conditions that precede and shape it. In other words, every event is the one and only possible consequence of all the events that have preceded it, given the laws of nature.

If determinism is true, then although we may entertain alternative courses of action when confronted with what seem to be genuinely accessible options surrounding some decision or choice event, only one such option is genuinely open—the one and only one that was uniquely determined by the laws of nature and all the conditions that preceded the choice moment. This is not to say that deliberation, desire, belief, effort, and so forth do not play a causal role in determining that single option: they may, and typically/probably do. However, each of those prechoice items itself is the one and only one that was uniquely determined by all relevant preceding causal conditions, and so on for all still prior conditions—and here's the stinger—all the way back to before you were conceived, if not all the way back to the Big Bang (or whatever the equivalent cosmic origins were, if any).

One way to drive home the sting of this deterministic view is to imagine a being like God who could (hypothetically) rewind cosmic history, like rewinding a DVD, to the start and replay it infinitely many times, leading to exactly the same events/choices each time. That infinitely repetitive image doesn't bode well for the idea that we have free will because no alternative ever happens. Intuitively, free will seems to be the ability to be the ultimate cause and origin of our own choices, not merely the latest link in an infinitely long causal chain that necessarily knocks over the domino reflecting your choice in one, and only one, way. Free will seems to be the ability to either do or not do whatever it is we are deliberating about doing, say, x or not-x. If we have free will, many think, we may have done x, but we could have not done x: we were free to not do x—we *could have done otherwise* than we did. However, if determinism is true, it seems, the impression that we have the ability to do either of two alternatives—that we are able to do otherwise—seems false. Only one of the two "alternatives" was ever really physically possible.

If determinism is true, our choices are all lawfully necessitated consequences of the series of conditions that predate our existence, there are no alternatives, and thus there is no free will. That's the Consequence Argument for incompatibilism between free will and determinism.[6] "Hard Determinists" are incompatibilists who think that determinism is true, and thus there is no free will.

There is another powerful argument for Hard Determinism that may be seen as an adjunct or alternative to the Consequence Argument, and that is the Manipulation Argument; versions of this have been proposed by a number of philosophers, but the most powerful one is the Four-Case Argument formulated by Pereboom. In the first case, imagine a chip secretly implanted in your brain that is connected to a program controlled by your manipulator, such that all subsequent thoughts, intentions, and decisions that occurred in your mind seemed to be yours but were completely caused by the manipulator. Surely you would be unfree when you choose and do x. In the second case, manipulation involves prior genetic programming that leaves all else alone but guarantees that you do x. In the third case, you are brainwashed as a child to do x. Finally, determinism is true, and you do x for natural reasons. Pereboom argues that there is no principled difference between any of these cases and determinism, in which case "Soft Determinism," the view that determinism is true and is compatible with free will, is false. "Compatibilism" is simply the logical view that determinism is consistent with free will, regardless of whether determinism is true or we have free will.

For the purposes of the Optimist's Dilemma, we may consider the Consequence and Manipulation Arguments joined, insofar as they share the same conclusion: Incompatibilism (which implies that if determinism is true, then so is Hard Determinism).

INDETERMINISM AND THE FREE WILL PROBLEM

"Libertarians" are incompatibilists who think that we have free will (for various reasons), so determinism must be false—indeterminism must be true, and not every event is causally necessitated by prior events in accordance with laws of nature. The main reasons for libertarianism are that it seems to capture our pretheoretical intuitions about free will, to comport with the phenomenology of volitional experience, and to be required for full-blooded ascriptions of moral responsibility, particularly the intuition that a person is not morally responsible for doing something if they were unable to do otherwise. (Many have challenged this latter idea, as we shall see shortly.) There are problems with indeterminism, however.

The free will skeptic objects to the idea that indeterminism will really help support optimism about free will because if choices are utterly random, then they are not really under our control or up to us in a way that we can be considered to author them. This has been called the "Mind Argument" (due to its prominence in the journal *Mind*) but may also be called the "Randomness Argument." One way to grasp the force of this objection is to imagine that indeterminism is true, and compare the following two scenarios: In scenario A, a random quantum occurrence *inside* one's brain triggers a sequence that culminates in a decision between two otherwise equal alternatives; and in scenario B, a random quantum occurrence *outside* one's brain (say, in the air in one's nose) triggers a sequence that culminates in a decision between two otherwise equal alternatives. The argument is as follows:

1. Surely one is not the author of the decision in scenario B.
2. There is no principled difference between scenarios A and B.
3. Thus, surely one is not the author of the decision in scenario A.

Kane argues, however, that this argument fails to afford the libertarian the most charitable interpretation.[7] According to Kane, the role of the indeterminacy is not to randomly generate some nonvolitional (quantum-to-neural) sequence that culminates in a decision, but rather to invalidate the Consequence Argument; and, more important, where the indeterminacy is located makes all the difference in the world. In Kane's model, the agent has volitions/reasons for action in support of two competing choices, both of which she intends, where tension generates the indeterminacy that invalidates the Consequence Argument, but her will lends itself to one of the alternatives over the other. According to Kane, the will of the agent is what makes the decision, so it is the agent herself who has caused or brought about the decision—not some random quantum fluctuation.

One problem with this is that it is difficult to flesh out just what the agent is doing or how she is doing it: if the decision favoring x over not-x is not a function of the strength of her overall reasons for x, then x's coming about from the agent's will seems indistinguishable from x's coming about randomly; if it is a function of the strength of her overall reasons for x, then it is arguably determined. If the action potentials of x and not-x are truly equal, how could some further action potential for x emerge if not randomly? Further, there is little empirical evidence in support of this, and arguably what we do know about how the brain works does not seem to support it. In any case, it seems a slim basis on which to rest belief in libertarianism.

EITHER WAY, THERE'S NO FREE WILL

The Optimist's Dilemma, recall, fuses the Consequence (Manipulation) and Mind (Randomness) arguments together, concluding that whether determinism is true or indeterminism is true, there is no free will. To summarize, either choices are lawfully necessitated consequences of ancient causal conditions or they are purely random, but in either case, they are not under our control, we do not author them, and they are not up to us, and thus we are not free.

THE IMPOSSIBILITY ARGUMENT

Just as the Manipulation Argument augments the Consequence Argument, Strawson's Impossibility Argument augments the Optimist's Dilemma.[8] Whereas the Optimist's Dilemma separately assumes the truth of determinism and of indeterminism to show that each leads to unfreedom, the Impossibility Argument sets aside the question about whether the nature of causation is deterministic or indeterministic, directing attention to features of the moment of choice itself (particularly the mental state that one is in at that moment). Strawson argues rather intuitively that whatever we choose, it must be a function of the mental state that we are in at, and perhaps immediately prior to, the moment of choice. Intuitively, the mood or state of mind that an individual is in just before and at the moment of choice conditions what the person chooses, regardless of whether the nature of that conditioning is deterministic, indeterministic, or otherwise. No choice is made, in other words, in some sort of totally unconditioned mental state—in a mental state vacuum, so to speak. Thus, no choice is ever made absent such conditioning, and thus no choice is ever one for which the agent is ultimately totally responsible.

Strawson adds that every mental state is conditioned by the previous mental state together with whatever other factors (biological, environmental, social, and others) conditioned that prior mental state, and so on for every previous and subsequent mental state. Unless one could somehow create one's own mind, one's own first mental state, without any conditions—unless, that is, one could create oneself ex nihilo, mysteriously as a *causa sui*, which is logically impossible (because one would already have to exist to be able to do anything, much less create one's own first mental state)—then it is impossible to be free in the sense required to be genuinely morally responsible for one's choice. Thus, free will is impossible.

The Impossibility Argument thus has the same effect as the Optimist's Dilemma—namely, that free will is impossible regardless of whether determinism or indeterminism is true, but it does so without reasoning on the basis of the assumption of the truth of either.

Compatibilism, Soft Compatibilism, and Semi-Compatibilism

Some philosophers have argued that one or more of these skeptical arguments is unsound, and thus determinism, indeterminism, or both may be compatible with free will.[9] I'll discuss only some of the more prominent examples. "Compatibilism" originally meant that free will is compatible with determinism because the problem of free will and determinism dominated the earlier modern free will literature, but in light of the more recent Optimist's Dilemma, which says that free will is incompatible with both determinism and indeterminism (the latter view is called "Hard Incompatibilism"), the term "Compatibilism" may also be taken to mean that free will is compatible with either determinism or indeterminism. I call the latter, inclusive sense of the term "Soft Compatibilism" to make this explicit.

Frankfurt famously argued for Compatibilism by noting that agents who lack alternatives and thus could not do otherwise (say, because a manipulator was standing by ready to block any such attempt on their part to do so), but who do as they do of their own accord, such that the manipulator plays no causal role in their choice (which implies that they would have done as they did even if they could have done otherwise), act freely in a sense sufficient to consider them morally responsible for what they do.[10] This is a counterexample to the idea that access to alternative possibilities (and thus the ability to do otherwise) is required for free will. Determinism threatens free will because it rules out alternative possibilities, but if Frankfurt's counterexample is cogent, then alternatives are unnecessary, and thus the fact that determinism precludes them removes the nonalternatives' threat to free will. Philosophers are still debating whether the many so-called Frankfurt cases that have subsequently dominated the free will literature are cogent.

Frankfurt went on to develop a positive account of morally responsible free agency according to which *actions* are free if they accord with the agent's will, and the *will* is free if it accords with the agent's higher-order will (i.e., if they have the sort of will they want to have).[11] Conversely, if a lower-order desire that they disapprove of manages to issue an action, they maintain freedom of action because they acted on their own desire, but not freedom of will because they willed not to act on that desire but did anyway. Critics have noted that both lower- and higher-order desires are determined, but also that if what makes a desire free is its being endorsed by a higher-order desire, what makes the higher-order desire free would have to be a still-higher-order one, and so on, threatening an infinite hierarchical regress. Frankfurt's hierarchical account has not been as popular as his counterexample.

Watson suggested that our deeper self and core values could avoid the regress problem.[12] However, this move would not avoid the objection that these too are determined. Only the

Libertarian seems able to claim that we can be responsible for our deeper self and core values.

A more promising compatibilist direction based on Frankfurt's counterexample differentiates between the compatibilist and incompatibilist senses of free will, each of which involves a different conception of control on the one hand, and moral responsibility on the other. Fischer argues that the Libertarian or incompatibilist sense of control, which he calls "regulative control," requires that an agent be able to bring about each of two or more alternatives in any choice situation, and that is obviously impossible in a deterministic world lacking any alternatives. Because the world is likely deterministic, it is doubtful that we possess the sort of control for this stronger sort of free will. However, as shown by Frankfurt's counterexample and many similar Frankfurt cases that Fischer and others have designed, agents in deterministic worlds can still act of their own accord despite lacking alternatives, exhibiting what Fischer calls "guidance control," the sort that is in play when a driver's voluntary handling of their car's steering wheel mechanism is what determines the direction of the vehicle. If such agents are able to recognize, deliberate about, and respond rationally/appropriately to moral reasons, thus exhibiting both "reason-responsiveness" and guidance control, Fischer argues that such agents possess a form of free will that is weaker, but strong enough to be considered morally responsible for their choices and actions.

Fischer's view, that deterministic agents lack strong, Libertarian free will but may possess weak (compatibilist) free will and moral responsibility, is called "Semi-Compatibilism." To some, Semi-Compatibilism is just a slightly more nuanced form of Compatibilism. However, Semi-Compatibilists may be credited with acknowledging that our pretheoretical sense of free will is the Libertarian's and that we lack that robust sort of freedom, but maintaining that we possess a weaker one that is nonetheless sufficient for why we mainly care about free will at all: moral responsibility. But whereas Semi-Compatibilism might plausibly be thought to escape the sting of the Consequence Argument, Pereboom's Four-Case Argument seems to undermine the idea that determined agents are any different from manipulated ones.

Western Conclusions

In summary, the Consequence Argument, augmented by the Manipulation Argument and linked with the Mind or Randomness Argument to form the Optimist's Dilemma, further augmented by the Impossibility Argument, all suggest that whether determinism or indeterminism is true, and indeed regardless of whether either of them is, we do not have the sort of free will that would be required to be appropriately considered as genuinely or ultimately morally responsible for our choices and actions. There are other free will skeptical arguments as well, of which I'll mention only a small sample. For example, some think that neuroscience shows that consciousness is causally impotent and there is no such thing as mental-to-bodily causation whatsoever, much less free will. Others argue that neuroscience suggests that there is no such thing as a self, no "homunculus" or "ghost in the machine" of the mind, no executive controller, or, more strongly, that consciousness is an illusion altogether, that the mind is just a shadow of the brain. Still others argue that the more we learn about behavior from neuroscience, cognitive science, and the social sciences, the more we see that mind is fraught with biases, cognitive errors, illusions, and the like, so much so that the idea that we are ever really the way we think we are and take ourselves to be—conscious agents relatively controlling our own behavior—is not only probably utterly false, but in light of the current state of knowledge, extremely naive. The conjunction of all these views may be called "free will skepticism."[13] Free will skepticism appears to be increasingly dominating the philosophical literature, to the point where, for many contributors to the discussion, the focus has moved on to whether we should eliminate the term "free will," or revise it, and many have also moved to exploring the consequences of not believing in free will.

FREE WILL FROM THE BUDDHIST PERSPECTIVE

I mentioned in the last section that neuroscience seems to undermine the idea that there is even a self: any sort of integrated, stable, enduring psychological/neural networks or mechanisms that could serve as the basis of agency or selfhood. Among philosophers in the modern West, Hume came to a similar conclusion, claiming that when he looks within, all he sees are momentary impressions, thoughts, sensations, feelings, and perceptions, but no enduring impression that remains unchanged throughout the changing series that could unite them; in the contemporary period, Parfit did as well, for similar but more nuanced reasons.[14] However, the Buddha first claimed this well over two millennia ago, as well as the claim that the self-illusion is the primary confusion at the root of all our suffering, the eradication of which illusion constitutes nirvana, or enlightenment.[15]

Thus, it would appear on the surface that if there is *no agent/self* in Buddhism, there cannot be any *autonomous agent/self* (free will) in Buddhism. This is exactly what at least one Buddhist philosopher, Goodman, argues explicitly,[16] and what others either assume[17] or argue implicitly.[18]

However, as I have argued by analogy,[19] if there were no *red apples*, that would not imply that *nothing* is red. Consider another analogy: the idea that there is no real self might imply that there is no real *speaker*, but not that there is no real *speech*.

Is it possible to have free action or free agency without an agent? Some Buddhist philosophers think it is; some think it is not. In fact, just as there are different forms of Western philosophy, and even different forms of empiricism, so are there different forms of Buddhism. There is even disagreement among Buddhists about the *history* of Buddhist thinking about free will. Some Buddhists claim that the subject of free will never arose in Buddhist history prior to its recent encounters with Western philosophy;[20] others locate discussion of the subject right in the beginning, with the Buddha's own words.[21]

However, unlike their Western counterparts, Buddhist philosophers did not go through an initial period where the term "free will" explicitly entered the philosophical lexicon, as occurred when Augustine introduced it to solve his theodicy problem.[22] Thus, Buddhist history did not face any consequent theological free will problem concerning divine omniscience or omnipotence, not only because it lacked the terminology of "free will," but also because Buddhists disbelieve in a creator God to begin with. There is a related issue concerning the Buddhist claim that the Buddha is omniscient,[23] but I cannot devote space to that problem here.

Historical and Contemporary Buddhist Views of Free Will

Buddhists are, by definition, centrally committed to the denial of the autonomous agent/self.[24] It stands to reason that a philosophy/religion that revolves around the attempt to attain enlightenment upon the realization that *the agent/self is an illusion* should have no interest in defending belief in an autonomous agent. Moreover, the Buddha generally restricts his philosophical analyses to soteriological issues, specifically to clarifications that promote enlightenment, and refuses to engage in nonsoteriologically-relevant discussions, such as about the origins of the world or what happens to an enlightened being after death.[25] The term "free will" does not even appear in any Buddhist texts prior to the contemporary period; it comes up only when Buddhist philosophers attempt to explain what they think the Buddhist view would be on the subject, in light of Western philosophical interest in Buddhism.[26]

However, philosophers from different Buddhist traditions disagree about what exactly is being denied when Buddhism denies the ultimate reality of the agent/self,[27] and one prominent form of early Indian Buddhism, then constituting the largest minority, that of the Pudgalavādins (person-theorists), disbelieved in the reality of the *self* but believed in the reality of the *person*.[28] Consequently, complex disputes arose between the various camps on whether consciousness is (1) inherently self-illuminating, in the way that a flame is itself visible, and thus *self-conscious*, revealing a subject of experience, a self; or (2) only other-illuminating, in the way that a flame makes other objects visible, among other conceptions. These arguments and their suggestive metaphorical models (e.g., that a knife cannot cut itself) are extremely subtle and often difficult to differentiate.[29]

However, we need not resolve the proper Buddhist understanding of the self to preempt the Buddhist free will issue. The Buddha himself spoke in a way strongly suggesting that he believed in some form of free will: he not only explicitly rejected some of the *opposites* of free will—what I have described as belief in "inevitable causation" by gods, fate, matter, and chance[30]—but he ridiculed these fatalistic ideas.[31] In doing so, he seems to have rejected challenges to free will from divine will, the fatalism Aristotle considered, determinism, and indeterminism. This could sufficiently explain why there was no subsequent discussion of the subject until Buddhism encountered a philosophical tradition that is curious to know what it thinks about free will—Western philosophy's central, enduring puzzle. Indeed, most of the sophisticated philosophical positions that have been articulated in Buddhism were constructed precisely in response to non-Buddhist Indian philosophical challenges.[32]

The Buddha also rejected the idea of inevitable causation by karma, but I treat the issue of karma separately from the list of the Buddha's rejected fatalist concepts already discussed because *nonfatalistic* karma is asserted in Buddhism, although on analysis, it is unclear whether it may be subsumed under (or distributed across) the concepts of determinism and indeterminism: the Buddha and subsequent Buddhist philosophers treat karmic causation in a highly nuanced—but clearly nonfatalistic—way throughout the history of Buddhism. Indeed, the first wave of "early-period") contemporary Buddhist philosophers to examine the Buddhist understanding of free will revolved their discussions around their understanding of karma.[33]

Thus, Rāhula,[34] Story,[35] Kalupahana,[36] Gómez,[37] and Harvey,[38] for example, interpret both karmic causation and agency in ways that resist purely deterministic and purely indeterministic parsings, a difficult view that I have described as wiggly determinism.[39] In this view, which the Buddha significantly endorsed, *cetanā* (volition) is karma (action), and thus volition and action are voluntary.[40] It cannot be purely deterministic, for if it were, liberation would be impossible (for the same reasons that the Incompatibilist cites). Nor can it be purely indeterministic, for if it were, again, liberation could not be brought about by bringing about the right causal conditions that lead to it,[41] which, on analysis, resembles the Hard Indeterminist view that indeterminism cannot ground free will because random events cannot be controlled).[42] But, contra the Hard Incompatibilist, these early-period contemporary Buddhists seem to be grasping for some sort of Semi-Compatibilism or Soft Compatibilism, for they implicitly reject both Hard Determinism and Hard Indeterminism, notwithstanding the relatively noncommittal, inchoate nature of their accounts.

Some subsequent Buddhist philosophers discussing free will tend to move beyond this initial wiggly compatibilism, taking more bold positions. Relying on the Buddhist two-truths distinction between ultimate-reality-level and conventional-reality-level discourses, Siderits asserts a more nuanced form of paleo-compatibilism,[43] according to which, at the ultimate reality level, determinism is true, everything is atomistic and impersonal, there are no wholes made of parts, and there is no such thing as free agency, whereas at the conventional level, there are whole persons who have libertarian free will.[44] The two-truths distinction resembles Sellars's distinction between the scientific image of the world and the manifest (common sense, pragmatic) image, with a parallel insofar as both the scientific view and the ultimate reality are considered accurate.

The *locus classicus* for the way that this Buddhist distinction plays out is in the dialogue between the Buddhist monk Nagasena and the Bactrian king Menander ("Milinda") in *Questions to King Milinda* (*Milindapañha*). There, Milinda asks who bears the name "Nagasena" and similar common-sense questions that seemingly reveal contradictions in the Buddhist view. Nagasena asks in return whether Milinda's chariot exists in addition to, independent of, or identical with its parts, their configuration, or both, to which Milinda admits the term "chariot" is just a convenient designator for the configured collection for which we have a use. Nagasena concludes that his name functions similarly. Ultimately, there is no independently existing chariot-thing, nor any self, but conventionally, pragmatically, we speak *as if* there is. If this is Siderits's view, it is an *as if* view of free will, not a substantive view.

While there is much to be said in favor of the two truths, I have the sense that there is more to this issue than mere semantics, as Nagasena suggests, and that the reason that the early Pudgalavādin Buddhists rejected the no-self view is that more needs to be said here; Thompson seems to agree.[45] Aronson also agrees, asserting that while there may be no substantive metaphysical entity that is a self, the empirical/psychological entity (self) is a highly functional, highly integrated causal/psychological system, and that otherwise, pathology would result.[46]

Arguing along lines more attuned to Aronson's view, Harvey,[47] Federman,[48] and Wallace[49] argue for what I have described as a Buddhist form of Semi-Compatibilism.[50] For slightly different reasons, each accepts the ultimate metaphysical unreality of a self but argues that the individual nonetheless has enough self-reflective, deliberative, volitional abilities to constitute a legitimate form of causal/functional self-regulative control to ground the sort of practical free will necessary to progress along the Buddhist path to liberation. I have argued extensively along similar lines.[51]

Indeed, the eightfold soteriological path—the path to Buddhist salvation, enlightenment—that the Buddha prescribed (in his "Fourth Noble Truth") makes clear that to attain nirvana, an individual must bring under their complete control their own views/beliefs, intentions/volitions, speech, actions, efforts, awareness and attentional focus,[52] to a degree of self-mastery that I have described as that possessed by a mind-body-controlling virtuoso.⁵³ The Buddha describes the Buddhist path to nirvana as requiring the individual's sustained, disciplined effort, success at which leads to a level of control over their own mind that he described as being able to think and not think whatever thoughts they wish to think or not think, among many other mental powers that would make the libertarian's "ability to do otherwise" seem relatively minimal: indeed, the Buddha describes certain psychic abilities attendant upon soteriological progress that appear to be at least supramundane, if not supernatural and/or titanic.⁵⁴

We need not pursue this line of thought further here. The point is the obvious fact that there is agency in Buddhism, but how to interpret it is precisely the question. I have addressed those issues elsewhere,⁵⁵ so here I will say only a few general things about Buddhist views of free will, and thereafter focus on my own views, according to which not only can there be Buddhist free will in the absence of an agent/self, but Buddhist thought actually makes possible the formulation of one powerful counterargument against all the skeptical arguments discussed in the section "The Free Will Problem in Western Philosophy," earlier in this chapter.

I have acknowledged that there are Buddhist free will skeptics primarily because nonself suggests nonagency, but there are also Buddhist free will optimists. Buddhism divides somewhat loosely into earlier and later traditions; among the earlier traditions, the only surviving one is Theravāda, the Way of the Elders, but there are many living variations on later, Mahāyāna Buddhism. Considerations of space prevent further elaboration here, but suffice it to say, simplifying greatly, that Theravāda is committed to a kind of atomistic reductionist foundationalism, whereas Mahāyāna embraces a nonfoundational and significantly antirealist sort of holism. There are many significant variations within these divisions—too many to even sketch out here. Earlier and later Buddhists also embrace the two-truths doctrine, but they interpret it differently. Most Theravādins argue for a conventional-level acceptance of free will and an ultimate-level rejection,[56] whereas most Mahāyānists tend to reject free will altogether.[57]

While most Western philosophers are certainly interested in what particular philosophers in another tradition *have* said, what is more interesting from the Western philosophical perspective is what they *can* say, given their doctrinal and other commitments. Both subjects matter, but Buddhists can say an awful lot more than what they have said to date. Thus, I shall hereafter set aside what particular Buddhists *have* said about free will and focus on what they *can* say.[58]

A Possible Buddhist Counterargument

Thus, Buddhists can argue that if *the core belief* of Buddhism is plausible (namely, that the meditation virtuoso can attain enlightenment),[59] then it follows that even an unenlightened but highly advanced adept, which Buddhists call an *ārya* ("noble one"), can embody and enact the defeat of all the free will skeptical arguments set forth in the section "The Free Will Problem in Western Philosophy," in one simple move: she is able to completely detach from her current mental state and all its actual and possible conditioning influences just prior to and at the moment of choice, *regardless of whether that mental state was produced manipulatively, deterministically, indeterministically, or otherwise.*

Indeed, the Buddha describes the moments just prior to his own enlightenment as involving his being tempted by supernatural beings in possession of titanic, if not godlike, psychic powers of deception (e.g., Mara, the Buddhist equivalent of Satan, among others). He was uninfluenced by them. Arguably, it would not matter to an *ārya* if they happened to be a brain in a vat or a digital being in a simulated world: if they cultivated the powers that the Buddhist path prescribes, they could still attain nirvana. In fact, the word "Buddha" means "awakened," and upon awakening or enlightenment, the Buddha spoke about the mind/body/world as if it was equivalent to one of these illusions—as dreamlike.

If this seems too easy, perhaps it is. It requires the non-Buddhist to accept certain basic premises that the Buddhist presupposes, such as that there is such a thing as mental causation—indeed, very powerful forms of it—despite there being no real self. The one form of free will skepticism to which the Buddhist so far remains theoretically vulnerable here is from the epiphenomenalist, who denies mental causation altogether; however, few philosophers of mind, cognitive scientists, and neuroscientists still take epiphenomenalism seriously. As for the ubiquity of cognitive errors being uncovered by recent science, Buddhism is certainly not threatened by them, as it has been a champion of the central cognitive error for millennia—that of our dearest self—not to mention its embrace of the unreality of wholes (composing everything else in the world), or of a creator, among others.

In conclusion, Buddhists have disagreed over whether it makes more sense for them to reject free will outright; to embrace some form of two-tiered conventional/ultimate view, according to which there is free will at the conventional but not the ultimate level; or at both levels. However, the Buddha himself not only rejected and ridiculed the main opposites of free will concerning inevitable causation by gods, fate, matter, and chance (divine determinism, fatalism, physical determinism, and indeterminism, respectively), as well as by karma, but he prescribed practices that apparently enhance agential effectiveness to virtuoso levels on the path to the realization that there is no real agent/self. I have described this as "agentless agency."[60]

An "agent" is a *thing*, while "agency" involves *abilities* and is a *process*. One of the fundamental insights of the Buddha's enlightenment is that everything is impermanent, in constant flux—all processes, no things. Nothing lasts long enough—more than a moment—to count as an agent/thing. But this no more entails that there is no agency than it entails—to use an awkward but effective analogy I've used before—that there is no difference between those who are continent and those who are not.[61] Regardless of whether there is a self and whether the world is deterministic, the continent can control the release of their bladders, whereas the incontinent cannot; the latter is governed by purely hydraulic factors in the bladder, whereas the former involves a feedback loop through conscious volitional centers.

I said earlier in this chapter that the fact that there is no static agent/self might entail that there is no static entity that is the "speaker," but that does not entail that there is no speech, nor that speech just happens, without volition. Intuitively, it is psychologically if not logically impossible for true speech—which is intentional and meaningful, not mere sounds—to occur without consciousness and/or volition. Speech alone involves agency. The Buddha spoke rather intentionally, and quite masterfully. How to explicate agentless agency is a task for another time, but surely the Buddha *spoke*. Were that not so, there would be no Buddhism.

NOTES

1. Owen Flanagan, "Negative Dialectics in Comparative Philosophy: The Case of Buddhist Free Will Quietism," in *Buddhist Perspectives on Free Will: Agentless Agency?*, ed. R. Repetti (London: Routledge, 2016), 59–71.
2. J. Garfield, "Just Another Word for Nothing Left to Lose: Freedom, Agency and Ethics for Mādhyamikas," in *Free Will, Agency, and Selfhood*

in Indian Philosophy, ed. Matthew R. Dasti and Edwin F. Bryant (New York: Oxford University Press, 2014), 164–85.

3. There are several reasons to doubt the Augustinian account in the text: children possess many of the free will–type intuitions numbered in the text; at a certain age, they shift from thinking that free will involves being able to do what you want to thinking that it involves being able to *not* do what you want. See T. Kushnir, A. Gopnik, N. Chemyak, E. Seiver, and H. M. Wellman, "Developing Intuitions about Free Will between Ages Four and Six," *Cognition* 138 (2015): 79–101. Also, pre-Augustinian biblical passages suggest a belief in free will regarding divine punishment for our choices; and the pre-Augustinian Buddha presupposed abilities we associate with free will, although he lacked the term and disbelieved in any creator deity, and thus lacked any theodicy-based need for free will.

4. For an insightful collection on the problem of divine foreknowledge and free will, see J. M. Fischer, ed., *God, Foreknowledge, and Freedom* (Stanford, CA: Stanford University Press, 1989). For an analysis of ways that various forms of free will skepticism (concerning the timelessness of truth values, divine foreknowledge, and determinism) share basic logical features, see R. Repetti, *The Counterfactual Theory of Free Will: A Genuinely Deterministic Form of Soft Determinism* (Saarbrücken, Germany: LAP Lambert Academic, 2010).

5. We could use the inclusive sense of "or," which permits both determinism and indeterminism to be true, but they would have to be true in two different domains (i.e., macro and micro, respectively), but the result would be the same (viz., that determinism is not universally true of "every" event). Some philosophers, such as Honderich, argue that it doesn't matter because indeterminism at the quantum level is so infinitesimal that its influence cannot affect a single neuron, but this unestablished *empirical* prediction ignores the fact that compatibilism is a *logical* claim. T. Honderich, *How Free Are You?* (New York: Oxford University Press, 1993).

6. P. van Inwagen, *An Essay on Free Will* (Oxford: Oxford University Press, 1983).

7. R. Kane, *The Significance of Free Will* (New York: Oxford University Press, 1996). There are other forms of libertarianism, but space

considerations prevent discussion of them here, and Robert Kane's is arguably the best representative of them.
8. G. Strawson, "The Impossibility of Moral Responsibility," *Philosophical Studies* 75, no. 1–2 (1994): 5–24.
9. R. Repetti, "I Could Have Done Otherwise, Had I Wanted To," in *Clarity and Vision: An Introduction to Philosophy*, 2nd ed., ed. Ben Abelson, Marie Friquegnon, and Raziel Abelson (Dubuque, IA: Kendall Hunt, 2018), chap. 6.
10. H. Frankfurt, "Alternate Possibilities and Moral Responsibility," *Journal of Philosophy* 66, no. 23 (1969): 829–39.
11. H. Frankfurt, "Freedom of the Will and the Concept of a Person," *Journal of Philosophy* 68, no. 1 (1971): 5–20.
12. G. Watson, ed., *Free Will: Oxford Readings in Philosophy* (New York: Oxford University Press, 2003).
13. For a fairly representative collection of such free will skeptical views, see G. D. Caruso, ed., *Exploring the Illusion of Free Will and Moral Responsibility* (Lanham, MD: Lexington Books, 2013).
14. D. Parfit, *Reasons and Persons* (New York: Oxford University Press, 1987).
15. J. Garfield, *Engaging Buddhism: Why It Matters to Philosophy* (Oxford: Oxford University Press, 2015).
16. C. Goodman, "Resentment and Reality: Buddhism on Moral Responsibility," *American Philosophical Quarterly* 39, no. 4 (2002): 359–372.
17. See the essays by G. Strawson and by S. Blackmore in R. Repetti, ed., *Buddhist Perspectives on Free Will: Agentless Agency?* (London: Routledge, 2017).
18. See also the essays by J. Garfield, O. Flanagan, and M. T. Adam in Repetti, *Buddhist Perspectives on Free Will*.
19. R. Repetti, "Buddhist Reductionism and Free Will: Paleo-Compatibilism," *Journal of Buddhist Ethics* 19 (2012).
20. "Flanagan, "Negative Dialectics in Comparative Philosophy"; Garfield, "Just Another Word for Nothing Left to Lose."
21. A. Federman, "What Kind of Free Will Did the Buddha Teach?," *Philosophy East and West* 60, no. 1 (2010): 1–19; P. Harvey, "'Freedom of the Will' in the Light of Theravāda Buddhist Teachings," *Journal of Buddhist Ethics* 14 (2007): 35–98; R. Repetti, "Meditation and Mental

Freedom: A Buddhist Theory of Free Will," *Journal of Buddhist Ethics* 17 (2010cb): 166–212; Repetti, "Agentless Agency: The Soft Compatibilist Argument from Buddhist Meditation, Mind-Mastery, Evitabilism, and Mental Freedom," in Repetti, *Buddhist Perspectives on Free Will*, 193–206; Repetti, *Buddhism, Meditation, and Free Will: A Theory of Mental Freedom* (London: Routledge, 2019). For a variety of such views, see Repetti, *Buddhist Perspectives on Free Will*.

22. Garfield, "Just Another Word for Nothing Left to Lose."
23. P. Harvey, "Psychological versus Metaphysical Agents: A Theravāda Buddhist View of Free Will and Moral Responsibility," in Repetti, *Buddhist Perspectives on Free Will: Agentless Agency?*, 158–70.
24. Goodman, "Resentment and Reality."
25. C. Gowans, "Why There Was No 'Problem of Freedom and Determinism' in Indian Buddhism," in Repetti, *Buddhist Perspectives on Free Will*, chap. 1.
26. For a series of articles reviewing the recent discussions of free will within Buddhism, see R. Repetti, "Meditation and Mental Freedom: A Buddhist Theory of Free Will," *Journal of Buddhist Ethics* 17 (2010): 166–212; R. Repetti, "Earlier Buddhist Theories of Free Will: Compatibilism," *Journal of Buddhist Ethics* 17 (2010): 279–310; R. Repetti, "Buddhist Reductionism and Free Will: Paleo-Compatibilism," *Journal of Buddhist Ethics* 19 (2012): 33–95; R. Repetti, "Buddhist Hard Determinism: No Self, No Free Will, No Responsibility," *Journal of Buddhist Ethics* 19 (2012): 130–97; and R. Repetti, "Recent Buddhist Theories of Free Will: Compatibilism, Incompatibilism, and Beyond," *Journal of Buddhist Ethics* 21 (2014): 279–352. See also R. Repetti, "Buddhist Meditation and the Possibility of Free Will," *Science, Religion and Culture* 2, no. 2 (2015): 81–98; R. Repetti, "Agentless Agency: The Soft Compatibilist Argument from Buddhist Meditation, Mind-Mastery, Evitabilism, and Mental Freedom," in R. Repetti, ed., *Buddhist Perspectives on Free Will*, 193–206; and indeed the entire Repetti, *Buddhist Perspectives on Free Will*.
27. Aronson attempts to reconcile the two major opposing interpretations by way of the "two truths" distinction, between conventional, pragmatic-reality-level discourse and ultimate-reality-level discourse. Harvey B. Aronson, *Buddhist Practice on Western Ground: Reconciling Eastern Ideals and Western Psychology* (London: Shambhala, 2004).

28. L. Priestley, *Pudgalavāda Buddhism: The Reality of the Indeterminate Self* (Toronto: Centre for South Asian Studies, University of Toronto, 1999).
29. For an excellent collection of representative essays on the various leading positions within this area of inquiry and how they compare with positions in both Indian and contemporary analytic philosophy and phenomenology, see M. Siderits, E. Thompson, and D. Zahavi, eds., *Self, No Self? Perspectives from Analytic, Phenomenological, and Indian Traditions* (Oxford: Oxford University Press, 2011). For an in-depth argument in support of the self-reflexive model of consciousness, see Christian Coseru, *Perceiving Reality: Consciousness, Intentionality, and Cognition in Buddhist Philosophy* (New York: Oxford University Press, 2012); for his argument against the Buddhist rejection of free will and the self on the grounds that such a conception cannot bear the weight of Buddhist ethics, see Christian Coseru, "Freedom from Responsibility: Agent-Neutral Consequentialism and the Bodhisattva Ideal," in Repetti, *Buddhist Perspectives on Free Will*, 92–112.
30. Repetti, "Agentless Agency"; Repetti, *Buddhism, Meditation, and Free Will*.
31. See Harvey, " 'Freedom of the Will' in the Light of Theravāda Buddhist Teachings," 35–98; Asaf Federman, "What Kind of Free Will Did the Buddha Teach?"; and B. A. Wallace, "A Buddhist View of Free Will: Beyond Determinism and Indeterminism," *Journal of Consciousness Studies* 18, no. 3–4 (2011): 217–33, reprinted in Repetti, *Buddhist Perspectives on Free Will*, 113–22.
32. Garfield, *Engaging Buddhism*.
33. Repetti, "Meditation and Mental Freedom."
34. W. Rāhula, *What the Buddha Taught* (New York: Grove Press, 1974).
35. F. Story, *Dimensions of Buddhist Thought: Essays and Dialogues* (Kandy, Sri Lanka: Buddhist Publication Society, 1976).
36. D. J. Kalupahana, *Buddhist Philosophy: A Historical Analysis* (Honolulu: University Press of Hawaii, 1976); Kalupahana, *A History of Buddhist Philosophy: Continuities and Discontinuities* (Honolulu: University of Hawaii Press, 1992); Kalupahana, *Ethics in Early Buddhism* (Honolulu: University Press of Hawaii, 1995).
37. L. O. Gómez, "Some Aspects of the Free Will Question in the Nikāyas," *Philosophy East and West* 25 (1975): 81–90.

38. Harvey, "'Freedom of the Will' in the Light of Theravāda Buddhist Teachings,"
39. Repetti, "Meditation and Mental Freedom."
40. Harvey, "'Freedom of the Will' in the Light of Theravāda Buddhist Teachings"; Federman, "What Kind of Free Will Did the Buddha Teach?"; N. F. Gier and P. Kjellberg. "Buddhism and the Freedom of the Will: Pali and Mahayanist Responses," in *Freedom and Determinism*, ed. Joseph Keim Campbell, Michael O'Rourke, and David Shier (Cambridge, MA: MIT Press, 2004), 277–304.
41. Story, *Dimensions of Buddhist Thought*; Gómez, "Some Aspects of the Free Will Question in the Nikāyas"; Kalupahana, *Buddhist Philosophy*; Kalupahana, *A History of Buddhist Philosophy*; Kalupahana, *Ethics in Early Buddhism*.
42. See Repetti, "Earlier Buddhist Theories of Free Will: Compatibilism," for a critical review of these early-period discussions of free will among Buddhist philosophers.
43. M. Siderits, "Buddhist Paleocompatibilism," in Repetti, *Buddhist Perspectives on Free Will: Agentless Agency?*, 133–47.
44. See Repetti, "Buddhist Reductionism and Free Will: Paleo-Compatibilism," for a critique of this view.
45. E. Thompson, *Waking, Dreaming, Being: Self and Consciousness in Neuroscience, Meditation, and Philosophy* (New York: Columbia University Press, 2015).
46. Aronson, *Buddhist Practice on Western Ground*.
47. Harvey, "'Freedom of the Will' in the Light of Theravāda Buddhist Teachings"; Harvey, Harvey, "Psychological versus Metaphysical Agents."
48. Federman, "What Kind of Free Will Did the Buddha Teach?"
49. Wallace, "A Buddhist View of Free Will."
50. Repetti, "Agentless Agency."
51. Repetti, "Meditation and Mental Freedom"; Repetti, "Buddhist Meditation and the Possibility of Free Will"; Repetti, "Agentless Agency"; R. Repetti, "What Do Buddhists Think About Free Will?," in *A Mirror Is for Reflection: Understanding Buddhist Ethics*, ed. J. H. Davis (New York: Oxford University Press, 2017), 257–75; Repetti, "I Could Have Done Otherwise, Had I Wanted To"; Repetti, *Buddhism, Meditation, and Free Will*; R. Repetti, "A Defense of *Buddhism, Meditation, and Free Will*: A

Theory of Mental Freedom," *Zygon* 55, no. 2 (2020): 540–64; R. Repetti, "Freedom of the Mind: Buddhist Soft Compatibilism," *Philosophy East and West* 70, no. 1 (2020): 174–95.

52. Repetti, "Meditation and Mental Freedom"; Repetti, "Buddhist Meditation and the Possibility of Free Will"; Repetti, "Agentless Agency"; K. Meyers, "Free Persons, Empty Selves: Freedom and Agency in Light of the Two Truths," in *Free Will, Agency, and Selfhood in Indian Philosophy*, ed. M. Dasti and E. F. Bryant (New York: Oxford University Press, 2014), 41–67; Meyers, "Grasping Snakes: Reflections on Free Will, Samādhi, and Dharmas," in Repetti, *Buddhist Perspectives on Free Will: Agentless Agency?*, 182–92.
53. Repetti, "Agentless Agency": Repetti, "What Do Buddhists Think About Free Will?"; Repetti, "I Could Have Done Otherwise, Had I Wanted To"; Repetti, *Buddhism, Meditation, and Free Will*; Repetti, "A Defense of *Buddhism, Meditation, and Free Will: A Theory of Mental Freedom*"; Repetti, "Freedom of the Mind."
54. Meyers, "Free Persons, Empty Selves"; Meyers, "Grasping Snakes."
55. See Repetti, *Buddhist Perspectives on Free Will*.
56. See Mark Siderits, "Buddhist Paleocompatibilism," in Repetti, *Buddhist Perspectives on Free Will*, 133–47, for a reductionist compatibilism; also see Harvey, "'Freedom of the Will' in the Light of Theravāda Buddhist Teachings; and Federman, "What Kind of Free Will Did the Buddha Teach?"
57. Garfield, "Just Another Word for Nothing Left to Lose." Cf. Wallace, "A Buddhist View of Free Will"; and E. McRae, "Emotions and Choice: Lessons from Tsongkhapa," in Repetti, *Buddhist Perspectives on Free Will*, 170–81.
58. The interested reader can explore most of these issues in Repetti, *Buddhist Perspectives on Free Will*; "Meditation and Mental Freedom"; "Earlier Buddhist Theories of Free Will: Compatibilism"; "Buddhist Reductionism and Free Will: Paleo-Compatibilism"; "Recent Buddhist Theories of Free Will"; and "Buddhist Meditation and the Possibility of Free Will."
59. Repetti, *Buddhism, Meditation, and Free Will*.
60. Repetti, "Agentless Agency."
61. Repetti, "Meditation and Mental Freedom"; Repetti, *Buddhism, Meditation, and Free Will*.

BIBLIOGRAPHY

Aronson, H. B. *Buddhist Practice on Western Ground: Reconciling Eastern Ideals and Western Psychology*. London: Shambhala, 2004.

Caruso, G. D., ed. *Exploring the Illusion of Free Will and Moral Responsibility*. Lanham, MD: Lexington Books, 2013.

Coseru, C. "Freedom from Responsibility: Agent-Neutral Consequentialism and the Bodhisattva Ideal." In *Buddhist Perspectives on Free Will: Agentless Agency?*, ed. R. Repetti, 92–112. London: Routledge, 2016.

Coseru, C. *Perceiving Reality: Consciousness, Intentionality, and Cognition in Buddhist Philosophy*. New York: Oxford University Press, 2012.

Federman, A. "What Kind of Free Will Did the Buddha Teach?" *Philosophy East and West* 60, no. 1 (2010): 1–19.

Fischer, J. M., ed. *God, Foreknowledge, and Freedom*. Stanford, CA: Stanford University Press, 1989.

Flanagan, Owen. "Negative Dialectics in Comparative Philosophy: The Case of Buddhist Free Will Quietism." In *Buddhist Perspectives on Free Will: Agentless Agency?*, ed. R. Repetti, 59–71. London: Routledge, 2016.

Frankfurt, H. "Alternate Possibilities and Moral Responsibility." *Journal of Philosophy* 66, no. 23 (1969): 829–39.

Frankfurt, H. "Freedom of the Will and the Concept of a Person." *Journal of Philosophy* 68, no. 1 (1971): 5–20.

Garfield, Jay L. *Engaging Buddhism: Why It Matters to Philosophy*. Oxford: Oxford University Press, 2015.

Garfield, J. "Just Another Word for Nothing Left to Lose: Freedom, Agency and Ethics for Mādhyamikas." In *Free Will, Agency, and Selfhood in Indian Philosophy*, ed. Matthew R. Dasti and Edwin F. Bryant (New York: Oxford University Press, 2014), 164–85; reprinted in *Buddhist Perspectives on Free Will: Agentless Agency?*, ed. R. Repetti, 45–58. London: Routledge, 2016.

Gier, N. F., and P. Kjellberg. "Buddhism and the Freedom of the Will: Pali and Mahayanist Responses." In *Freedom and Determinism*, ed. Joseph Keim Campbell, Michael O'Rourke, and David Shier, 277–304. Cambridge, MA: MIT Press, 2004.

Gómez, L. O. "Some Aspects of the Free Will Question in the Nikāyas." *Philosophy East and West* 25 (1975): 81–90.

Goodman, C. "Resentment and Reality: Buddhism on Moral Responsibility." *American Philosophical Quarterly* 39, no. 4 (2002): 359–72.

Gowans, Christopher. "Why There Was No 'Problem of Freedom and Determinism' in Indian Buddhism." In *Buddhist Perspectives on Free Will: Agentless Agency?*, ed. R. Repetti, chap. 1. London: Routledge, 2016.

Harvey, P. "'Freedom of the Will' in the Light of Theravāda Buddhist Teachings." *Journal of Buddhist Ethics* 14 (2007): 35–98.

Harvey, P. "Psychological versus Metaphysical Agents: A Theravāda Buddhist View of Free Will and Moral Responsibility." In *Buddhist Perspectives on Free Will: Agentless Agency?*, ed. R. Repetti, 158–70. London: Routledge, 2016.

Honderich, T. *How Free Are You?* New York: Oxford University Press, 1993.

Kalupahana, David J. *Buddhist Philosophy: A Historical Analysis*. Honolulu: University Press of Hawaii, 1976.

Kalupahana, David J. *Ethics in Early Buddhism*. Honolulu: University Press of Hawaii, 1995.

Kalupahana, David J. *A History of Buddhist Philosophy: Continuities and Discontinuities*. Honolulu: University of Hawaii Press, 1992.

Kane, R. *The Significance of Free Will*. New York: Oxford University Press, 1996.

Kushnir, T., A. Gopnik, N. Chemyak, E. Seiver, and H. M. Wellman. "Developing Intuitions About Free Will Between Ages Four and Six." *Cognition* 138 (2015): 79–101.

McRae, E. "Emotions and Choice: Lessons from Tsongkhapa." In *Buddhist Perspectives on Free Will: Agentless Agency?*, ed. R. Repetti, 170–81. London: Routledge, 2016.

Meyers, K. "Free Persons, Empty Selves: Freedom and Agency in Light of the Two Truths." In *Free Will, Agency, and Selfhood in Indian Philosophy*, ed. M. Dasti and E. F. Bryant, 41–67. New York: Oxford University Press, 2014.

Meyers, K. "Grasping Snakes: Reflections on Free Will, *Samādhi*, and *Dharmas*." In *Buddhist Perspectives on Free Will: Agentless Agency?*, ed. R. Repetti, 182–92. London: Routledge, 2016.

Parfit, D. *Reasons and Persons*. New York: Oxford University Press, 1987.

Priestley, L. *Pudgalavāda Buddhism: The Reality of the Indeterminate Self*. Toronto: Centre for South Asian Studies, University of Toronto, 1999.

Rāhula, Walpola. *What the Buddha Taught*. New York: Grove Press, 1974.

Repetti, R. "Agentless Agency: The Soft Compatibilist Argument from Buddhist Meditation, Mind-Mastery, Evitabilism, and Mental Freedom." In *Buddhist Perspectives on Free Will: Agentless Agency?*, ed. R. Repetti, 193–206. London: Routledge 2016.

Repetti, R. "Buddhist Hard Determinism: No Self, No Free Will, No Responsibility." *Journal of Buddhist Ethics* 19 (2012): 130–97.

Repetti, R. *Buddhism, Meditation, and Free Will: A Theory of Mental Freedom.* London: Routledge, 2019.

Repetti, R. "Buddhist Meditation and the Possibility of Free Will." *Science, Religion, and Culture* 2, no. 2 (2015): 81–98.

Repetti, R., ed. *Buddhist Perspectives on Free Will: Agentless Agency?* London: Routledge, 2016.

Repetti, R. "Buddhist Reductionism and Free Will: Paleo-Compatibilism." *Journal of Buddhist Ethics* 19 (2012): 33–95.

Repetti, R. *The Counterfactual Theory of Free Will: A Genuinely Deterministic Form of Soft Determinism.* Saarbrücken, Germany: LAP Lambert Academic, 2010.

Repetti, R. "A Defense of *Buddhism, Meditation, and Free Will: A Theory of Mental Freedom.*" *Zygon* 55, no. 2 (2020): 540–564.

Repetti, R. "Earlier Buddhist Theories of Free Will: Compatibilism." *Journal of Buddhist Ethics* 17 (2010): 279–310.

Repetti, R. "Freedom of the Mind: Buddhist Soft Compatibilism." *Philosophy East and West* 70, no. 1 (2020): 174–195.

Repetti, R. "I Could Have Done Otherwise, Had I Wanted To." In *Clarity and Vision: An Introduction to Philosophy*, 2nd ed., ed. Ben Abelson, Marie Friquegnon, and Raziel Abelson, chap. 6. Dubuque, IA: Kendall Hunt, 2018.

Repetti, R. "Meditation and Mental Freedom: A Buddhist Theory of Free Will." *Journal of Buddhist Ethics* 17 (2010): 166–212.

Repetti, R. "Recent Buddhist Theories of Free Will: Compatibilism, Incompatibilism, and Beyond." *Journal of Buddhist Ethics* 21 (2014): 279–352.

Repetti, R. "What Do Buddhists Think About Free Will?" In *A Mirror Is for Reflection: Understanding Buddhist Ethics*, ed. J. H. Davis, 257-275. New York: Oxford University Press, 2017.

Siderits, Mark. "Buddhist Paleocompatibilism." In *Buddhist Perspectives on Free Will: Agentless Agency?*, ed. R. Repetti, 133–47. London: Routledge, 2016.

Siderits, M., E. Thompson, and D. Zahavi, eds. *Self, No Self? Perspectives from Analytic, Phenomenological, and Indian Traditions*. Oxford: Oxford University Press, 2011.

Story, F. *Dimensions of Buddhist Thought: Essays and Dialogues*. Kandy, Sri Lanka: Buddhist Publication Society, 1976.

Strawson, G. "The Impossibility of Moral Responsibility," *Philosophical Studies* 75, no. 1–2 (1994): 5–24.

Thompson, E. *Waking, Dreaming, Being: Self and Consciousness in Neuroscience, Meditation, and Philosophy*. New York: Columbia University Press, 2015.

Van Inwagen, P. *An Essay on Free Will*. Oxford: Oxford University Press, 1983.

Wallace, B. A. "A Buddhist View of Free Will: Beyond Determinism and Indeterminism." *Journal of Consciousness Studies* 18, no. 3–4 (2011): 217–33; reprinted in R. Repetti, ed., *Buddhist Perspectives on Free Will: Agentless Agency?* 113–22. London: Routledge, 2016.

Watson, G., ed. *Free Will: Oxford Readings in Philosophy*. New York: Oxford University Press, 2003.

6

WHY DO BAD THINGS HAPPEN TO GOOD PEOPLE?

"And None of Us Deserving the Cruelty or the Grace": Buddhism and the Problem of Evil

AMBER D. CARPENTER

The Indian theory of karma is, according to Max Weber, the most perfect solution to the problem of evil.[1] This judgment has cast a long shadow over scholarly discourse in the twentieth century, with partisans lining up on one side or the other on the question of whether karma does or does not solve the problem of evil.[2] Weber's claim was intended, and taken by some who endorsed it, to be true of any theory of karma (e.g., Buddhist, Hindu, Jaina) in spite of substantial differences,[3] in virtue of what they all have in common—namely, the idea that good or ill befalls a person according to the good or evil of their deeds.

One might well wonder, however, whether the Buddhism—or indeed any worldview incorporating karma—has a problem of evil to solve in the first place. In its classic formulation, the problem of evil is pegged to belief in a god of a very specific sort. The *locus classicus* for the problem is Job, who was upright and honored God, and who precisely for that reason was made to suffer the appalling loss of wealth, friends, family, and health. How could a god who is supremely good and just, and who moreover has it in His power to make it otherwise, allow this to happen? And is it not just Job. The wicked have power, as Psalm 35 observes, and flourish like a green bay tree; the just do not always fare so well. The problem of evil is a problem of proportion and commensurability—not simply that "the world is full of suffering,"[4] but that this suffering is *undeserved*, or wildly out of all proportion with the moral qualities of the sufferer. This is indeed the heart of Ivan Karamazov's famous complaint, and what makes it so compelling.[5] Such conspicuous and grotesque mismatch of moral worth to natural flourishing impugns either God's power or His goodness—or else His very existence.[6] But since Indian Buddhists will quite happily endorse the lattermost option—there simply is no creative, controlling power organizing reality—the flourishing of the wicked and suffering of the virtuous do not so much pose a problem, we might think, as simply describe the nature of things. Such an outlook might have been shared by the archaic Greeks, as that world is evoked by Homer in the *Iliad* and the *Odyssey*. There are gods, of course; but none of them has the monopoly on power together with the reliable goodness necessary to make the flourishing of the wicked and the suffering of the virtuous a *problem*.

It may be, however, that the disbeliever cannot be rid of the problem of evil so easily—at least so several in the European tradition have thought, and Weber is evidently one of them.[7] Although formulated most sharply in terms of an all-powerful and benevolent God, the problem of evil, they would insist, challenges all of us. It is, quite simply, intolerable that we should dwell in a condition in which the consequences of our actions are wildly unfitting or disproportionate. If we truly believed there was no fit or proportion between the quality of our actions and the results, we would find ourselves incapable of acting—at least, incapable of prosecuting consistently any project over time, committing ourselves to principle, and on the whole acting *for reasons*. And any other such so-called action is mere behavior, not action at all.

Thus Plato and Aristotle—neither of whom believed in a creator-god capable of affecting the course of events in daily life—both have the problem of evil. For both, we are to understand our own actions by relation to the larger, rational, and providential order of the universe. But if the universe is well arranged—that is, arranged in such a way that we can make sense of what is good for us and good to do in light of that arrangement—then why do the wicked flourish and the good sometimes suffer miserable fates here and now? Many of Plato's myths look designed to address this human need for moral order and proportion in the world within which our actions take place.[8] Many Chinese philosophers, it has been argued, have the same basic problem, without commitment to the creator-god of the Mediterranean monotheisms.[9]

On this view, only something like the "tragic" worldview of Sophocles may be immune to the classic problem of evil since there is no expectation that the world should be fair—with goods distributed according to moral or ethical merit—in the first place. It is the lamentable but simple fact of the matter that there is no proportion between actions and their consequences. But while insisting there is nothing for it but to accept this hard fate, Sophocles also (and relatedly) observes darkly, "It is best for a man that he should never be born; second-best, having been born, that he should return whence he came—and quickly."[10] While a bit of bracing pessimism may be salutary, many find such acceptance difficult to maintain once outside the amphitheater. To find reason to go on, to act in the world and to value and care, we must be able to hope that a fair and measured arrangement is possible. That such fair arrangement is not evident in our daily lives *just is* the problem of evil. This is a problem of evil that we all have, regardless of our theistic convictions.

Nevertheless, in what follows I shall argue that the Buddhists, on the whole, did not have the problem of evil and, in particular, they often did not use the doctrine of karma to justify suffering or render it explicable and tolerable to reason. But this is not for reasons of Sophoclean pessimism. Rather a much more salutary lesson is to be drawn regarding the fact of suffering and our aversion to it. While karma is indeed invoked—or deliberately *not* invoked—to address effectively this psychological "problem of suffering," it does so by undermining the core presumption underlying the problem of evil: namely, that suffering is something *deserved*, that such desert could ever function as an adequate explanation, and that this sort of explanation is something we ought to be demanding in the first place.

KARMA AND SUFFERING EVIL IN BUDDHISM

If the doctrine of karma is seen as the perfect solution to the problem of evil, it is because the doctrine just is a commitment to the perfect fit between the moral quality of one's actions and the felt quality of one's subsequent experiences. There are variations across both Buddhist and non-Buddhist doctrines about the exact fit—is it the deed, the consequence, or the intention behind it that matters more in determining the quality of the consequences for the agent? Are the results experienced primarily as external, nonmoral goods and evils, as positive and negative internal states, or perhaps as the accretion of a spiritually inhibiting substance about one's person? Does a commitment to such a doctrine of karma require a commitment to literal rebirth? But one shared point in all such doctrines of karma is that there is no judge or adjudicator of actions standing serenely above all of the manifold actions and results; no god or gods *implement* karmic results, so there is no agent punishing or rewarding the actions of human beings (or indeed of nonhuman beings).[11] The fit between action and result is perfect because it is simply the natural unfolding of events according to their kind. On the karma principle, no one *blames and punishes* you for stealing a sheep; your sheep-stealing itself gives rise to the suffering that befalls you somewhere down the road.

But this can solve the problem of evil only if *all* the misery that befalls a person can be traced to some previous wicked deed—otherwise there is still unexplained, apparently undeserved suffering, and that is precisely the problem of evil. Yet the Buddhists, at least, do not hold that *all* suffering is to be traced back to a previous misdeed. Take the *Milindapañha* (*Milinda's Questions*), a text from about the first century CE that purports to be a record of a lengthy encounter between the Greek king Menander (Pāli: *Milinda*), who reigned in Bactria (today's Afghanistan) in the second century BCE, and the Buddhist monk Nāgasena (possibly historical, possibly an invention of the text). In it, the king interrogates Nāgasena extensively on points of Buddhist thought, and the monk replies equally extensively, often by offering metaphors or similes that should indicate the correct, usually unanticipated, ways of considering the matter under examination. Often the king offers objections or dilemmas which Nāgasena must resolve or dissolve, as in this passage from *Milindapañha* IV.1.viii.

The Buddha, King Milinda reminds us, is said to have "burnt up all *kamma*."[12] It is constitutive of attaining enlightenment that all previous intentional acts have had their result, and no more such acts have set anything further in motion. This is what it means for the cycle of *saṃsāra*—the endless fluctuation of good and evil fortune—to have ceased. How is it then, the king asks, that the Buddha nevertheless suffered pain when someone dropped a stone on him, and required medical attention for dysentery? If he suffered injury, pain, or illness, surely this must indicate that there was at that point some previous unexpiated bad action of his own at the root of it. Nāgasena's reply is, perhaps, surprising:

> "Sire," he says, "not all that is experienced is rooted in *kamma*. What is experienced, sire, arises from eight (material) causes by reason of which many beings experience feelings. What are the eight? Some things that are experienced here, sire, arise originating in winds (of the body), [135] arise originating in bile . . . originating in phlegm . . . arise resulting from a union of the humours of the body . . . arise from a change of season . . . arise from the stress of circumstances . . . arise suddenly, some things that are experienced here, sire, arise born of the maturing of *kamma*."

That is, while every wicked deed is sure to result eventually in suffering of some kind for the perpetrator, not every episode of suffering can be traced back to some previous ill deed. For any given episode of natural or human-caused suffering, it *may* be that previous actions of the current sufferer caused it—but it may just as easily not be. The Buddha's foot was injured when his jealous cousin, Devadatta, tried to assassinate him by dropping a boulder on him from above, and the injury was painful. But this pain was not the fruition of some previous bad deed of the Buddha's—it is just the sort of thing that happens sometimes, due in this case to Devadatta's jealousy and having nothing in particular to do with the Buddha at all.[13]

The venerable Nāgasena is no radical free-thinker here. The claim he will repeat later in his conversations with the king (at MP 303) is based on passages in the Pāli canon of the Buddha's discourses, some of the oldest Buddhist material that has come down to us. In the *Sivaka Sutta* (SN 36.21), when asked whether he agrees with the claim that "whatever a person experiences, be it pleasure, pain or neither-pain-nor-pleasure, all that is caused by previous action,"[14] the Buddha offers the same manifold causes that Nāgasena offered the king:

> Some feelings, Sīvaka, arise here originating from bile disorders. . . . Some feelings, Sīvaka, arise here originating from phlegm disorders . . . from wind disorders . . . from an imbalance (of the three) . . . [some are] produced by change of climate . . . by careless behaviour . . . caused by assault . . . [some are] produced as the result of kamma. . . . [This] one can know for oneself, and that is considered to be true in the world.
>
> Now when those ascetics and brahmans hold such a doctrine and view as this, "whatever a person experiences, whether it be pleasant or painful or neither-painful-nor-pleasant, all that is caused by what was done in the past," then they overshoot what one knows by oneself and they overshoot what considered to be true in the world. Therefore, I say that this is wrong on the part of these ascetics and brahmins.[15]

Not just illness and injury, but even death can occur adventitiously, due to causes other than previous bad deeds. Although the text is confused about whether premature death that *is* a result of previous bad action should be "untimely," the *Milindapañha* is clear that there is such a thing as untimely death due to an assortment of physical causes, distinguished from previous karma. Nāgasena even quotes a verse of what he presumably took to be the Buddha's words, articulating this position: "From hunger, from thirst, if bitten by a snake, and from poison, by fire, water, a knife it is that one dies untimely. From winds, bile, phlegm, a union and the seasons, from stress, suddenly . . . it is that one dies untimely."[16]

The *Milindapañha* and the *Connected Discourses of the Buddha* are not obscure texts. Given this, it seems odd that several scholars have supposed that—for Buddhists as well as Hindus—the so-called doctrine of karma offers the perfect solution to the problem of evil,[17] with one contemporary scholar citing the "karmic principle of justice" as answering Job's problem in particular.[18] A more recent debate disputes how successful a solution it is, but both sides agree it is supposed to be one.[19]

But on the Buddhist view, karma cannot be an apt place to look for either a formulation of the problem of evil or its solution. For although bad action surely brings misfortune, some misfortune arises without a bad action for its cause; there may well be other causes of suffering—mundane, physical causes, not admitting of any further, meaningful explanation. Who is more "innocent" than the Buddha? And yet he got dysentery. Sometimes "the famished man, not obtaining any food . . . dies untimely even though there is a further (portion) of his lifespan" (MP 302)—not because he starved someone in a previous life, but simply because he could not get food in this one. The Buddhist will not insist, like Job's facile friends, that there must after all have been some vicious deed he committed in the past that is responsible for his current misery. Even supposing "you deserved it" *were* a global answer to the problem of evil, it is not one the Buddhist view of karma is in position to offer.[20]

It is also, I shall try to show, not the sort of answer a Buddhist would be inclined to give, could she be made to feel "the problem" in the first place. There is a structural reason for this, and an ethical one.

The structural reason is that the Buddhists had a rather uneasy relationship with karma from the first. Operating in a milieu in which denying that wicked deeds resulted in misery for the evildoer was considered a free license to wanton transgression, the Buddha incorporates appeals to karma throughout his teachings. Causing misery brings misery on oneself; causing happiness brings happiness, inexorably. This recourse to the principle of karma persists through the next several centuries of development of Buddhist thought in India; indeed, the denial of karma is often regarded as a wrong view, tantamount to the egregiously wrong view of nihilism.[21] But it does not sit altogether comfortably within a Buddhist framework.

The ethical reason is simply the first noble truth—the ubiquity of suffering—which is simply to be understood (SN 56.11). Understanding that suffering penetrates all of existence undermines the very distinction between "deserved" and "undeserved" suffering, or indeed the notion that suffering is the sort of thing that is *deserved*. If we are concerned *explain* suffering in some way that should trace it back to a fault in someone's actions, then we have failed to adopt the appropriate stance toward the basic fact of suffering, and thus to make the ethical transformation Buddhism advises.

CRACKS IN THE KARMA-RESULT STRUCTURE WITHIN BUDDHISM

The highest Buddhist aim is nirvana—the cessation of suffering. Mahāyāna Buddhism proposes we take the universal cessation of suffering as our aim; but whatever differences this may introduce in other respects, for the purposes of this discussion it amounts to much the same. Nirvana, individual or universal, is a cessation so complete that there is no more desire, action or effect, pleasant or unpleasant. Indeed, this is why King Milinda thought that the Buddha, fully awakened, should suffer no illness or injury.

The suffering characteristic of existence, through all its ups and downs, may be typically traced back to three roots—craving, aversion, and confusion; but confusion about the self is paramount. Cessation is achieved only through realizing the impersonality of our condition: "I do not see any doctrine of self," says the Buddha, "that would not arouse sorrow, lamentation, pain, grief, and despair in one who clings to it" (MN 22.22).

In particular, every conceivable candidate for the role of "myself" is transient and vulnerable, dependent upon countless factors for its nature, its arising, and its passing away. There is nothing that persists or controls, and thus nothing capable and *worthy* of being a self (MN 22.26)—of being gratified and aggrandized. This is a metaphysical antiholism that resists all teleology: there is nothing with respect to which the parts become meaningful, nothing in virtue of which something can become good.[22] When we have thoroughly understood that we are not persistent entities—enduring agents and subjects of experience—then the craving and clinging that inevitably cause suffering in its various forms will also cease. Without a self to protect and promote, the story goes, much of the motive for unwholesome behavior evaporates. With practice at seeing oneself and others as selfless, one's interest becomes turned toward the badness of suffering itself, with no distinction for whose suffering it is.[23]

Such psychological and practical changes do not happen easily, or instantly upon drawing the conclusion to a valid argument that there is no self. The habits of mind—of thinking and feeling—that we build up around the self are very deep and very persistent. It takes a great deal of patience and mental practice to begin to uproot the nest of emotive energy entangled in the conception of ourselves as independent agent-subjects (or substances), and to replace this with a recognition of the transient and mutually interdependent and conditioned nature of all things. Many mental and practical exercises, as well as endless similes and stories, are constructed with the aim of enabling us to make this understanding a thoroughgoing perspective shift. The principle of karma, however, seems to directly undermine this effort in two significant ways.

First, to the extent that karma is twinned with a belief in rebirth, it encourages us to trace out distinct individuals and regard each as the same enduring thing over time. This is not the ancient objection that karma (and the rebirth implied in it) is metaphysically incompatible with no-self; for this objection is perfectly resolvable by substituting a continuous succession of momentary entities for endurance of a single thing over time.[24] But even if we formally replace endurance with continuity, the karma principle requires us to individuate these continuities, and attend to their distinctness from one another as well as to their specific internal connectedness. Indeed even without literal rebirth, anything like the principle of karma would seem to require us to strongly differentiate and isolate one particular enduring entity—or determinate chain of continuity—as *the* cause, distinct from everything else. More extremely, if karma is to be a system of reward and punishment, then some individual or another has to be picked out as the *guilty party*—still "the same person" later, in whatever sense necessary to receive their just deserts. The evident incompatibility of this with a metaphysical ethics of no-self was pointed out by a minority Buddhist position (known as *pudgalavāda*), which cited it as a reason for positing "the person" as ultimately existing.[25]

The second tension between karma and the practice of seeing no-self arises when we suppose that karma is taken as an incentive: do good things now to get good things in the future; avoid evil deeds now to prevent evil befalling you in the future.

This simple and prevalent thought is in tension with the Buddhist view that we ought to give up our craving for and attachment to such goods as are ordinarily thought to come from karma. This is not to say, of course, that Buddhists eschew all such appeals in practice, or that such appeals *must* undermine the aims of the no-self claim.[26] But in the ordinary cases of which we might think in the context of solving the problem of evil, if the incentive works, it is because I am not yet seeing things at all correctly; and when I act under such incentives, I reinforce the perspective from which such goods are to be sought and such evils to be avoided.

These tensions have prompted some contemporary Buddhist scholars to recommend naturalizing the principle of karma[27]—not without some basis in the early literature[28]—while others suspect that karma was not in fact part of the *Buddha's* own view at all (again, perhaps not entirely without ground).[29] But references to karma pervade Indian Buddhist thought,[30] and insofar as they do, karma would seem—so far from solving any problem of evil—to undermine the specifically Buddhist solution to the problem of suffering. For according to the Buddhist diagnosis, thinking in terms of self causes suffering and must be eliminated; yet that very same thinking in terms of self is required when conceiving a result as the *result* of some previous action, connected by a distinct and unified causal chain. *Just to the extent* that it explains current suffering by previous bad action, it encourages just that clinging to thinking in terms of self as originator of action and owner of experiences that the Buddhists claim must be dismantled if suffering is to be eliminated. This effect is only exacerbated when karmic consequences are invoked as incentives for good behavior.

This brings us, then, to the ethical incongruity in treating karma as a solution to the problem of evil in Buddhism.

At its core, the proposal mistakenly presumes that the Buddhist acknowledges a problem of evil that *would* be solved, if only those suffering were to blame for their own sorry state. But taking any such (causal) explanation as a *justification*—that is, supposing that there is or ought to be a system of reward and punishment, of blame and guilt, and that this would somehow redeem suffering by giving meaning to it—is wholly antithetical to the Buddhist ethical outlook. To shed light on this, let us consider how karma does (and does not) figure in stories of ordinary life meant to inform ordinary life with the Buddhist perspective.

AND NONE OF US DESERVING THE CRUELTY OR THE GRACE

The sayings of the *Dhammapada* were collected across the subcontinent over several centuries. It has been observed that in many of these verses, there may be nothing particularly *Buddhist* about the moral advice offered. Some have doubted whether all of it was in fact originally Buddhist at all, or whether it was a collection of precepts in common currency, picked up and appropriated by whatever was the dominant religious view of the day. But a text is not just its words; it is also what is done with it. And certainly in what was done with the *Dhammapada*, it is a decidedly Buddhist text.

For instance, in order to illustrate the sage advice given in the verses and make it more alive, stories—sometimes several embedded within each other—were associated with each observation. Quasi-historical, these stories are full of a variety of characters and incidents from everyday life, often featuring monastics, and special guest appearances by the Buddha, who is said to have told the tales originally as part of his teachings.

In fifth-century Sri Lanka, these stories—which had been accumulated and circulating over more than 400 years—were translated into Pāli as the *Dhammapada-aṭṭakathā*, the *Commentary on the Dhammapada*.

We start in the middle of a lengthy and complicated tale illustrating the verse that reads, "Even while a man is gathering flowers and is absorbed in pleasure, death comes and carries him off, even as a mighty flood overwhelms a sleeping village." The fact that so complicated a tale is told to illustrate this verse is indeed very much to the point: in explicating loss, there is no straightforward "evil done then, evil suffered now"; it is always more involved, and more compromising.

Bandhula, a friend of King Pasenadi and commander-in-chief of his army, is a fair and honest judge, which wins him the enmity of powerful men. These men pour poison regarding Bandhula in the king's ear. Believing the slander, the king arranges the treacherous massacre of Bandhula, together with his thirty-two sons. His wife, Mallikā, receives the news while hosting the sangha's daily meal: " 'Your husband's head has been cut off and likewise the heads of your sons.' When she learned the news, she said not a word to anyone, but put the letter in a fold of her dress and ministered to the Congregation of Monks as if nothing had happened."[31] Shortly after, a servant drops a jar of ghee in front of the Elders, but

> the Captain of the Faith [Sariputta] said, "No notice should ever be taken of the breaking of anything that is capable of being broken." Thereupon Mallikā, drawing the letter from the fold of her dress, said, "They have just brought me this letter: 'The head of your husband has been cut off and the heads of your two and thirty sons likewise.' Yet even when I heard this, I took no thought. Much less, therefore, am I likely to take thought of the breaking of a mere jar, Reverend Sir."

Later, she advises her thirty-two widowed daughters-in-law:

> "Your husbands were free from guilt and have merely reaped the fruit of misdeeds in previous states of existence. Grieve not, nor lament. Cherish no resentment against the king." The king's spies listened to her words and went and told the king that they cherished no hatred of him. The king was overcome with emotion, went to Mallikā's residence, asked Mallikā and her daughters-in-law to forgive him, and granted Mallikā a boon. "I accept," said she.

Her request that the widows all be allowed to return to their families is granted.

Notice first the apparently paradoxical nature of Mallikā's consolatory words: "Your husbands were free from guilt and have merely reaped the fruit of misdeeds in previous states of existence."[32] There is a curious fluidity of identity at work here. Their *husbands* are the persons who were born at a particular time and place to Mallikā and Bandhula, were boys and grew into the adult men they married. *These* persons are guilt-free, the crimes for which they were killed were fabricated—and their wives should take some solace in that. These persons are also, however, direct inheritors-by-continuity of previous existences and the deeds that constituted them. Those previous deeds set in motion a chain of causes that would eventually have issued in some such circumstance as the current one. For each wife, the man she married both is and is not the person who committed misdeeds in a previous life.

"Reaping the fruit" is not the language of retribution, nor of desert.[33] It is natural cause and effect that is being appealed to here: the wives are being encouraged to see their innocent husbands' deaths as, in a way, the coming to fruition of the larger, extended and beginningless personal factors that are directly, though distantly, responsible for the men's births in this life.³⁴ They are at the same time, then, being explicitly *diverted* from looking at the human agents—the king's men acting under orders, or the slanderers, or the king himself—as the relevant cause of their husbands' deaths. This is not to say that the king did no wrong—and we will come back to this, as the story itself does. But each wife is being advised to attend instead to other causes that belonged properly to her husband in such a way that his untimely death was not to be avoided. She is not advised to *look for* specific causes, or the particular misdeed—it is an important part of the perspective to be adopted that such looking would be futile and relatively uninformative. This "opacity of karma"³⁵ is integral to the perspective-shift being recommended. Rather than an invitation to determine *the* culprit, it is a gesture toward the infinite embeddedness, dependency, and consequently compromised nature of whatever—and whomever—we take to be a discrete entity.

Mallikā herself, notice, does not need such consolation, nor such diversion. She immediately sees that a mortal has died—something breakable has broken. One is reminded here of Cicero's story of Anaxagoras's reaction to news of his son's death: "I knew all along that I had begotten a mortal."³⁶ This does not mean that Mallikā does not feel her husband's absence, or feel sorrow at the loss of her sons. But she immediately accepts that what is a standing possibility for every human being has happened now, in this way, for her husband and sons, and she does not indulge in excessive grief. What has come together comes apart, and she was under no illusion that she or they or anyone had ultimate control over this.

Giving her daughters-in-law vague appeals to karma approximates this perspective. It makes available to them her alternative way of relating to their husbands' deaths, and thus prepares the way for the next and perhaps most important part of her advice: rejecting the expected, "normal" reaction of indignation against the king who ordered the massacre. "Cherish no resentment against the king." This rejection of resentment, which opens up space for a different kind of response to the situation, is absolutely central to Buddhist morality—for hatred, anger and resentment are particularly virulent forms of aversion, one of the three fundamental roots of suffering.[37]

The opening of the *Dhammapada* offers opportunity for multiple elaborations on this theme of appropriate reactions to violence:

> "He abused me, he struck me, he defeated me, he robbed me;"
> If any cherish this thought, their hatred never ceases. ||3||
> "He abused me, he struck me, he defeated me, he robbed me;"
> If any cherish not this thought, their hatred ceases. ||4||
> For not by hatred are hatreds ever quenched here in this world.
> By love rather are they quenched. This is an eternal law. ||5||

The story illustrating the last verse is particularly colorful.[38] A wife who was barren encourages her husband to take a second wife; but she is immediately jealous when the younger wife conceives a child. She secretly gives the second wife an abortifacient, and she does the same again the next time the young wife conceives. Wising up, the second wife does not announce her third pregnancy. But when she is too far along to hide it, the jealous first wife eventually finds a way to slip poison into the pregnant woman's food. The second wife dies in childbirth along with the child, earnestly wishing, "When I have passed out of this existence may I be reborn as an ogress able to devour *your* children" [48]. She is reborn as a cat, while the husband beats and abandons the first wife, who soon dies of her injuries.

Notice there is no mention anywhere of anyone having deserved any of what befell them in virtue of their behavior in this, or any previous life. An everyday moral sensibility might suppose that being beaten and cast out is simply what the murderous first wife deserves. The text does not present it this way; instead this eventuality is simply what, perhaps predictably, this man did when he found out his wife had killed his other wife and their unborn child. The first wife's unhappy death is *not* the moral of the story.

The first wife is reborn as a hen, whose chicks are three times devoured by the cat before she is similarly devoured, earnestly wishing that in the next life she may do the same to the cat. The pair are then reborn as a leopardess and a deer, with the same predictable pattern, and the same dying wish. In each rebirth, the women get what they wished for—not what they "deserved." Finally, the leopardess is reborn as "a young woman of station," the deer as an ogress. After having her first two children eaten by the ogress, the young woman runs with the third to the monastery where the Buddha is teaching, the ogress close behind.

The young wife lays her boy at the feet of the Buddha, saying "I give you this child; spare the life of my son." The Buddha has the ogress, held at the gate, summoned within, and before them both says, in effect, "*Why are you doing this?*" and quotes what we have as verse 5 of the *Dhammapada*. The ogress gets the point. In the longer thirteenth-century Sinhala vernacular version, the *Saddharmaratnāvaliya*, the Buddha has to say a bit more to get her there: "As spit, snot, and so on, are washed off with clean water . . . so hatred that burns on the fuel of justifications must be drenched with the water of compassion, not fed with the firewood of reasons and causes . . . Good, founded on compassion, destroys malice and puts out the fire of enmity."[39]

The Buddha tells the young mother to let the ogress hold the child. Entrusted with the child, the ogress caresses him, and gives him back. Then she cries because, she says, now that she is no longer eating human flesh, she will starve.[40] So the Buddha tells the mother to invite the ogress into her home and feed her with the best rice-porridge.

The story goes on.[41] But this is enough to see that it is not karma that fuels the misadventures, but rather hatred, anger, and resentment. There is no suggestion that the barren wife of the first incarnation has behaved anything but appallingly; yet she is not considered to have "got what she deserved," either in being beaten to death, or when reborn as a hen in the house of a chick-devouring cat. The husband's domestic misfortune is not credited to some foul deed in this or some previous life. Nor is the misfortune of the fruitful wife attributed to any previous misconduct of her own.[42] At the end of the tale, the ogress is to be allowed to hold the child not because she has *earned* it, or because her eating the first two infants is inconsequential, but because this is the only way out of the ongoing cycle of suffering caused by the perfectly "well-grounded," "justified" mutual resentment these two women have cultivated toward each other. The new mother has to be willing not to consider questions of guilt and desert, but instead look to the hunger of the ogress and invite her into her home to assuage that hunger. This is the only real prophylactic against more baby-devouring.

The Buddha is not acting in this story as a *judge* (perhaps it is interesting to contrast in this respect the tale of wise king Solomon searching for the best and fairest way to decide the competing claims of two women over an infant child). There is no apportioning of blame when the rivals come to the temple, no weighing of conduct in the balances. Obviously, if indignation is ever righteous, then the new mother has every justification for her resentment toward the ogress. What more reason could one possibly need? Likewise, the doe has every reasonable ground to be angry with the leopardess; the hen is entitled to her fury with the cat; and the young woman, brought into the household by the first, barren wife only to have her children killed in the womb, has ample ground for complaint. The Buddha does not inquire into any of this, nor give either party the opportunity to recite all the good reasons she has for calling the other to the punishment she so richly deserves.[43] This indeed is the crux of the whole story.[44]

In the tale of the murder of Bandhula along with his thirty-two sons, Mallikā—the widow and bereaved mother—sees the pointlessness of anger, and more importantly, sees how important it is so to see things. From the first intimation of her loss, she does not frame things—for herself, or for her daughters-in-law—in such a way that anger would reasonably and naturally arise. Instead she frames things in a way that the reasonable and authentic response is, "This violence stops here." And so it does. The power of her thus taking responsibility for nonproliferation so moves the king that he asks her forgiveness, and returns her gesture by allowing her to name what she wants from him.

In the tale, Mallikā's response is directly contrasted with its opposite. The now remorseful king goes to visit the Buddha, entrusting the symbols of royal power to the care of Kāyāyana, a nephew of the murdered man, who has been given his uncle's post. This nephew, however, thinks of the king as "the man who treacherously murdered my upright uncle and blameless cousins," and accordingly wants to punish him. Kārāyaṇa makes off with the royal symbols of power, and gives them to Prince Viḍūḍabha, who claims the throne. Upon discovering the usurpation, the king, remorseful but still unwilling to give up power, rushes headlong back to the city, where he promptly dies of exhaustion, alone, outside the city gates.

In a way, the king does in fact die as a result of his unjust killing of Bandhula. But there are no non-natural agents or impersonal natural forces at work. His crime set in motion both his remorse, and so his journey to the Buddha, *and* the nephew's desire for retribution. He contributes, moreover, a desire to hold onto the kingdom that leads him to take the exhausting journey that kills him. The nephew, having acted out his revenge, creates the circumstances for the new king, Viḍūḍabha, to recall his own thirst for retribution against slights the neighboring Sākiyas showed him years ago. The very next line is: "When Viḍūḍabha became king, he remembered his grudge."

But before seeing where this leads, we should not leave the old king without noting how nothing is said about his sorry fate being due to his crime, nor about what became of him postmortem on account of it. "Retribution" is something carried out by human beings suffering under a confusion that presents such action as the right, even the necessary, thing to do—much for the worse for all concerned. Mallikā's way is the only way to whatever happiness is yet to be won for us.

The new king's old grudge leads him to slaughter his kinsmen, the Sākiyas, while they—out of honor—do not fight but put up only a show of doing so. On the way back from their bloody victory, the king and his men bed down for the night in and around a riverbed. There is a flash flood, and half the men, including the king, are washed away.[45]

The local Buddhist monks speculate about this before the Buddha. "The slaying of the Sākiyas was unjust," they say (Dhp-a 360). "It was not right to say, 'The Sākiyas must be killed,' and to smite them and kill them." The Buddha replies with a clairvoyance about previous misdeeds not ordinarily available: "Monks, if you regard only this present existence, it was indeed unfitting [*ayutta*] that the Sākiyas should die in such wise.

What they received, however, was entirely fitting, considering the bad deed [*pāpakamma*] they committed in a previous state of existence . . . [when] they conspired together and threw poison into the river."[46]

Finally, we have just the sort of invocation of karma that people expect: it's okay that someone suffered, because it is actually punishment for an earlier crime. But that is not quite what the Buddha says. He says that the Sākiyas' being killed was *indeed* unjust (or more precisely, "unfitting"); but it was *also* fitting and only to be expected that they would suffer unjust death because they had set in motion the conditions for such a result some time ago. This also means that those who killed the Sākiyas *acted unjustly*—they are not the instrument of natural justice. Their intention was bad, and it will set in motion that sort of effect for themselves in the future.

Once again, we are diverted from casting the situation simply in terms of just deserts. There is this life, in which they were unjustly killed; and there is the endless succession of lives (an unwhole totality), with reference to which they justly died; but no preference is given for the long view over the short—the endless, nonteleological succession of lives is no proper whole with claim to be the "real truth of the matter." If, then, we are not to think, "They deserved it. He had it coming to him," how *are* we to think of it? This is modeled for us by the monks, who turn immediately from wondering about the justice of the slaying to sympathy for the perpetrators washed away in the flood after their victory. "Viḍūḍabha slew all those Sākiyas," they say (Dhp-a 361) "and then, before the desire of his own heart had been fulfilled, he and his numerous company were swept out to sea and became food for fishes and tortoises." To which the Buddha replies, "Monks, or ever the desire of these living beings be fulfilled, even as a mighty flood overwhelms a sleeping village, so the Prince of Death cuts short their lives and plunges them into the four oceans of suffering."

Here would be an excellent opportunity to say that Viḍūḍabha is being punished for his injustice against the Sākiyas. But that is exactly what the Buddha does *not* say. Instead he encourages the opposite outlook: rather than consoling the monks that, after all, Viḍūḍabha only got what he deserved, he points out that Viḍūḍabha got what all of us get, at some (least expected) point. The Buddha encourages us to reflect: We are all in his position.[47] We set our hearts on something, order—and disorder—our priorities and perspective for the sake of it; we do (and fail to do) any number of things in pursuit of this end to which we have become so attached. And then—something intervenes; a flood comes and washes the whole business away. This is a condition we all share, each day of our lives.

IS THERE A PROBLEM OF EVIL TO SOLVE?

What is Job's complaint? It is not that there is suffering, or even that there is innocent suffering. When he, upright as he is, loses his children and all his property, he "fell down upon the ground, and worshipped; And said, Naked came I out of my mother's womb, and naked shall I return thither: the LORD gave, and the LORD hath taken away; blessed be the name of the LORD" (Job I:20–21). It is only when he himself is struck with a repulsive and debilitating disease—when, as we later hear, his condition has become one in which he is cast out from any possibility of human relations—that he curses not God, as predicted, but the day he was born.

What does it *mean* to "curse the day that you were born"? There is not much within the biblical text from which to build an interpretation. But it seems at least that "it was a black day that saw me born" must mean something like "there is no conceivable good to anyone, or to the universe, that I was born."

But the Buddhist is likely to be perplexed at this point. Whatever put it into your head that there was supposed to be any good to anyone—yourself or others or the order of reality as a whole—in your being born? Where did this expectation come from that one's having been born ought to have some modicum of good in it, or reason? That there must be some purpose served, or else it was an especially *black* day? We are all conceived and born in the usual way, due to familiar causes—there is desire, there is physiology and biology and physics. All these factors are entangled in suffering, in psychological suffering, in the metaphysical suffering of vulnerability and dependence.[48] Where does this expectation come from that there is some amount or kind of suffering that is *too much*, or the *wrong kind*? Suffering is just the nature of reality—this is the first of the four Noble Truths.[49] Indeed, our inability to accept this—our insistence that there must be some more permanent reality to hold onto—is just what leads to greater suffering. If there is a *problem* of suffering (rather than a problem of evil), it is in our resistance to this fundamental truth, and Buddhist teaching, theoretical and practical, devotes considerable resources and ingenuity to addressing this. One may think here of the much-recounted tale of the woman who had lost a child, and was utterly bereft.[50] The Buddha advises her to bring him a mustard seed from a house that has known no loss. When she has suffered terrible loss, the woman is not offered karma as consolation—she is encouraged to look beyond her own immediate loss, or to see it in the context of the human condition, and the community of fellow sufferers.

To feel pained at the ultimate meaninglessness of one's life, at the futility and lack of overarching justificatory narrative, is to be caught up in a false metaphysical view—one that supposes *real* reality is one of well-formed wholes, a fitting and valuable order to things, and that our experience is therefore to be evaluated according to how it measures up to this standard. It supposes that there is some end whose goodness—rightness, appropriateness—would or could make sense of the series of changes, give them meaning and purpose. But if there are no wholes, no greater order, no promise of unity and meaning—if the whole of reality is just "from this, that arises; from that, this arises"— the question "Why was I ever born?" just cannot arise in the same way.[51] When Job asks, "Why?" he is looking for the final cause, not the efficient or material cause. And on the Buddhist view, there simply are none of those to be found in the order of reality. Final causes are introduced only in the intentional thought and actions of living beings, and they go out of existence with them. It is in fact our attachment to these final causes—"my life will be meaningless unless . . ."— that is, on the Buddhists' diagnosis, responsible for unnecessary suffering that we generate independently of other causes. This is not Sophoclean pessimism, because there is no cause for dismay at the lack of meaning in suffering—it is the thought that suffering *could* be redeemed or redemptive, but is not, that does the damage.

WHY IS LIFE SO HARD?

It is not as if the Buddhists are tongue-tied in the face of this question, or that they refuse to acknowledge it. In this, I think they were less pessimistic than the Greeks.[52] But they do not confuse the fact of suffering with any supposed problem of evil. The idea that evil is a special *problem* comes from the expectation that the distribution of pleasures and pains *ought* to be just, but is not; and it comes, especially in its secular version, from the related idea that we could not make sense of having projects at all if we thought that the distribution of positive and negative results was only arbitrarily connected to the virtuous effort we bring to life and our conduct through it. But such expectations are, on the Buddhist view, symptoms of precisely the sort of confusion they take to be at the root of suffering. The only "problem of suffering" is quite simply that there is suffering and we do not like it. But that we do not like it is not something in need of an explanation; and how it in fact arises is something amenable to perfectly ordinary sorts of explanation. There are traceable, discernable causes of suffering, and it is in fact this which holds out hope for its amelioration.

Ultimately, suffering comes from our ignorance or confusion, and from the confused and misguided feelings and desires and aversions that therefore arise. Generally, where there is suffering, there is some confusion, some craving and attachment somewhere, as part of its conditions; and conversely, the need and inflexibility that come from confused ways of grasping our condition result inevitably in suffering. There is tremendous benefit in understanding this, and in tracing out the particular paths through which our insistence on the specialness and priority of ourselves leads to suffering for ourselves and others.

But if suffering comes down to our ignorance, does this mean that we are *to blame* for our suffering? That we are only "getting what we *deserve*"?

On the contrary. On this point, Ivan Karamazov is exactly right: "there is suffering and none are guilty." As the Buddhist view is not particularly concerned with *innocence* as opposed to guilt, we might say that the question of blame and desert is simply taken off the table.[53] The categories of guilt and blame, justice and desert are the wrong ones to bring to the situation at hand.[54] *Saṃsāra*, with its endless ups and downs, is not the sort of thing anyone *deserves*. And no one is *to blame* for the human condition—for the fact of ignorance, or the fact that ignorance causes confusion, craving, grasping, clinging; for the fact that grasping at what is fleeting is therefore a futile, Sisyphusian enterprise that sets people against each other and makes them callous or incognizant of the suffering their actions cause. It is a desperate, pitiable condition. The more we recognize it, the more heartbreaking it is to see, the more urgently we seek to interrupt this self-perpetuating process, to eliminate suffering by eliminating the causes of suffering.

NOTES

ABBREVIATIONS

Dhp-a	*Dhammapada-aṭṭkathā*, see Burlingame, *Buddhist Legends*
JS	*Jaina Sūtra*, see Jacobi, *Jaina Sūtras*
MN	*Majjima Nikāya*, see Ñāṇamoli and Bodhi, *Middle Length Discourses of the Buddha*
MP	*Milindapañha*, see Horner, *Milinda's Questions*
SN	*Samyutta Nikāya*, see Bodhi, *Connected Discourses of the Buddha*
AN	*Aṅguttara Nikāya*, see Nyanaponika and Bodhi, *Numerical Discourses of the Buddha*
Vism	*Visuddhimagga*, see Ñāṇamoli, *The Path of Purification*

My thanks are due to the Einstein Forum, at whose invitation I first prepared an earlier version of these thoughts for their multidisciplinary conference on the figure of Job, and to the audience and other speakers for their insightful discussion.

1. Indeed, "the most consistent theodicy ever produced by history." Max Weber, *The Religion of India*, trans. and ed. Hans H. Gerth and Don Martindale (New York: Free Press, 1958), 121.
2. See, among more recent iterations of this debate, John Hick, *Philosophy of Religion*, 3rd ed. (Englewood Cliffs, NJ: Prentice-Hall, 1983, chap. 10), as taken up by Roy Perrett in "Karma and the Problem of Suffering," *Sophia* 24, no. 1 (1985): 4–10; and Whitley Kaufman ("Karma, Rebirth, and the Problem of Evil," *Philosophy East and West* 55, no. 1 [2005]: 15–32) on the one hand, and Monima Chadha and Nick Trakakis ("Karma and the Problem of Evil: A Response to Kaufman." *Philosophy East & West* 57, no. 4 (2007): 533–56), on the other.
3. Thus Weber calls the Brahamanical "combination of caste legitimacy with the *karma* doctrine, thus with the specific Brahmanical theodicy . . . a stroke of genius" (*Religion of India*, 131), while Buddhists challenged the legitimacy of caste; but the figuring of the karma doctrine as the perfect solution to the problem of evil remains (*Religion of India*, 206–7).
4. As G. Schlesinger has it in his proposed dissolution of the problem of evil ("The Problem of Evil and the Problem of Suffering," *American Philosophical Quarterly* 1, no. 3 [1964]: 244–47). Perrett offers an astute examination of whether there can be said to be a problem of *suffering* at all—though he adds only parenthetically that the suffering under consideration is "apparently unmerited" ("Karma and the Problem of Suffering," 9). As he observes, our *dislike* of suffering, and our wish to escape it, constitute a separate problem, and one addressed in the Hindu tradition by "a plethora of diverse answers . . . presupposing and yet transcending the logically satisfactory answered by the doctrine of karma" (where "logically" means "causally explanatory," "Karma and the Problem of Suffering," 9). See also in this context Wendy Doniger O'Flaherty, *The Origins of Evil in Hindu Mythology* (Berkeley: University of California Press, 1976), the first chapter of which gives an excellent introduction to and orientation in the problem of evil as it relates to Hindu thought in particular.
5. Dostoyevsky has Ivan Karamazov saying,

> If [children] suffer, they must suffer for another's sins; but that reasoning I don't understand. The innocent must not suffer for another's sins! . . . Why should [man] know evil when it costs so

much? The whole of knowledge is not worth that child's prayer to 'dear, kind God'! I say nothing of the suffering of grown-up people! But these little ones! . . . I understand nothing . . . I don't want to understand. I want to stick to the fact. I made up my mind long ago not to understand. If I try to understand anything, I shall be false to the fact . . . I took children only to make my case clearer. I cannot understand why the world is arranged as it is. With my pitiful understanding, all I know is that there is suffering and none are guilty . . . and I can't consent to live by it. I must have justice"; and then, "While there is still time, I want to renounce the higher harmony altogether. It's not worth the tears of one tortured child! It's not worth it because those tears must be atoned for, or there can be no harmony. But how? How are you going to atone for them? . . . By their being avenged? But what do I care for avenging them, . . . since the children have already been tortured?

(FYODOR DOSTOYEVSKY, *THE BROTHERS KARAMAZOV*, TR. CONSTANCE GARNETT [MINEOLA, NY: DOVER PUBLICATIONS, 2005], 215–21)

6. This anxiety already finds terse articulation in Thomas Aquinas's thirteenth-century *Summa Theologica*, Question 2, Article 3: "It seems that there is no God. For if, of two mutually exclusive things, one were to exist without limit, the other would cease to exist. But by the word 'God' is implied some limitless good. If God then existed, nobody would ever encounter evil. But evil is encountered in this world. God therefore does not exist." *Summa Theologiae*, tr. Timothy McDermott, OP (Garden City, NY: Doubleday, 1969).

7. "The resultant problem of theodicy," Weber writes in *Sociology of Religion* (trans. Ephraim Fischoff, with introduction by Talcott Parsons [Boston: Beacon Press, 1963], 139), "is found in ancient Egyptian literature as well as in Job and in Aeschylus . . . All Hindu religion was influenced by it . . . ; even a meaningful world order that is impersonal and supertheistic must face the problem of the world's imperfections." In his introduction, Parsons highlights the source of the problem of

evil for Weber in the "discrepancies between expectation systems which are institutionalized in normative orders and the actual experiences people undergo," since "*regardless of the particular content of the normative order*, a major element of discrepancy is inevitable"; people's experiences are, consequently,

> frustrating in the very specific sense, not merely that things happen and contravene their "interests," but that things happen which are "meaningless" in the sense that they *ought* not to happen. Here above all lie the problems of suffering and of evil, not merely the existence of phenomena defined in these terms, but also the prevalence of the suffering of those who do not morally deserve to suffer, the prevalence of the exposure to evil of the morally just, who thus are punished rather than rewarded for their pains.

(WEBER, *SOCIOLOGY OF RELIGION*, XLVII, EMPHASIS IN ORIGINAL)

For a more contemporary articulation of this line of thought, see Susan Neiman, *evil in modern thought* (Princeton, NJ: Princeton University Press, 2002), and Charles Taylor's *sources of the self* (Cambridge, MA: Harvard University Press, 1989), which insists that life be rationally organized around some ultimate good in order for it, and the actions comprising a life, to be meaningful.

8. See, for instance, myths at the end of the *Phaedo*, of the *Gorgias*, and in Book X of the *Republic*.
9. Franklin Perkins, *Heaven and Earth Are Not Humane: The Problem of Evil in Classical Chinese Philosophy* (Bloomington: Indiana University Press, 2014).
10. *Oedipus at Colonnus* 1225–27; according to Herodotus (8.138), Sophocles is here sharing a bit of common wisdom that was given to King Midas by a silenus.
11. Amber D. Carpenter, "Illuminating Community: How to Learn from India's Lack of a Category for Non-Human Animals," in *Oxford Philosophical Concepts: Animals*, ed. P. Adamson and F. Edwards (Oxford: Oxford University Press, 2018, 63–85), has discussion and further

references regarding the actions of animals and their liability to attract results according to their quality.

12. MP 134, Division IV (Dilemmas) 1.viii. Quotes from the *Milindapañha* follow the translation of I. B. Horner (Oxford: Pali Text Society, 1963) unless noted otherwise.

13. J. P. McDermott points out that this particular bit of the Buddha's post-enlightenment suffering, unlike the dysentery, is ascribed by Nāgasena to chance elsewhere in the *Milindapañha* (*Development in the Early Buddhist Concept of Kamma/Karma* [New Delhi: Munshiram Manoharlal, 1984], 116).

14. Translations from the Pāli canon are those published by Wisdom Publications as the *Discourses of the Buddha*, unless otherwise noted.

15. Cf. also SN 36.21; AN ii.87–88; AN iii.131. The *Vibhaṅga* (367) also speaks out against considering all prosperity and adversity . . . to be the result of deeds done in past lives (McDermott, *Development*, 92); and the old view is retained in the current Theravāda (Ledi Sadaw, "Some Points of Buddhist Doctrine," *Journal of the Pali Text Society* 7 1913–1914, 119).

16. MP VIII.6. Max Müller, in his *Sacred Texts of the East* translation, notes that this verse has not been traced in the *piṭakas*; and I. B. Horner makes no note of a possible source at all. Since many texts of diverse canons have been lost, it is not unlikely that Nāgasena here quotes from what was taken at the time to be the Buddha's words. Where I have put ellipses, Müller has nothing, but Horner has "and from *kamma*." Horner's version is strange because the text has just said that of these, only that which is due to *kamma* is "in due season"—although Horner's translation of this preceding passage is very complicated, evidently making distinctions so as to reconcile it with what is said in the verse. Is muddle here perhaps to do with the fact that the untimely death of an *arhat* was disputed among Buddhists themselves? (McDermott cites *Kathāvatthu* XVII.2 in *Development*, 100.)

17. O'Flaherty observes, "It has been argued that 'the most complete formal solution to the problem of theodicy is the special achievement of the Indian doctrine of *karma*, the so-called belief in the transmigration of souls.' This doctrine, simply stated, 'solves' the problem by blaming evil on itself: one's present experience is the direct result of the action (karma), good and bad, accumulated in past lives and affixed to the

transmigrating soul" (*Origins of Evil in Hindu Mythology*, 14). The quote is from Weber (*Sociology of Religion*, chap. 9), who goes on to note that "guilt and merit within this world are unfailingly compensated by fate in the successive lives of the soul . . . What may appear from the viewpoint of a theory of compensation as unjust suffering in the terrestrial life of a person should be regarded as atonement for sin in a previous existence" (*Sociology of Religion*, 145). In his clear and careful study of karma in early Buddhist thought, McDermott observes that multiple causes, and in particular chance—which seems to be the explanation of the splinter of rock hitting the Buddha's toe (MP 181)—"undermines any sense of universal justice as being operative through the principle of kamma" (*Development*, 116). But old habits die hard—see notes 18 and 19.

18. "In the schema of time-space structured existence embodied in sentient existence," writes Winston King, "at all levels and in all forms (human, sub-human, super-human) the *karmic principle of justice* rules without exception or hindrance. There is no such thing as unexplained, causeless suffering, Job to the contrary" (Winston King, "Judeo-Christian and Buddhist Concepts of Justice," *Journal of Buddhist Ethics* 2 [1995]: 67–82; emphasis added).

19. Kaufman ("Karma, Rebirth, and the Problem of Evil") treats karma—in Buddhism and Hinduism indifferently—as *supposed to be* a "solution" to the problem of evil, by positing perfect justice in punishments and rewards, but finds it wanting in this respect. Chadha and Trakakis respond to the objections, but without noting that—for the Buddhist at least—karma could not possibly play this role since there is suffering that is not caused by previous actions. In fact, they say that "it is more accurate to conceive of the karma theory as providing a model of impersonal or cosmic justice" ("Karma and the Problem of Evil," 538).

20. This does not mean that *no* current evils were ascribed to bad karma, of course. In MN 135, differences in fortune that one is born into are ascribed to previous deeds having their effects. One is inclined, as in other cases in the Buddha's discourses, to search for contextual clues for why *this particular answer* is given to *this particular questioner*.

21. Cf. *Ratnāvalī* I.9, 43.

22. I explore this understanding of the no-self claim in more detail in *Indian Buddhist Philosophy*, chap. 1; and consider the ethical implications of

the rejection of teleology in "Metaphysical Suffering, Metaphysics as Therapy." In *On Suffering: An Inter-Disciplinary Dialogue on Narrative and the Meaning of Suffering*, ed. N. Hinerman and M. Sutton (Oxford: ID Press, 2012), 3–10.

23. This is especially evident in the Mahāyāna (Madhyamaka) tradition, particularly in the *Bodhicaryāvatāra*.
24. Vasubandhu, *AKBh*. IX
25. See J. P. McDermott, *Development of the Early Buddhist Concept of Karma/Kamma*, 84–86; and for a more detailed discussion of the possible philosophical motivations of the *pudgalavāda*, see my "Persons Keeping Their *Karma* Together," in *The Moon Points Back: Analytic Philosophy and Asian Thought*, ed. Koji Tanaka, Yasuo Deguchi, Jay L. Garfield, and Graham Priest (New York: Oxford University Press, 2015), 1–44.
26. Here is an attempt to incorporate an interest in action and its fruits within the project of aiming at an enlightenment which recognizes no distinct agents or subjects, and sees the vanity of the sorts of goods and evils to be won by wholesome and unwholesome acts: "(someone) doing demerit is remorseful and says, 'An evil deed was done by me'—therefore evil does not increase. But (someone), sire, doing merit, is not remorseful. Rapture is born of the absence of remorse, joy is born of rapture, the body of one who is joyful is impassible, when the body is impassible, he experiences happiness, the mind of one who is happy is concentrated, and he who is concentrated comprehends as it really is—in this way merit increases" (MP 84, Division II.6.vii). There are a few other such attempts in the oldest forms of Buddhism. J. P. McDermott cites two in his "*Nibbāna* as a Reward for *kamma*" (*Journal of the American Oriental Society* 93, no. 3 [1973]: 344–47): the first is also in the *Milindapañha*, in a colorful description of 'the Buddha's bazaar' (MP 341); the other is the *Nidhikaṇḍasutta* of the *Khuddakapāṭha*, which describes nirvana as something gained by merit accumulated by wholesome actions. One finds a similar incorporation of good action and result within the path to enlightenment in Nāgārjuna's *Ratnāvalī* (treated in detail in my "Aiming at Happiness, Aiming at Ultimate Truth—in Practice," in *Moonpaths: Ethics and Emptiness*, ed. The Cowherds [New York: Oxford University Press, 2016]), 21–42.
27. That is, turning it entirely into a claim about the intrinsic effect on the *psyche* of certain sorts of intentional states—see especially Dale

Wright's "Critical Questions towards a Naturalized Concept of Karma in Buddhism," *Journal of Buddhist Ethics*, On-line Conference on "Revisioning Karma," vol. 11, 2005, http://blogs.dickinson.edu/buddhistethics /2010/04/27/conference-revisioning-karma; but also Damien Keown's "Karma, Character, and Consequentialism" and Christian Coseru's "Karma, Rebirth and Mental Causation", in the same volume.

28. McDermott recalls Aung and Rhys Davids' comment that "result of actions was . . . conceived of as *feeling* experienced by the agent," and adds "it is thus only subjective experience resulting from kamma which is properly termed '*vipaka*' [fruit]" (*Development*, 87) And conversely, "a man's character, as a whole, is a most significant element in determining how the effects of any given act will be experienced" (*Development*, 20).

29. See Stephen Batchelor, *Confessions of a Buddhist Atheist* (New York: Spiegel & Grau, 2010).

30. See Naomi Appleton, *Narrating Karma and Rebirth* (Cambridge: Cambridge University Press, 2014) for details on the treatment of karma in Buddhist and Jaina narrative literature. The *Sūtrakṛtāṅga* II.6 of the *Jaina Sūtras* (trans. by Herman Jacobi. *Sacred Books of the East* 45, [Varanasi: Motilal Banarsidass 1964 (orig. Clarendon 1895)], 414–15) captures the disputes between them over karma in its farcically grotesque caricature of the Buddhist view. The *Milindapañha* captures conflicting views at MP 84 and MP 159 regarding whether witting or unwitting wrong attracts the worse karma—which is surprising since the *Anguttara Nikāya* iii.415 declares that "intention (volition) is *kamma*." McDermott calls it "generally accepted that an emphasis on the role of cetanā in the action of kamma was the Buddha's contribution to the concept of kamma," (*Development*, 28). Dan Lusthaus, *Buddhist Phenomenology* (London: RoutledgeCurzon, 2002) and, in a different way, Jonathan Gold, *Paving the Great Way* (New York: Columbia University Press, 2014) both take karma to be central to Buddhist philosophical and soteriological thought.

31. Translations of *Dhammapada-aṭṭakathā* are taken from Eugene Watson Burlingame, *Buddhist Legends, Translated from the Original Pali Text of the Dhammapada Commentary* (Harvard Oriental Series, vols 28–30, Cambridge, MA: Harvard University Press, 1921), with occasional minor revisions.

32. My attention was originally called to this tale by the excellent discussion by Charles Hallisey and Anne Hansen, "Narrative, Sub-Ethics,

and the Moral Life: Some Evidence from Theravāda Buddhism" (*Journal of Religious Ethics*, 24, no. 2 [1996]: 305–27), who make much of this striking line.

33. Contrary to how Chadha and Trakakis speak of it, even as they too note its naturalistic connotations.

34. The way narratives work to place our actions in a much broader temporal perspective is illuminatingly discussed in chapter 4 of Maria Heim's *Forerunner of All Things* (New York: Oxford University Press, 2014).

35. Hallisey and Hansen use this phrase with marvelous sensitivity in "Narrative, Sub-Ethics, and the Moral Life," 319. "The opacity of karma displayed in the narrative," they write, "profoundly configures moral life by undermining any confidence we might have in our ability to identify the karmic results of any particular action that we plan to do. In other words, the story seems to preclude an attempt to describe an ethical intention as good by recourse to the perceived results that it will have for oneself."

36. *Tusculan Disputations* 3. 30).

37. Candrakīrti famously says "all anger felt towards a *bodhisattva* destroys within an instant merits that arise through discipline and giving of a hundred *kalpas*; there is no other evil similar to wrath" (*Madhyamakāvatāra* III.6); and Śāntideva comments at length on the evils of all forms of hatred and anger in the sixth chapter of his *Bodhicārāvatāra*. See also Buddhaghosa's *Visuddhimagga* IX.14–39.

38. See *Dhammapada-aṭṭakathā* I.5. This tale is also discussed by Ranjini and Gananath Obeyesekere, in "The Tale of the Demoness Kali: A Discourse on Evil," *History of Religions* 29 (1990): 318–34.

39. Quoted by Obeyesekere and Obeyesekere, "The Tale of the Demoness Kali," 325–26.

40. Obeyesekere and Obeyesekere speculate that "the child in her arms releases her own frustrated maternal love and (*we* might add though no peasant listener would) her guilt" ("The Tale of the Demoness Kali," 328); but the substantial difference between my reading and theirs is that I think "we" would be quite wrong to supplement with what "no peasant listener would"—the language of guilt and its associates is not the language and the categories of the story (at least not of the Pāli). The Buddha is not fishing for expressions of guilt; becoming "established in

the fruit of conversion," as the ogress does, is all the "act of contrition" that is required.

41. A simplified variant of the tale is recounted at *Dhammapada-aṭṭakathā* xxi.2, without the barren background, with reference to *Dhammapada* 291: "Whoever by causing suffering to others seeks to win happiness for himself, becomes entangled in the bonds of hate; such a man is never freed from hatred."

42. Her sufferings are "*not* configured karmically as the consequence of some previous misfortune on her part," as Heim illuminatingly says of Uppalavaṇṇā, whose story is found in the *Dhammapada* commentary, *Buddhist Legends*, Story V.10 (*Forerunner of All Things*, 197n24).

43. "By the time we reach the middle of the story," write Oberyesekere and Obeyesekere, "we have lost track of who is good, who bad, who originally guilty, and who the wronged one. The text deliberately blurs the distinctions. The question then is, how to stop the spiral of hate unleashed by vengeance?" ("The Tale of the Demoness Kali," 333). Apparently, this eschewing of righteous indignation persists in at least some Buddhist cultures. Pen Khek Chear writes, "The practices of restorative *and* retributive justice, in a Western context, accept the expression of anger by victims . . . Theravada Buddhism acknowledges that people will feel angry, however, people are discouraged from harboring anger and expressing it . . . The Buddhist ideal suggests that the betterment of oneself and others can be achieved without expression or thought of anger"; this should in part explain why "the Cambodian community, on the other hand, has not responded with the same fervor for justice and the prosecution of the Khmer Rouge" as nongovernmental organizations, and the international community generally ("Restorative Justice in the Cambodian Community: Challenges and Possibilities in Practice," Khmer Institute, Articles, 2011, http://www.khmerinstitute.com/articles/art14restorative .html; accessed January 18, 2021).

44. "Punishment is in itself regarded as an evil institution (grouped with theft and lying)," writes O'Flaherty, "rather than a satisfactory answer to the problem of the evil nature of man which results from various wicked dispositions from former births" (*Origins of Evil in Hindu Mythology*, 34).

45. At *Dhammapada-aṭṭakathā* 360, there is a lot of bother about who is lying down where: those who had committed a misdeed in a previous

existence lie in the way of the flood; those who did not lie upground. So this looks like a standard invocation of karma to explain away the apparent arbitrariness of natural evil (which afflicts the righteous along with the wicked).

46. Dhp-a 360, modifying the translation of Burlingame, *Buddhist Legends*, Part 2 (Harvard Oriental Series vol. 29), 45.

47. As Pen Khek Chear writes, "where no beings are exempt from *kamma*, there is no victim or offender. The victim does not suffer any more than the offender" ("Restorative Justice").

48. "That the only genuine problem of evil relates to the challenge of explaining why the world contains 'such a strange mixture of good and evil'," write Chadha and Trakakis, "may be correct from a Judeo-Christian perspective, but it utterly fails to appreciate the uniqueness of the Hindu and Buddhist view of the human predicament, according to which life itself is nothing more than suffering and misery." I disagree, however, when they go on to say further that "if this bleak view of our predicament is accepted, the problem of evil does not disappear, but takes on an ever-greater significance" ("Karma and the Problem of Evil," 544), for on the Buddhist view, I think, the problem becomes an entirely *practical* one of how suffering is best eliminated, and is no longer a *philosophical* problem at all. Chadha and Trakakis, who advise us to "appreciate fully the strong practical dimension of the theory of karma" (551), may not disagree.

49. Roy Perrett writes, "Now the Indian answer to this will be that, while individual instances of suffering are explicable by reference to karma, the fact that suffering exists in our world at all (given there are possible worlds in which it does not) is just a brute fact about our world. And this reply seems perfectly reasonable" ("Karma and the Problem of Suffering," 7). While mistaken that the Buddhist explains all suffering by reference to karma instead of other incidental causes, Perrett is essentially right about the profound difference regarding what as seen as *needing* explanation, and what explains.

50. Kisā Gotamī's story is told in *Dhammapada-aṭṭakathā* viii.13 (Burlingame, *Buddhist Legends, Part 2*, Harvard Oriental Series vol. 29, pp. 257–260).

51. In "Theodicy, Sin and Salvation in a Sociology of Buddhism," in *Dialectic in Practical Religion*, ed. Edmund R. Leach (Cambridge Papers in

Social Anthropology, no. 5, [Cambridge: Cambridge University Press, 1968]), Gananath Obeyesekere writes, "In a culture which possesses a theory of suffering like that of *karma* the problem of explaining unjust suffering simply cannot arise" (11).

52. Though for fun, compare Sophocles's "best is never to have been born, second-best to die soon" with *Dhammapada* 113: "Though one should live one hundred years and never see the rise and set of beings, yet it were better far to live out but a single day and see the rise and set of beings."
53. For more detailed discussion of the eschewal of blame and its significance in Buddhist ethics, see Amber D. Carpenter, "Ethics without Justice," in *A Mirror Is for Reflection: Understanding Buddhist Ethics*, ed. Jake H. Davis (New York: Oxford University Press, 2017), 315–335.
54. And not seeing *this* is the source of Karamazov's own suffering; for all that he insists on not hiding from the facts, he still needs there to be some *justice* in the suffering, or some reasonable payoff.

BIBLIOGRAPHY

Appleton, Naomi. *Narrating Karma and Rebirth*. Cambridge: Cambridge University Press, 2014.

Aquinas, Thomas. *Summa Theologica*. Trans. Timothy McDermott, OP. Garden City, NY: Doubleday, 1969.

Batchelor, Stephen. *Confessions of a Buddhist Atheist*. New York: Spiegel & Grau, 2010.

Bodhi, Bhikkhu, trans. *The Connected Discourses of the Buddha*. Boston: Wisdom, 2005.

Buddhaghosa, *Visuddhimagga*. see Ñāṇamoli, tr.

Burlingame, Eugene Watson. *Buddhist Legends, Translated from the Original Pali Text of the Dhammapada Commentary*. Harvard Oriental Series, vols. 28–30. Cambridge, MA: Harvard University Press, 1921.

Carpenter, Amber D. *Indian Buddhist Philosophy*. Durham: Acumen (now Routledge), 2014.

Carpenter, Amber D. "Aiming at Happiness, Aiming at Ultimate Truth—in Practice." In *Moonpaths: Ethics and Emptiness*, ed. The Cowherds, 21–42. New York: Oxford University Press, 2016.

Carpenter, Amber D. "Ethics without Justice." In *A Mirror Is for Reflection: Understanding Buddhist Ethics*, ed. Jake H. Davis, 315–35. New York: Oxford University Press, 2017.

Carpenter, Amber D. "Illuminating Community: How to Learn from India's Lack of a Category for Non-Human Animals." In *Oxford Philosophical Concepts: Animals*, ed. P. Adamson and F. Edwards, 63–85. Oxford: Oxford University Press, 2018.

Carpenter, Amber D. "Metaphysical Suffering, Metaphysics as Therapy." In *On Suffering: An Inter-Disciplinary Dialogue on Narrative and the Meaning of Suffering*, ed. Nate Hinerman and Matthew Sutton, 3–10. Oxford: Inter-Disciplinary Press, 2012.

Carpenter, Amber D. "Persons Keeping Their *Karma* Together." In *The Moon Points Back: Analytic Philosophy and Asian Thought*, ed. Koji Tanaka, Yasuo Deguchi, Jay L. Garfield, and Graham Priest, 1–44. New York: Oxford University Press, 2015.

Chadha, Monima, and Nick Trakakis. "Karma and the Problem of Evil: A Response to Kaufman." *Philosophy East & West* 57, no. 4 (2007): 533–56.

Coseru, Christian. "Karma, Rebirth and Mental Causation." *Journal of Buddhist Ethics* 11 (2005); http://blogs.dickinson.edu/buddhistethics/2010/04/27/conference-revisioning-karma. Accessed January 18, 2021.

Gold, Jonathan. *Paving the Great Way*. New York: Columbia University Press, 2014.

Hallisey, Charles, and Anne Hansen. "Narrative, Sub-Ethics, and the Moral Life: Some Evidence from Theravāda Buddhism." *Journal of Religious Ethics* 24, no. 2 (1996): 305–27.

Heim, Maria. *Forerunner of All Things: Buddhaghosa on Mind, Intention, and Agency*. New York: Oxford University Press, 2014.

Hick, John. *Philosophy of Religion*. 3rd ed. Englewood Cliffs, NJ: Prentice-Hall, 1983.

Hopkins, Jeffrey, trans. *Nāgārjuna's Precious Garland (Ratnāvalī)*. Ithaca, NY: Snow Lion, 2007.

Horner, I. B., trans. *Milinda's Questions (Milindapañha)*. Oxford: Pali Text Society, 1963.

Jacobi, Herman, trans. *Jaina Sūtras. Sacred Books of the East* 45. Varanasi: Motilal Banarsidass, 1964 (orig. Clarendon 1895).

Kaufman, Whitley. "Karma, Rebirth, and the Problem of Evil." *Philosophy East and West* 55, no. 1 (2005): 15–32.

Keown, Damien. "Karma, Character, and Consequentialism." *Journal of Buddhist Ethics* 11 (2005); http://blogs.dickinson.edu/buddhistethics/2010/04/27/conference-revisioning-karma. Accessed January 18, 2021.

King, Winston. "Judeo-Christian and Buddhist Concepts of Justice." *Journal of Buddhist Ethics* 2 (1995): 67–82.

Lusthaus, Dan. *Buddhist Phenomenology*. London: RoutledgeCurzon, 2002.

McDermott, J. P. *Development in the Early Buddhist Concept of Kamma/Karma*. New Delhi: Munshiram Manoharlal, 1984.

McDermott, J. P. "*Nibbāna* as a Reward for *Kamma*." *Journal of the American Oriental Society* 93, no. 3 (1973): 344–37.

Nāgārjuna, *Ratnāvalī*. See Hopkins.

Ñāṇamoli, Bhikkhu, trans. *The Path of Purification* (Buddhaghosa's *Visuddhimagga*), 3rd ed. Kandy, Sri Lanka: Buddhist Publication Society, 2011.

Ñāṇamoli, Bhikkhu, and Bhikkhu Bodhi, trans. *The Middle Length Discourses of the Buddha*. Boston: Wisdom, 1995.

Neiman, Susan. *Evil in Modern Thought*. Princeton, NJ: Princeton University Press, 2002.

Nyanaponika Thera, and Bhikkhu Bodhi, trans. *Numerical Discourses of the Buddha*. Walnut Creek, CA: Altamira, 1999.

Obeyesekere, Gananath. "Theodicy, Sin and Salvation in a Sociology of Buddhism." In *Dialectic in Practical Religion*, ed. Edmund R. Leach, Cambridge Papers in Social Anthropology, no. 5, 7–40. Cambridge: Cambridge University Press, 1968.

Obeyesekere, Ranjini, and Gananath Obeyesekere. "The Tale of the Demoness Kali: A Discourse on Evil." *History of Religions* 29 (1990): 318–34.

O'Flaherty, Wendy Doniger. *The Origins of Evil in Hindu Mythology*. Berkeley: University of California Press, 1976.

Pen Khek Chear. "Restorative Justice in the Cambodian Community" Khmer Institute, Articles, 2011, http://www.khmerinstitute.com/articles/art14restorative.html. Accessed January 18, 2021.

Perkins, Franklin. *Heaven and Earth Are Not Humane: The Problem of Evil in Classical Chinese Philosophy*. Bloomington: Indiana University Press, 2014.

Perrett, Roy. "Karma and the Problem of Suffering." *Sophia* 24, no. 1 (1985): 4–10.

Sadaw, Ledi. "Some Points of Buddhist Doctrine." *Journal of the Pali Text Society* 7, (1913–14): 115–64.

Weber, Max. *The Religion of India*. Trans. and ed. Hans H. Gerth and Don Martindale. New York: Free Press, 1958.

Weber, Max. *The Sociology of Religion*. Trans. Ephraim Fischoff. Boston: Beacon Press, 1963.

Wright, Dale. "Critical Questions towards a Naturalized Concept of Karma in Buddhism." *Journal of Buddhist Ethics*, On-line Conference on "Revisioning Karma," vol. 11, 2005, http://blogs.dickinson.edu/buddhistethics/2010/04/27/conference-revisioning-karma. Accessed January 18, 2021.

7

HOW MUCH IS ENOUGH?

Greed, Prosperity, and the Economic Problem of Happiness: A Comparative Perspective

STEVEN M. EMMANUEL

It has become fashionable in recent decades to assert that greed is good—or more accurately that greed is a productive force for good. This is not a new idea. In fact, the earliest glimmers of it appeared in the seventeenth century, when philosophers began to speculate that the human propensity for vice might serve a larger purpose in advancing the development of civil society.[1] Writing in 1670, the French Jansenist theologian Pierre Nicole observed that "men full of cupidity are worse than tigers, bears, or lions. Each of them wishes to devour the others; and yet by means of laws and police, these ferocious beasts are so tamed that one draws from them all the human services one might draw from the greatest charity."[2] In the eighteenth century, the Italian philosopher Giambattista Vico noted the way that society channels the vices of "ferocity, avarice, and ambition" into "national defense, commerce, and politics," which are necessary for civil happiness.[3] However, the fullest expression of the idea was presented by the political philosopher and satirist Bernard Mandeville, who provoked moral outrage with his scandalous assertion that "private vices" yield "publick benefits."[4] Mandeville laid special emphasis on the way that avarice, vanity, and the desire for luxury conspire to promote industry, prosperity, and an improved standard of living for the poor.

Mandeville's seminal idea was taken up later by the Scottish Enlightenment philosopher and political economist Adam Smith, who pointed to self-love as the driving force behind economic growth and progress. Unlike Mandeville, however, Smith did not regard all expressions of self-love as vicious. "Regard to our own private happiness and interest," he wrote in *Theory of Moral Sentiments* (1759), is in many situations a "very laudable" principle of action (TMS 359). Smith saw nothing wrong with accumulating wealth for the purpose of "bettering our condition." Indeed, the law-abiding merchant who steadily increases his wealth through hard work and prudent management of his resources is, in Smith's view, not only a model of respectability in commercial affairs but also a boon to society.

At the same time, however, Smith warned that we should not expect the "benevolent affections" of generosity, humanity, kindness, or compassion from the merchant. This point came through clearly in his better-known work *The Wealth of Nations* (1776), where he described the nature of commercial transactions as follows:

> Give me that which I want, and you shall have this which you want, is the meaning of every such offer; and it is in this manner that we obtain from one another the far greater part of those good offices which we stand in need of. It is not from the benevolence of the butcher, the brewer, or the baker that we expect our dinner, but from their regard to their own interest. We address ourselves, not to their humanity but to their self-love, and never talk to them of our own necessities but of their advantages. (WN 26–27)

Although Smith regarded benevolence as a supreme virtue[5] and the key to creating a truly flourishing and happy society,[6] he understood that individuals in the marketplace are motivated by a much narrower concern for their own interests. But this was not such a bad thing, in his view, for in the "system of natural liberty" that he advocated, the merchant would be incentivized to make the most efficient use of his energy, talents, and capital; and even though he might have "only his own gain" in view, his industry and productivity would nevertheless contribute to the prosperity of society as a whole. Operating within the limits of justice and prudence, the self-regarding merchant would be "led by an invisible hand to promote an end which was no part of his intention" (WN 456).

Needless to say, Smith's attempt to defend commercial society by appealing to the logic of unintended consequences would do little to dispel the concerns of traditional moralists, who not only saw benevolence as a moral duty but also regarded the practice of usury and the accumulation of wealth for its own sake as blatant forms of greed. The constraints imposed by law and the forces of market competition did not eliminate selfishness or the desire for power and social status, nor did the increased productivity created by the division of labor prevent gross inequalities of income and wealth in society.[7] Indeed, Smith readily acknowledged that those who work the hardest get the least, noting that the poorest laborer who "supports the whole frame of society and furnishes the means of the convenience and ease of all the rest is himself possessed of a very small share and is buried in obscurity."[8]

Yet whatever concerns Smith may have had about the "oppressive inequality" that he witnessed in society, he was not much inclined to restrict the liberty of individuals in the lawful pursuit of their own economic interests. Despite the glaring disparity of wealth, he hastened to point out that even "the lowest and most despised member of civilized society" enjoys a higher standard of living than "the most respected and active savage can attain to."[9]

For Smith, inequality was not only compatible with the idea of "universal opulence" but also a seemingly inevitable by-product of human progress and the advancement of civilization. As he noted in *Theory of Moral Sentiments*, the desire for "wealth and greatness" is what first prompted people "to cultivate the ground, to build houses, to found cities and commonwealths, and to invent and improve all the sciences and arts, which ennoble and embellish human life" (TMS 214–15). Appealing once again to the metaphor of the "invisible hand," Smith went on to explain how the "vain and insatiable" desire for luxury caused the wealthy proprietors of his day to make steady improvements to their land, thereby redoubling its natural fertility and creating a surplus that maintained "thousands" in productive labor.[10] Despite their "natural selfishness and rapacity," the rich are thus

> led by an invisible hand to make nearly the same distribution of the necessaries of life, which would have been made, had the earth been divided into equal portions among all its inhabitants, and thus without intending it, without knowing it, advance the interest of the society, and afford means to the multiplication of the species. (TMS 215–16)

By Smith's reckoning, inequality was a small price to pay for a system that enabled the poorest members of society to enjoy the peace of mind associated with having their most important material needs satisfied. Indeed, with regard to "the real happiness of human life," the laboring poor were "in no respect inferior to those who would seem so much above them" (TMS 216).

Smith's "invisible hand" would eventually become a cornerstone of modern economic liberalism. But it was not until the latter half of the twentieth century that economists openly embraced the word "greed." This rhetorical shift was largely a response to moral concerns about the excesses of corporate capitalism and the growing disparity of wealth and power separating the world's richest and poorest nations. A pivotal moment in the debate came in 1979, when economist Milton Friedman was asked in a nationally televised interview whether he had ever had a "moment of doubt" about an economic system that runs on greed. Friedman met the challenge head on, saying, "Is there some society you know that doesn't run on greed? You think Russia doesn't run on greed? You think China doesn't run on greed? What is greed? Of course, none of us are greedy, it's only the other fellow who's greedy."[11]

Echoing Smith, Friedman went on to say that the "great achievements of civilization have not come from government bureaus," but rather from the hard work and enterprise of individuals "pursuing their separate interests." Indeed, the only places where the masses have been able to escape from grinding poverty, he argued, are those "where they have had capitalism and largely free trade." When pressed to explain why there was still so much poverty in the United States, Friedman replied: "Nirvana is not for this world. There is no paradise. Of course, we've got a lot of people who are poorly off. But if you look at it over time . . . the well-being of ordinary people has been the main thing that has been improved by . . . economic growth and development."

Like most economists, Friedman normally preferred the anodyne term "self-interest,"[12] which he used not merely as a shorthand expression for selfish profit-seeking, but for "whatever it is that interests the participants, whatever they value, whatever goals they pursue."[13] In addressing the heart of the moral argument against capitalism, however, he affirmed three key points: first, that greed is a pervasive feature of capitalist and noncapitalist societies alike; second, that when properly constrained by law and the forces of market competition, greed is an unparalleled engine of economic prosperity; and finally, that while a free enterprise system inevitably results in unequal distributions, it gradually improves the material conditions of the poorest members of society over time, and it does so more effectively than systems that promote equality at the expense of economic growth.[14]

Friedman's defense of greed was amplified in a provocative ABC News special, *Greed with John Stossel*.[15] Stossel and his guests were eager to distinguish the prosperity-generating kind of greed from acts of theft, fraud, and coercion—all of which constitute a violation of individual rights. So long as trade is voluntary, they reasoned, there is no limit to how much anyone is morally entitled to have, even if this results in large-scale inequalities in society, because the prosperity created by the most industrious individuals redounds to the benefit of everyone in the form of wealth, investment, and jobs.

Greed, according to this line of reasoning, produces greater benefits for society than caring or charity. As a test case for this claim, Stossel posed a provocative question: who did more for the world, the "greedy junk bond king" Michael Milken or Mother Teresa?[16] According to David Kelley, a guest on the program, the answer was obvious: "Milken far surpassed the benefits that she provided." This may seem surprising, given that Mother Teresa dedicated her life to alleviating the suffering of the poorest of the poor, while Milken was dedicated solely to self-enrichment, earning in excess of a billion dollars during a four-year stretch in the mid-1980s.[17] But by revolutionizing the way that capital markets work, the Wall Street financier arguably helped to create an enormous pool of wealth and jobs that enabled people to become economically independent and enjoy the satisfaction of being self-responsible agents. Thus, according to Kelley, while charity may seem a more noble activity than making money, the capitalist approach offers both a more respectful and a more sustainable solution to the problem of poverty.

GREED AND THE ECONOMIC PROBLEM OF HAPPINESS

While economists assume that economic behavior is motivated by individual interests and desires, the incessant striving to get as much as we can for ourselves hardly seems conducive to the tranquility or inner contentment that philosophers have traditionally associated with happiness. Adam Smith was keenly aware of this problem. Although he saw nothing wrong with the pursuit of personal gain, he discerned a clear threat to happiness in the restless striving for riches, power, and social status.

In his *Theory of Moral Sentiments*, Smith offered some lengthy observations on the psychology of human acquisitiveness. "To what purpose," he asked,

> is all the toil and bustle of this world? what is the end of avarice and ambition, of the pursuit of wealth, of power, and preheminence? Is it to supply the necessities of nature? The wages of the meanest labourer can supply them. We see that they afford him food and clothing, the comfort of a house, and of a family.... From whence, then, arises that emulation which runs through all the different ranks of men, and what are the advantages which we propose by that great purpose of human life which we call bettering our condition? (TMS 61)

The answer, in short, is human vanity—the desire to be "the object of attention and approbation," to be applauded and admired for one's material success:

> The rich man glories in his riches, because he feels that they naturally draw upon him the attention of the world.... At the thought of this, his heart seems to swell and dilate itself within him, and

he is fonder of his wealth, upon this account, than for all the other advantages it procures him. (TMS 61–62)

But this ego-driven striving for wealth and greatness inevitably fails to bring us any ultimate satisfaction. Indeed, it tends to undermine our real happiness, which consists chiefly in tranquility (TMS 174). By "tranquility," Smith meant first and foremost a state of inner contentment or peace of mind—free from stress and worry, free from the disturbing passions of hatred and anger,[18] free from the guilt of wrongdoing, and free from the anxiety and restlessness of incessant desire. Without this tranquility, he said, "there can be no enjoyment; and where there is perfect tranquillity there is scarce any thing which is not capable of amusing" (TMS 172).

Although Smith's understanding of happiness was influenced by his reading of Stoic philosophy, the kind of tranquility he had in mind was not the perfect equanimity of the sage. He rejected the Stoic ideal of *apatheia*—the complete detachment from all "private, partial, and selfish affections"—on the ground that it renders us "altogether indifferent . . . in the success or miscarriage of every thing which Nature has prescribed to us as the proper business and occupation of our lives" (TMS 345). Instead, Smith proposed a less perfect but meaningful and satisfying kind of happiness that is compatible with the acquisition and enjoyment of external goods—namely, the peace of mind that people experience when they achieve a proper balance between their needs and their wants. As he explained it, the individual who is content to live "within his income," satisfied with "small accumulations," is

> enabled gradually to relax, both in the rigour of his parsimony and in the severity of his application; and he feels with double satisfaction this gradual increase of ease and enjoyment, from having

felt before the hardship which attended the want of them. He has no anxiety to change so comfortable a situation, and does not go in quest of new enterprises and adventures, which might endanger, but could not well increase, the secure tranquillity which he actually enjoys. (TMS 252)

According to this view, happiness is not about getting more for ourselves, but rather knowing when we are well (TMS 174).

All the self-inflicted suffering caused by the restless pursuit of wealth could easily be avoided if people had fewer desires and knew how to be content with what they have. This is the wisdom of Smith's "prudent man," who sacrifices the frivolous and self-indulgent pleasures of luxury and vanity (TMS 252) for the sake of his long-term economic well-being and happiness: "In the bottom of his heart he would prefer the undisturbed enjoyment of secure tranquillity . . . to all the vain splendour of successful ambition" (TMS 253).

Yet in commercial society, we see "the respectful attentions of the world more strongly directed towards the rich and the great, than towards the wise and the virtuous" (TMS 72). Living under the sway of vanity and ambition, we are disposed "to admire, and almost to worship, the rich and the powerful, and to despise . . . persons of poor and mean condition" (TMS 72). This is illustrated in Smith's parable of the "poor man's son," who longs for the luxuries and conveniences afforded by great wealth, believing that these things represent the "means of happiness" (TMS 213). But whatever pleasures may be derived from such "trinkets of frivolous utility," they surely do not add to the stock of *real* human happiness, and often they become the very source of our unhappiness:

> Power and riches appear then to be, what they are, enormous and operose machines contrived to produce a few trifling

conveniencies to the body, consisting of springs the most nice and delicate, which must be kept in order with the most anxious attention, and which in spite of all our care are ready every moment to burst into pieces, and to crush in their ruins their unfortunate possessor. (TMS 213)

For all their allure, power and riches leave us just as exposed, if not more so, to anxiety, fear, and disappointment, and to sickness, danger, and death. "What could be added," Smith wondered, "to the happiness of the man who is in health, who is out of debt, and has a clear conscience? To one in this situation, all accessions of fortune may properly be said to be superfluous" (TMS 55).

Contemporary research on the economics of happiness confirms Smith's view. According to Richard Layard, there is "a paradox at the heart of our lives. Most people want more income and strive for it. Yet as Western societies have got richer, their people have become no happier."[19] Indeed, the pursuit of ever-greater wealth and social status has only increased the level of anxiety and restlessness that people feel. Layard notes the irony in the fact that "as we become richer, we also become less secure and more stressed." We would expect that "security and a quiet mind are goods that should increase, not decrease, as people become richer." The fundamental problem is "the lack of common feeling between people—the notion that life is essentially a competitive struggle. With such a philosophy the losers become alienated and a threat to the rest of us, and even the winners cannot relax in peace." So long as we remain "obsessed by status" and make material success the measure of our self-worth and our happiness, we will be condemned to a life of relentless striving, stress, and dissatisfaction.[20]

Smith surely would agree with Layard that people would be happier if they were able to "appreciate what they have, whatever it is" and "not always compare themselves with others" (71–72). But there is just one problem. As Smith observed in *Theory of Moral Sentiments*, economic growth is fueled by an ethical "deception" that causes people to admire wealth and greatness more than wisdom and virtue. The desire for the pleasures of vanity and superiority motivates people to work hard to better their condition:

> The pleasures of wealth and greatness . . . strike the imagination as something grand and beautiful and noble, of which the attainment is well worth all the toil and anxiety which we are so apt to bestow upon it.
>
> And it is well that nature imposes upon us in this manner. It is this deception which rouses and keeps in continual motion the industry of mankind. It is this which first prompted them to cultivate the ground, to build houses, to found cities and commonwealths, and to invent and improve all the sciences and arts, which ennoble and embellish human life. (TMS 214–15)

In *Wealth of Nations*, Smith noted that the "uniform, constant, and uninterrupted effort of every man to better his condition" is the principle that accounts for the wealth and prosperity of a nation (WN 343; see also 345, 540). The basics of food, clothing, and lodging may suffice for the purposes of human happiness, but it is steady economic growth that brings these goods within the reach of more and more people in society. Hence Smith's remark that it is "in the progressive state, while the society is advancing to the further acquisition . . . that the condition of the labouring poor, of the great body of the people, seems to be the happiest and the most comfortable. It is hard in the stationary, and miserable in the declining state" (WN 99).

Scholars have wrestled with the seemingly paradoxical implications of Smith's discussion.[21] As Dennis C. Rasmussen succinctly puts it,

> According to Smith, the desire to better our condition is the main engine driving economic growth in commercial society, yet he admits that this desire also tends to disrupt people's tranquility, which he sees as the key component of all true happiness. . . . From Smith's point of view, then, the relationship between progress and happiness is a paradoxical and complicated one.

Ryan Patrick Hanley agrees, noting that the profound gains produced by commercial society—particularly for the poor—seem to come at a steep price. This is because in "a very real sense, the 'wealth of nations' is itself often bought at the cost of individual happiness."[22] Charles Griswold, too, notes the "comic irony" in Smith's suggestion that progress and civilization are made possible by a deception that plunges us into "the world of unceasing work, of 'bettering our condition,' and therefore of unhappiness." As Griswold reads Smith, the conditions of our "material prosperity" are inextricably linked to our "spiritual poverty."[23]

Modern critics of capitalism have long complained that it promotes economic growth at the expense of virtue and happiness. John Maynard Keynes famously lamented that the capitalist solution to the problem of poverty requires us to pretend "that fair is foul and foul is fair; for foul is useful and fair is not."[24] But does the capitalist model for alleviating poverty necessarily force us to choose between the useful and the good? Is some measure of unhappiness simply the price we have to pay for human progress?

Although it may seem an unlikely source, Buddhism offers a useful conceptual framework for thinking about this question. There are many places in the canonical literature where the

Buddha speaks directly to the benefits and the dangers of wealth acquisition as it pertains to the happiness of a householder. What emerges from these texts is an account of economic growth in which energetic striving for wealth is compatible with moral and spiritual growth. This account describes an ennobling form of economic activity aimed at promoting well-being and creating opportunities for human development, while at the same time weakening the destructive impulses of greed and selfishness that prevent a householder from realizing the ultimate goal of the Buddhist path: the complete and perfect happiness of nirvana. Before we examine the details of that account, however, it will be helpful to begin with a general overview of the Buddhist understanding of greed.

THE CONCEPT OF GREED IN BUDDHIST THOUGHT

In Buddhism, the concept of greed is expressed in a constellation of closely related terms. One of these is the Pāli term *lobha*, which indicates an intense, self-centered longing or desire that not only produces suffering in this life but creates the conditions for an unhappy rebirth in the next:

> Any action performed with greed—born of greed, caused by greed, originating from greed: wherever one's selfhood turns up, there that action will ripen. Where that action ripens, there one will experience its fruit, either in this very life that has arisen or further along in the sequence.[25]

In Buddhist teaching, greed (*lobha*), hatred (*dosa*), and delusion (*moha*) are identified as "unwholesome roots" or defilements of mind that give rise to unskillful moral actions. The element of greed is also expressed by the word *rāga*, which conveys the sense of lust or passion. Thus, in the *Ādittapariyāya Sutta* (fire sermon), the Buddha explains that suffering arises in those who burn "with the fire of passion, with the fire of aversion, with the fire of delusion" (SN 35.28). The terms *lobha* and *rāga* are very closely related to *abhijjhā* (covetousness) and *taṇhā* (craving, thirst). The Pāli lexicon lists all four terms as synonyms, and for good reason: all point to the same deep-seated longing or desire that drives the self-centered pursuit of worldly happiness.

The term *taṇhā* figures most prominently in the Buddha's foundational teaching on the Four Noble Truths, where it is identified as the proximate cause of all suffering (*dukkha*):

> And this, monks, is the noble truth of the origination of stress [*dukkha*]: the craving [*taṇhā*] that makes for further becoming—accompanied by passion & delight, relishing now here & now there—i.e., craving for sensual pleasure, craving for becoming, craving for non-becoming.[26]

The three manifestations of craving mentioned here indicate the breadth of the Buddhist concept, which refers, on the one hand, to the insatiable desire to experience sense pleasure, as well as the desire to be or become a certain kind of person; and on the other hand, the desire to be free from unpleasant experiences, as well as the desire not to be or become a certain kind of person (or not to exist at all).

A chief characteristic of craving is the "attachment" that people form to the objects of their desire. The Pāli word for attachment, *upādāna*, literally means "fuel," and in this context it refers to the fuel that sustains the "fires" of greed, hatred, and delusion.[27] As Rupert Gethin explains, attachment is the attempt to "take possession" of the things we desire, to "call them our own." In other words, attachment is the attempt to hold on to the experiences, objects, and people that make us who we are and constitute our happiness. But in this quest for lasting personal happiness, says Gethin, we become attached to things that are, by their very nature, "unreliable, unstable, changing, and impermanent."[28] Sense pleasures are by nature fleeting; material objects are subject to falling apart or being stolen or destroyed; and even the people we love and cherish are subject to aging, illness, and death. Thus, as the Buddha instructed, when a person who does not understand the impermanent nature of things is confronted with the "loss of relatives, loss of wealth, or loss through disease, he sorrows, grieves, & laments, beats his breast, becomes distraught."[29] In short, suffering arises because we want things to be other than the way they really are—we long for stability and permanence that do not exist in the realm of our experience.

It is important to notice how the idea of self is bound up with craving and attachment. As Gethin puts it, our sense of self arises from "the desire to identify or claim some part or parts of the universe as one's own, as one's possession, and say of them "this is mine, I am this, this is my self."[30] At the most basic level, this involves the attempt to take possession of the bodily and mental processes that constitute our experience. In Buddhism, these processes are described as "bundles" or "aggregates" of form (body), feeling, perception, mental formations, and consciousness. Without even thinking about it, we regard these things as "my body," "my feeling," "my perception," "my thoughts," and "my consciousness." Yet the identification of one's self with any of these aggregates must inevitably lead to suffering, and for the same reason that our attachment to objects and people leads to suffering: namely, they are impermanent and constantly changing. Thus, the person who identifies the self with body becomes anxious and distressed at seeing the process of change and decay that bodies inevitably undergo:

> With the change and alteration of form, his consciousness becomes preoccupied with the change of form. Agitation and a constellation of mental states born of preoccupation with the change of form remain obsessing his mind. Because his mind is obsessed, he is frightened, distressed, and anxious, and through clinging he becomes agitated.[31]

Here again, suffering is rooted in the desire for things to be different from the way they actually are. According to the Buddhist analysis, the idea of the self as an independent subject or "I" that endures unchanged through time is a delusion. Such an "I" is not to be found within our experience at any rate. The fact that the body constantly undergoes physical change is apparent in the natural process of aging. But careful observation of the mind, where we might hope to encounter the immutable essence of our selfhood, reveals nothing more than a perpetual succession of thoughts, ideas, and emotions.

The process of craving and self-making inevitably leads to conflict because, explains Gethin, it

> drives me to accumulate "possessions" . . . that define and reinforce my sense of my own selfhood as student, teacher, banker, lawyer, politician, craftsman, Buddhist monk—as some kind of person as opposed to some other kind of person. And when I feel that what I regard as my self, that what I regard as by rights mine, is in danger of being taken from me, I become angry, frustrated, fearful; I may even be driven to violence and kill.[32]

It takes only a little reflection to see how this prioritizing of the needs of the self in opposition to the needs of others fuels destructive competitiveness, acquisitiveness, exploitation, corruption, crime, civil strife, and war.

The cessation of suffering requires that we abandon craving once and for all—that we relinquish all possessions, including the physical and mental processes that we identify as our self. But letting go is easier said than done. As biological organisms, we are connected to the world through the medium of the senses, and our very existence depends on the satisfaction of basic material needs. The idea of self arises almost imperceptibly from the struggle for subsistence. Confronted by what we regard as a hostile world in which we must claim our share of what we need in order to live and to flourish, we come to see the protection and preservation of the self as both natural and right. Yet the more we labor under this egoistic view of things, the more entangled we get in the subtle web of craving and grasping that perpetuates the cycle of suffering and rebirth.

The Buddhist path to liberation therefore involves an inward transformation of the individual, in which the mental defilements of greed, hatred, and delusion are gradually overcome through the cultivation of nongreed (*alobha*), nonhatred (*adosa*), and nondelusion (*amoha*)—or in their positive formulations: generosity (*dāna*), lovingkindness (*mettā*), and wisdom (*paññā*). In practical terms, this means establishing oneself firmly in good ethical conduct (*sīla*) and developing a greater capacity to act with unselfish concern for the welfare of others. This is crucially supported by the practice of meditative concentration (*samādhi*), aimed at deepening one's insight into the truth of the Dhamma.

The path of liberation is said to be "born" in that person whose mind "becomes steady, settles down, grows unified and concentrated."[33] In this tranquil state, one is able to gain direct insight into the true nature of reality—to see clearly the impermanent, conditioned, and unsatisfactory quality of all things connected with form, feeling, perceptions, mental formations, and consciousness. With this insight, the meditator begins to *dis*identify with the various sensations, thoughts, and emotions that arise in the continuing flow of conscious experience, affirming, "This is not mine, this I am not, this is not my self."[34] Through this process of *dis*identification, the meditator gradually "wearies" of these things, and being wearied, the Buddha says,

> he becomes passion-free. In his freedom from passion, he is emancipated. Being emancipated, there is the knowledge that he is emancipated. He knows: "birth is exhausted, lived is the holy life, what had to be done is done, there is nothing more of this becoming."[35]

With the end of craving and self-making comes the end of the cycle of suffering and rebirth. With the fires of greed, hatred, and delusion thus finally extinguished, one experiences the complete and perfect happiness of nirvana (*nibbāna*).

WEALTH AND HAPPINESS IN THE PĀLI CANON

Some of the Buddha's followers sought liberation by embracing the monastic life of moral discipline and contemplation. Renouncing the distractions and temptations of a householder's life, they devoted themselves to the purification of the mind and the cultivation of insight through intensive meditation. But for the majority of people who remained to a greater or lesser degree attached to the pursuit of worldly pleasures, the Buddha offered clear practical guidance regarding the attainment of liberation. The canonical texts recount numerous conversations with householders from various walks of life, including bankers, merchants, farmers, and tradesmen. In speaking to this audience, the Buddha adopted a pragmatic approach. He did not criticize the acquisition of wealth; instead, he reinforced the importance of cultivating moral virtues conducive to happiness in this life and to a good rebirth in the next. He laid a particular emphasis on the virtue of *dāna* as an antidote to greed.[36] The general strategy was to encourage a way of relating to wealth that would gradually loosen the householder's attachment to it.

Commenting on the central importance of giving to the Buddhist conception of happiness, Bhikkhu Bodhi writes:

> To give is not only a way to reduce our greed and attachment, not only a way to acquire merit productive of future benefits, but a directly visible source of joy which provides immediate confirmation of the central pillar on which the entire Dhamma rests: that the path to happiness is one of relinquishment rather than one of accumulation.[37]

Thus, as the Buddha instructed the young householder Sigālaka, to be "liberal and unselfish," to be disposed to generosity, kindness, and compassion, and to work for the benefit of others in a spirit of impartiality are the keys to experiencing happiness in this life and a good rebirth in the next.[38]

The Pāli texts present a very clear and consistent account of the proper acquisition and uses of wealth for a householder. According to this account, wealth may be acquired so long as it is earned by honest means and does not involve the violation of basic moral precepts.[39] In the *Vaṇijjā Sutta*, lay followers are explicitly instructed to abstain from trading in weapons, meat, human beings, intoxicants, and poisons (AN 5.177). As to the proper uses of wealth, the Buddha instructed the lay disciple Anāthapiṇḍika[40] as follows:

> Here, householder, with wealth acquired by energetic striving, amassed by the strength of his arms, earned by the sweat of his brow, righteous wealth righteously gained, the noble disciple makes himself happy and pleased and properly maintains himself in happiness; he makes his parents happy and pleased and properly maintains them in happiness; he makes his wife and children, his slaves, workers, and servants happy and pleased and properly maintains them in happiness. This is the first utilization of wealth.[41]

Having made adequate provisions to protect against future loss from disaster or theft, the householder's generosity then expands to others by assisting "friends and companions," making appropriate "oblations" to "relatives, guests, ancestors, the king, and the deities," and perhaps most important of all, an "uplifting offering of alms" to the monastic community. The wise and virtuous householder who uses wealth in these ways is said to have made the best use of it and will have no regrets. By the same token, wealth used for any other purpose "is said to have gone to waste, to have been squandered, to have been used frivolously."[42]

Although there is nothing inherently wrong with being rich, the accumulation of great wealth is fraught with danger. As another prominent lay disciple of the Buddha, King Pasenadi of Kosala, observed: "Few are those people in the world who, when acquiring lavish wealth, don't become intoxicated & heedless, don't become greedy for sensual pleasures, and don't mistreat other beings."[43] A householder, therefore, should refrain from pursuing wealth either as an end in itself or merely for the purpose of satisfying the self-indulgent desire for sensual pleasure.[44]

BUDDHISM AND THE ECONOMIC PROBLEM OF HAPPINESS

In the *Anaṇa Sutta*, the Buddha describes four kinds of happiness, or "bliss" (*sukha*), which can be experienced by householders.[45] They are as follows:

1. The happiness of having material wealth (*atthisukha*), which is experienced by those who "earn" their wealth by hard work and perseverance. *Atthisukha* includes the satisfaction that one derives from the fruits of labor performed well and honestly, as well as the contentment that comes from knowing that one has enough. As Lily de Silva notes, "one could have great wealth, but if one does not experience a sense of contentment with what one has, one cannot really enjoy *atthisukha* or the pleasure of having. The amassing of wealth of such a person is like trying to fill a bottomless vessel."[46]

2. The happiness of enjoying material wealth (*bhogasukha*), which is experienced by those who use wealth wisely to promote well-being for themselves and others. This means avoiding the extremes of extravagance and miserliness and using wealth for the purposes of "making merit"—that is, being generous and open-handed, attending to those in need, and "delighting in the distribution of alms."[47]

3. The happiness of being debtless (*anaṇasukha*), which is experienced by those who conscientiously fulfill all their obligations to others, both financial and social. This means living within one's income and discharging any specific duties that one might have to family, friends, and the wider community.

4. The happiness of being blameless (*anavajjasukha*), which is experienced by those who, because of their generosity and good conduct, enjoy the deep satisfaction of having a clear conscience.

Anavajjasukha is considered the greatest of the four kinds of happiness because it derives from the virtue of one's character as exhibited in thought, speech, and action.

It is important to emphasize here that wealth, viewed from a Buddhist standpoint, should be pursued with a view to creating the material conditions for genuine well-being and spiritual growth. One must take special care to avoid watering the seeds of craving and grasping. In this respect, life in modern commercial society presents some formidable challenges, and especially so in a consumer-based economy where the appetite for consumption is constantly being stimulated by advertising and reinforced by sophisticated marketing strategies designed to exploit the desire to be or become a certain kind of person. In this environment, writes Bhikkhu Bodhi, we are led to believe that "by acquiring ownership over more and more goods, we thereby come closer to *the* good, to becoming happier, more contented, more deeply fulfilled human beings." But this "sleight-of-hand deception" only lures us deeper into the entanglement of craving and grasping:

> At the heart of the consumerist culture we find this puzzling paradox, that when we pursue wealth as an end in itself, instead of arriving at true happiness we only seem further removed from it.... Those who enjoy the most abundant wealth and exercise the greatest power are rarely models of contentment.[48]

From a Buddhist perspective, says Bodhi, the problem posed by consumerism is not one that can be solved by making "a limp compromise between indulgence and virtue." What is required is a "bold, decisive step in the direction of detachment, an inner renunciation that enables one to rise above the whole round of production and consumption even while living within its boundaries." To this end, the layperson is advised to heed the example of the monastics, who demonstrate that true happiness is found not in accumulation, but in the relinquishment of possessions. For those who are "still enmeshed in the demands of economic subsistence," the monastics model a simple, mindful way of living in which material needs are reduced to the barest necessities: food, clothing, shelter, and medicine.[49] Their happiness lies in having limited desires (*appicchatā*) and knowing how to be content with what they have (*santuṭṭhi*).

For the layperson, taking a more decisive step in the direction of detachment and renunciation does not mean giving up the pursuit of wealth or reducing one's material needs to the most basic necessities of life. This is neither a realistic nor even a desirable expectation, as it would quickly lead to social stagnation. It is for this reason, explains Lily de Silva, that Buddhism encourages the layperson "to be industrious, to forge ahead in his chosen blameless occupation," to invest in his business, to save for the future, and to lead a comfortable, balanced life "consonant with earning capacity."[50] Yet the virtues of contentment (being satisfied with what one has) and industriousness (working to better one's condition) seem to pull in opposite directions. How does Buddhism reconcile these apparently conflicting ideas?

In *Buddhist Economics: A Middle Way for the Market Place*, P. A. Payutto explains that the Buddhist concept of contentment (*santuṭṭhi*) does not entail the absence of desire, but rather the absence of a certain *kind* of desire (namely, *taṇhā*, the insatiable, self-centered craving for sensual pleasure). By its very nature, this craving "leads to restlessness and exhaustion in the individual, strife in society, and unsustainable consumption."[51] However, contentment is compatible with another form of desire (namely, *chanda*,[52] which in this context refers to the wholesome desire for well-being). Rather than chasing "artificial wants," *chanda* focuses on things that contribute to genuine flourishing, such as good nutrition, adequate housing, health care, education, and spiritual growth. According to Payutto, "the path to true contentment involves reducing the artificial desire for sense-pleasure, while actively encouraging and supporting the desire for quality of life."[53]

When economic activity is directed by *chanda*, says Payutto, "its objectives are clear and its activities are controlled. A natural balance or equilibrium is achieved." Whereas in classical economic theory consumption is limited by scarcity, in Buddhism it is limited by "an appreciation of moderation and the objective of well-being." Moderation in the Buddhist sense means knowing how much is enough. It is "an awareness of that optimum point where the enhancement of true well-being coincides with the experience of satisfaction."[54] In the canonical literature, this point is illustrated in the *Doṇapāka Sutta* (SN 3.13), where the Buddha instructs King Pasenadi in the benefits of moderation as it pertains to the consumption of food:

> When a person is constantly mindful,
> And knows when enough food has been taken,
> All their afflictions become more slender
> —They age more gradually, protecting their lives.

Whereas the feeling of hunger can be satisfied in a manner that supports good health and brings contentment, the desire of the glutton, being insatiable, leads only to ill health and distress. By focusing on the goal of well-being, mindfulness of consumption promotes not only a healthier and happier life, but also the spiritual goal of *reducing* one's greed and attachment to sense pleasures.

In their book *How Much Is Enough? Money and the Good Life*, Robert and Edward Skidelsky point out that in affluent Western societies, we are all, in principle, "capable of limiting our wants to our needs; the problem is that a competitive, monetized economy puts us under continual pressure to want more and more." Although the "material conditions for the good life already exist . . . the blind pursuit of growth puts it continually out of reach."[55] Writing from a Buddhist perspective, de Silva similarly notes the way that production and consumption feed each other in a vicious circle: "Each time a target has been reached, the limit to possible growth recedes further like a mirage. More and more is produced, more and more is consumed." However, this approach to economic growth "is severely antithetical to Buddhist values. Buddhism sets the limit at the other end: it advocates that we feed our needs and not our greeds."[56]

The Buddhist emphasis on moderation and contentment contrasts sharply with the explicit endorsement of consumerism that we find in the contemporary defense of greed. "Show me someone who doesn't want more of something, be it cars, houses, clothing, food," writes economist Walter E. Williams. "The fact that people want more is [what accounts] for most of the good things that get done."[57] The implication, of course, is that without such desire, people would consume less, which would have a negative impact on productivity and jobs. But if consumer desire really is the engine that drives growth and improves the prospects of the poorest members of society, is there perhaps a danger in encouraging people to be content with what they have?

Anticipating this challenge, Payutto notes that "traditional economists" are inclined to view contentment as inimical to economic growth, on the ground that "without desire, the whole economy would grind to a halt." But again, this view is based on a misunderstanding of contentment. We experience contentment when we limit our desire for sense pleasure and the gratification of the ego. But having fewer desires of this kind is fully compatible with working hard to create the material conditions for a good life. Indeed, when it comes to creating "skillful conditions"—the internal and external conditions conducive to liberation—the Buddha urged his followers to be diligent.[58]

The key point here is that Buddhism is not opposed to economic growth per se; instead, it encourages a skillful approach that is both socially and environmentally sustainable, providing people with opportunities to achieve well-being for themselves and contribute in meaningful ways to the well-being of others. Buddhism sees productivity and responsible consumption as social goods and is amenable to developing and using material and technological resources for the purpose of alleviating the suffering caused by poverty, hunger, homelessness, disease, and lack of opportunity for inward growth. At the same time, it discourages forms of production and consumption that are harmful and diminish the overall quality of life. This ethical approach to development might not generate the rapid growth made possible in economies that foster a consumerist mentality, but the result promises to be a more peaceful, just, and sustainable society.

From a Buddhist perspective, the capitalist solution to the problem of *material* poverty need not lead to *spiritual* poverty. However, it does require a different way of thinking about what it means to "better our condition"—one that is motivated not by the insatiable, self-centered desire for sense pleasure, but by *chanda*. If all economic activities were guided by the principle of moderation and a compassionate desire to promote the welfare of others, writes Payutto, "the result would be much more than just a healthy economy and material progress—such activities would contribute to the whole of human development and enable humanity to lead a nobler life and enjoy a more mature kind of happiness."⁵⁹

BUDDHISM, SMITH, AND HUMAN FLOURISHING

To bring the wheel full circle, we turn now to a few comparative reflections on the conditions for human flourishing in Buddhism and the writings of Adam Smith.

From a Buddhist perspective, there is nothing surprising in Smith's assertion that most people are deluded about the true source of their happiness. Human beings are naturally prone to greed—to desire what is pleasant (agreeable) and to hate what is unpleasant (disagreeable), to cling to the objects of their desires, and to define who they are through the accumulation of possessions. But greed and hatred, as well as the delusion that conditions them, are manifested in varying degrees. Greed may be all-consuming, so to speak. As the Buddha cautioned in the *Pattakamma Sutta*, those whose hearts are overcome by covetousness and unrighteous greed (*abhijjhāvisamalobhābhibhūtena*) spoil their happiness and their reputations by doing what should not be done and neglecting their duties (AN 4.61). The natural desire for pleasure, however, can be restrained through conscious moral effort. It is possible to enjoy sense pleasure to a moderate degree—that is, without falling victim to the *craving* desire that leads, in Payutto's words, to "restlessness and exhaustion in the individual, strife in society, and unsustainable consumption" (1994, 32).⁶⁰ Happiness grows in proportion to our ability to limit our "wants" and promote the conditions for true well-being; and it continues to grow as we expand our capacity for generosity, kindness, and compassion.

Smith's character sketch of the "poor man's son" in *Theory of Moral Sentiments* (TMS 211ff.) vividly illustrates the suffering caused by the delusory pursuit of happiness:

> Through the whole of his life he pursues the idea of a certain artificial and elegant repose which he may never arrive at, for which he sacrifices a real tranquillity that is at all times in his power, and which, if in the extremity of old age he should at last attain to it, he will find to be in no respect preferable to that humble security and contentment which he had abandoned for it. It is then, in the last dregs of life, his body wasted with toil and diseases, his mind galled and ruffled by the memory of a thousand injuries and disappointments . . . that he begins at last to find that wealth and greatness are mere trinkets of frivolous utility, no more adapted for procuring ease of body or tranquillity of mind than the tweezer-cases of the lover of toys.[61]

Driven by vanity, "that love of distinction so natural to man" (TMS 213), the unhappy social climber imagines that wealth and luxury will somehow bring him peace of mind and fulfillment. But his vanity causes him to stake his character—and his happiness—on a false foundation. He desires to be praised for things that neither are truly praiseworthy nor bring any ultimate satisfaction. What is worse, his restless craving for the pleasures of wealth and greatness brings him only ill-being and discontent.

Later in the book, Smith offers the reader a contrasting portrait of the "prudent man," who prefers "the undisturbed enjoyment of secure tranquillity . . . to all the vain splendour of successful ambition" (TMS 253). Patient and hardworking, he knows that thrift and good conduct are the keys to long-term well-being and happiness. Like the virtuous Buddhist householder, the prudent man is content to live within his income. He enjoys a balanced life, free from debt and the burden of a bad conscience (TMS 55, 252).

But while prudent concern for one's private interest and happiness is generally regarded as both "respectable" and "agreeable," Smith notes that it is neither "the most endearing" nor "the most ennobling" of human virtues (TMS 253). Prudence does not earn one the "ardent love or admiration" enjoyed by those who freely act from a spirit of benevolent concern for the welfare of others:

> The man who, ... from proper motives, has performed a generous action, when he looks forward to those whom he has served, feels himself to be the natural object of their love and gratitude. ... His mind ... is filled with cheerfulness, serenity, and composure. He is in friendship and harmony with all mankind, and looks upon his fellow-creatures with confidence and benevolent satisfaction, secure that he has rendered himself worthy of their most favourable regards. In the combination of all these sentiments consists the consciousness of merit, or of deserved reward. (TMS 100)

Thus, whatever happiness or tranquility may be gained through prudent self-restraint is greatly enhanced by cultivating the "social and benevolent affections" of generosity, humanity, kindness, compassion, friendship, and esteem. Indeed, Smith went as far as to say that "the chief part of human happiness" arises from the consciousness of being beloved and knowing that one deserves to be beloved (TMS 50, 132). Here, we see a clear parallel with the Buddhist concept of "blamelessness"—the consciousness of merit that arises from the practice of generosity, kindness, and compassion toward others. As noted earlier, the peace of mind associated with blamelessness is the highest form of happiness possible for a householder.

Benevolence figured prominently in Smith's understanding of the conditions for societal flourishing and happiness. "All the members of human society," he wrote,

> stand in need of each others assistance, and are likewise exposed to mutual injuries. Where the necessary assistance is reciprocally afforded from love, from gratitude, from friendship, and esteem, the society flourishes and is happy. All the different members of it are bound together by the agreeable bands of love and affection, and are, as it were, drawn to one common centre of mutual good offices. (TMS 100)

But this inspiring vision of a humane and enlightened social order was balanced by Smith's sobering account of the weakness and partiality of human benevolence (TMS 256ff.). According to Smith, we are naturally disposed to sympathize with the joys and sorrows of others. This sympathy is rooted in our innate ability to put ourselves in *their* shoes, to imagine how *they* must be feeling (TMS 11ff., 374). However, the degree to which we sympathize with others varies greatly. Nature inclines us to care first and foremost for ourselves. We extend this care to the members of our own family, and then perhaps to a handful of people we consider friends. But our concern for the welfare of others does not extend so easily to those we do not know. For Smith, the scope of our benevolence is defined mainly by familiarity.[62]

Smith also called attention to a certain asymmetry in our sentiments that leads us to sympathize more fully with joy than with sorrow (TMS 60ff.). Although we are able to enter into the suffering of the poor, our compassion for their misery tends not to be very great. Hence Smith's remark that the "mere want of fortune, mere poverty" actually "excites little compassion" in us. In fact, poverty is more likely to elicit our contempt: "We despise a beggar; and, though his importunities may extort an alms from us, he is scarce ever the object of any serious commiseration" (TMS 166). By contrast, we are always eager to sympathize with the situation of the "man of rank and distinction" and to enter fully into "that joy and exultation with which his circumstances naturally inspire him" (TMS 61).

As we noted in an earlier section, the desire to "pursue riches and avoid poverty" (TMS 60) is connected to a deep-seated psychological need to gain the attention and sympathy of others. Smith points to vanity as the motivating force. But vanity, which relates to the way other people view us, does not fully capture the underlying pain and isolation experienced by the poor:

> The poor man . . . is ashamed of his poverty. He feels that it either places him out of the sight of mankind, or, that if they take any notice of him, they have, however, scarce any fellow-feeling with the misery and distress which he suffers. He is mortified upon both accounts. For though to be overlooked, and to be disapproved of, are things entirely different, yet as obscurity covers us from the daylight of honour and approbation, to feel that we are taken no notice of, necessarily damps the most agreeable hope, and disappoints the most ardent desire, of human nature. (TMS 62)

This passage underscores the dehumanizing effect of poverty. The poor man is largely invisible to society; his suffering goes unacknowledged. Thus, when he sees that the rich man is "the object of the observation and fellow-feeling of every body about him," his motivation to endure all the toil, anxiety, and "mortifications" involved in the pursuit of wealth has a certain existential urgency about it.

There is an undeniably tragic element to this story, for according to Smith, the desire for wealth and greatness not only promotes selfishness and inauthenticity, but also erodes any compassion that we might otherwise have for the misery of the poor (TMS 266). Yet, in a move characteristic of his thinking, Smith suggests that nature "has wisely judged" that the peace and order of society should "rest more securely" upon our disposition to admire the rich and the great "than upon the invisible and often uncertain difference of wisdom and virtue" (TMS 266). Indeed, as Dennis Rasmussen points out, Smith seems to have regarded a certain amount of economic inequality as "positively useful," both as a means of "bolstering political stability" and as a stimulus to economic productivity.[63] These observations chime well with Smith's claim that the desire for wealth and greatness—with a generous assist from the invisible hand—results in a fortuitous, if unintended, distribution of "the necessaries of life" to the lowest ranks of society.

While it is true, therefore, that Smith envisioned the possibility of a truly flourishing and happy society whose members are "bound together by the agreeable bands of love and affection," the social and psychological forces he described seem to undermine that possibility at every turn. The sentiments that inspire us to "pursue riches and avoid poverty" not only promote economic growth, but also reinforce our lack of concern (if not outright contempt) for the poor and the wretched. Picking up on this point, Simon Blackburn notes that Smith "does not seem to have realized that alongside the invisible hand there will by his own lights be an invisible boot, whereby the resulting stratification [of society] breaks apart any sense of us being in things together, interdependent, beating in time, or welded into a genuine society."[64]

Furthermore, Smith's own account of the psychological pain and social isolation experienced by those who live in poverty seems to cut against his assertion that the poor are "in no respect inferior" to the rich when it comes to "the real happiness of human life" (TMS 216). As social beings, our happiness depends on more than just having our most basic needs met. It is also important that we are seen by others—that our presence makes a valued difference in the community. Meaningful social interactions are a crucial part of human well-being and must be counted among the prerequisites for flourishing. As Rasmussen correctly observes, extreme inequality "undermines the happiness of the poor by depriving them of the pleasure of mutual sympathy."[65]

Recognizing the harmful effects of poverty, the early Buddhist texts assign an important role to government in creating the conditions for human flourishing. In addition to a fair and impartial system of justice, there is a need for policies that reflect a humane concern for the well-being and prosperity of *every* member of society. This is a central theme in the *Cakkavattisīhanāda Sutta* (DN 26), which identifies poverty (*dāliddiya*) as a root cause of moral corruption and social decay. In this discourse, the reader is invited to imagine a society in a state of disintegration brought on by the failure of government to address the material needs of the people. The situation is made steadily worse by disastrous policies aimed at stopping poverty-driven theft—first, by simply giving property to individuals arrested for stealing, and when that fails, trying to deter theft by the extreme measure of executing offenders. The downward spiral into moral depravity and violence is finally stemmed when a few like-minded people begin to realize that their own flourishing depends on the flourishing of those around them. They undertake to form a new community based on a commitment to moral precepts and doing good for the sake of others. By dedicating themselves to the practice of generosity, kindness, and compassion toward their fellow beings, they gradually reestablish the conditions required for peace, prosperity, and happiness.

One of the major insights of the discourse, writes Peter Hershock, is that poverty "is not best alleviated through either state welfare or legal and technological controls that address only 'the poor.' Such efforts eventually only exacerbate the root conditions of poverty."[66] This is so because such measures identify poverty with the poor rather than with a breakdown of the relational patterns of mutual sympathy and generosity that constitute genuine community. In other words, poverty and social instability arise when people are unable to contribute to the welfare of others or to be the object of their reciprocal goodwill and assistance:

> As the sutta makes clear, both felt community and its objective expression in abiding social institutions . . . disintegrate with the breakdown of robust patterns of mutual contribution. Resisting or reversing such . . . disintegration cannot hinge on simply meeting individual (or even collective) needs or wants; success finally hinges on how these are addressed—that is, on the values underlying our strategies for redressing the erosion of relational capacity and effective offering. Successfully alleviating poverty is a function of realizing and sustaining patterns of interdependence that enhance the capabilities of both individuals and communities for relating freely in contributing to one another's welfare.[67]

From a Buddhist perspective, it is the responsibility of government to create real opportunities for work that is satisfying and enables people to support themselves and contribute in meaningful ways to the well-being of others.

In the eponymously titled *Kūṭadanta Sutta* (DN 5), the Buddha recommends to the brahmin a plan of economic development that provides avenues for people to work and flourish together. In addition to providing direct assistance to those with acute need, the plan includes measures such as providing seed and fodder for those who farm and raise livestock, providing subsidies to those who work in trade, and guaranteeing a fair wage and food for those employed in government service. According to this view, if people have the freedom to engage in work that is enriching and allows them to live with dignity and perform their duties, society will be peaceful, prosperous, and happy.[68]

We should bear in mind that the primary aim of the Buddha's teaching was not to effect social or political reform. The social and economic views presented in these canonical texts must always be understood in light of the overarching soteriological goal of liberation. That said, early Buddhist discussions of the conditions for spiritual awakening and social welfare acknowledge the usefulness of economic freedom for alleviating forms of suffering that trap people in the prison of greed, hatred, and delusion. The lack of basic capabilities such as good health, nutrition, and adequate shelter presents a serious impediment to the project of liberation. Freedom enables people to use their energy, talents, and creativity to transform the material conditions of their lives in ways that are both ennobling and mutually liberating.

The early Buddhist view thus agrees with Smith that no society "can surely be flourishing and happy, of which the far greater part of the members are poor and miserable." At the very least, people must be free to work and enjoy "such a share of the produce of their own labour as to be themselves tolerably well fed, cloathed and lodged" (WN 96). However, flourishing depends on more than individuals simply being free to pursue their own interests. As discussed earlier, Smith's idea of a truly flourishing and happy society is one whose members are "bound together" by mutual love and affection (TMS 100). It is only by restraining our selfish tendencies and caring more for others that we may hope to produce that "harmony of sentiments and passions" on which our mutual flourishing depends (TMS 30).

Whether a government should intervene in a free market economy, and to what extent, are questions that divide contemporary interpreters of Smith's thought. From a Buddhist perspective, however, one thing is abundantly clear: achieving his vision of a more humane and enlightened society requires that we move beyond the familiar libertarian nostrums that "greed is good, what's mine is mine, and whatever the market produces is fair."[69] Government works best not by creating a level playing field and letting the chips fall where they may, but by creating policies that reflect and encourage a compassionate concern for the well-being and happiness of every member of society. As Payutto explains,

> The ideal society is one in which human beings, training themselves in mind and intellect, although possessing differences, are nevertheless striving for the same objectives. . . . While absolute equality is impossible, governments should ensure that the four requisites are distributed so all citizens have enough to live on comfortably and can find honest work. Moreover, the economic system in general should lead to a harmonious community rather than to contention and strife, and material possessions used as a base for beneficial human development rather than as an end in themselves.[70]

The nonpartisan aspect of the Buddhist approach challenges us to move beyond the narrowly defined ideological positions—"liberal" and "conservative"—that dominate the current political debate. Such views may ultimately prevent us from seeing and skillfully addressing the suffering caused by poverty, inequality, and lack of opportunity for human development.

NOTES

1. Concise discussions of this history can be found in Edward Skidelsky, "The Emancipation of Avarice," *First Things* (May 2011); and John Paul Rollert, "Greed Is Good: A 300-Year History of a Dangerous Idea," *The Atlantic*, April 2014.
2. Pierre Nicole, "De la Grandeur" (1670), quoted in Rudi Verburg, "The Rise of Greed in Early Economic Thought: From Deadly Sin to Social Benefit," *Journal of the History of Economic Thought* 34, no. 4 (2012): 515.
3. Giambattista Vico, *The New Science* (1725, esp. Element VII, §132), quoted in Skidelsky, "The Emancipation of Avarice."
4. Mandeville first presented his ideas in the poem *The Grumbling Hive: or, Knaves Turn'd Honest* (1705), which was subsequently republished with commentary in *The Fable of the Bees: or, Private Vices, Public Benefits* (1714).
5. According to Smith, "to feel much for others and little for ourselves, . . . to restrain our selfish, and to indulge our benevolent affections, constitutes the perfection of human nature" (TMS 30).
6. See, for instance, TMS 100.
7. R. L. Meek, D. D. Raphael, and P. G. Stein, eds., *Adam Smith: Lectures in Jurisprudence* (Indianapolis: Liberty Fund, 1982), 340.
8. Meek et al., *Adam Smith: Lectures in Jurisprudence*, 341.
9. Meek et al., *Adam Smith: Lectures in Jurisprudence*, 564.
10. Smith offered a lengthier discussion of this economy in *An Inquiry into the Nature and Causes of the Wealth of Nations* (2 vols., ed. R. H. Campbell and A. S. Skinner; reprinted by Liberty Press, 1976 [1776]), 181–82.
11. *The Phil Donahue Show* (September 6, 1979), https://www.youtube.com/watch?v=6r2rhl8997A.
12. On the historical origins of this terminological preference, see A. O. Hirschman, *The Passions and the Interests* (Princeton, NJ: Princeton University Press, 1977).
13. Milton Friedman and Rose Friedman, *Free To Choose: A Personal Statement* (New York: Harcourt, 1980), 27.
14. On this point, see Milton Friedman, *Capitalism and Freedom* (Chicago: University of Chicago Press, 1962), 168–69.
15. This was broadcast on February 3, 1998.

16. Milken became famous for his high-yield bonds, which rescued some corporations and helped others get started. In 1990, he pleaded guilty to various counts of securities fraud and tax evasion. On the other hand, Mother Teresa, a Roman Catholic nun and founder of the Missionaries of Charity, was canonized (officially declared a saint) on September 4, 2016.
17. Kurt Eichenwald, "Wages Even Wall St. Can't Stomach," *New York Times*, April 3, 1989.
18. "Hatred and anger are the greatest poison to the happiness of a good mind. . . . which is best promoted by the contrary passions of gratitude and love" (TMS 46).
19. R. Layard, *Happiness: Lessons from a New Science* (New York: Penguin, 2005), 3–4. See, for example, Richard A. Easterlin, "The Economics of Happiness," *Daedalus* 133, no. 2 (2004): 26–33; Daniel Kahneman, *Well Being: The Foundations of Hedonic Psychology* (New York: Russell Sage Foundation, 2003); Daniel Kahneman et al., "Would You Be Happier If You Were Richer? A Focusing Illusion." *Science* 312, no. 5782 (2006): 1908–10; Daniel Kahneman and Angus Deaton, "High Income Improves Evaluation of Life but Not Emotional Well-Being," *Proceedings of the National Academy of Sciences* 107, no. 38 (2010): 16489–93; and John Helliwell, Richard Layard, and Jeffrey Sachs, *World Happiness Report 2017* (New York: Sustainable Development Solutions Network, 2017).
20. The quotes in this paragraph are to Layard, *Happiness*, 164, 163, and 162.
21. See, for instance, R. H. Coase, "Adam Smith's View of Man," *Journal of Law and Economics* 19, no. 3 (1976): 24–25; Charles Griswold, *Adam Smith and the Virtues of Enlightenment* (Cambridge: Cambridge University Press, 1999), esp. 217–27; Samuel Fleischacker, *On Adam Smith's Wealth of Nations: A Philosophical Companion* (Princeton, NJ: Princeton University Press, 2004); Dennis C. Rasmussen, "Does 'Bettering Our Condition' Really Make Us Better Off? Adam Smith on Progress and Happiness," *American Political Science Review* 100, no. 3 (2006): 309; Dennis C. Rasmussen, *The Problems and Promise of Commercial Society: Adam Smith's Response to Rousseau* (University Park: Pennsylvania State University Press, 2008); Douglas J. Den Uyl and Douglas B. Rasmussen, "Adam Smith on Economic Happiness," *Reason Papers* 32 (2010): 29–40; Dennis C. Rasmussen, "Adam Smith on Commerce and Happiness: A Response to Den Uyl and Rasmussen," *Reason Papers* 33

(2011): 95–101; and Ryan Patrick Hanley. *Adam Smith and the Character of Virtue* (Cambridge: Cambridge University Press, 2009).

22. Ryan Patrick Hanley, "Adam Smith, Markets, and Virtues," *Montréal Review* (March 2013).
23. Griswold, *Adam Smith and the Virtues of Enlightenment*, 222 (see also 225), 16.
24. J. Keynes, "Economic Possibilities for Our Grandchildren," in *Essays in Persuasion*, vol. 9, *The Collected Writings of John Maynard Keynes* (London: Macmillan, 1972), 331. Keynes's hope was that perhaps another hundred years of robust economic growth, spurred on by the "strenuous, purposeful money-makers of society," would create such an abundance of material wealth that people might finally be able to retire the gods of avarice and usury and turn their attention to the nobler business of living "wisely and agreeably and well" (328).
25. *Nidāna Sutta* (AN 3.33), trans. Thanissaro Bhikkhu, Access to Insight, https://www.accesstoinsight.org/tipitaka/an/an03/an03.033.than.html.
26. See *Dhammacakkappavattana Sutta* (SN 56.11), trans. Thanissaro Bhikkhu, Access to Insight, https://www.accesstoinsight.org/tipitaka/sn/sn56/sn56.011.than.html. For a comprehensive discussion of this discourse, see Peter Harvey's "*Dukkha*, Non-Self, and the Teaching on the Four 'Noble Truths,'" in *A Companion to Buddhist Philosophy*, ed. Steven M. Emmanuel (Malden, MA: Wiley-Blackwell, 2013), 27–29.
27. See R. F. Gombrich, *How Buddhism Began: The Conditioned Genesis of the Early Teachings* (London: Athlone Press, 1996), 66–68.
28. R. Gethin, *The Foundations of Buddhism* (New York: Oxford University Press, 1998), 71, 74.
29. Trans. Thanissaro Bhikkhu, Access to Insight, https://www.accesstoinsight.org/tipitaka/an/an04/an04.192.than.html.
30. Gethin, *The Foundations of Buddhism*, 146–47.
31. *Upādāparitassanā Sutta* (SN 22.7), trans. Bhikkhu Bodhi, Sutta Central, https://suttacentral.net/sn22.7/en/bodhi.
32. Gethin, *The Foundations of Buddhism*, 1447.
33. *Yuganaddha Sutta* (AN 4.170), trans. Thanissaro Bhikkhu, Access to Insight, https://www.accesstoinsight.org/tipitaka/an/an04/an04.170.than.html.
34. *Anattalakkhaṇa Sutta* (SN 22.59), trans. N.K.G. Mendis, Access to Insight, https://www.accesstoinsight.org/tipitaka/sn/sn22/sn22.059.mend.html.

35. *Anattalakkhaṇa Sutta* (SN 22.59), trans. N.K.G. Mendis, Access to Insight, https://www.accesstoinsight.org/tipitaka/sn/sn22/sn22.059.mend.html.
36. *Pattakamma Sutta* (AN 4.61), trans. Bhikkhu Bodhi, Sutta Central, https://suttacentral.net/an4.61/en/bodhi.
37. Bhikkhu Bodhi, "Walking Even Amidst the Uneven," *Access to Insight* (Legacy Edition), June 5, 2010, http://www.accesstoinsight.org/lib/authors/bodhi/bps-essay_33.html.
38. *Sigālovāda Sutta* (DN 31), trans. Narada Thera, Access to Insight, https://www.accesstoinsight.org/ati/tipitaka/dn/dn.31.0.nara.html. The Buddha delivers the same message to the householder Dīghajāṇu in the discourse that bears his name (AN 8.54).
39. In particular, the Five Precepts (*pañcasīla*): the commitment to refrain from harming living beings, theft, sexual misconduct, lying, and intoxication.
40. A wealthy merchant and banker, Anāthapiṇḍika is recognized in Buddhist literature as the preeminent patron of the Buddha. He is remembered, among other things, for having donated the monastic residence in Jeta's Grove, where the Buddha delivered many of the Dhamma teachings that were later recorded in the Pāli texts. See chapter 9 in Nyanaponika Thera and Helmuth Hecker, *Great Disciples of the Buddha: Their Lives, Their Works, Their Legacy* (Boston: Wisdom, 2003), 335–60.
41. *Ādiya Sutta* (AN 5.41), trans. Bhikkhu Bodhi, Sutta Central, https://suttacentral.net/an5.41/en/bodhi.
42. *Pattakamma Sutta* (AN 4.61), trans. Bhikkhu Bodhi, Sutta Central, https://suttacentral.net/an4.61/en/bodhi.
43. *Appaka Sutta* (SN 3.6), trans. Thanissaro Bhikkhu, Sutta Central, https://suttacentral.net/an5.41/en/bodhi.
44. This is the central message of the *Aputtaka Sutta* (SN 3.19), which tells of a wealthy moneylender who lived like a pauper and died without having used any of his wealth to good purpose.
45. *Anaṇa Sutta* (AN 4.62), trans. Thanissaro Bhikkhu, Access to Insight, https://www.accesstoinsight.org/tipitaka/an/an04/an04.062.than.html.
46. Lily de Silva, "One Foot in the World: Buddhist Approaches to Present-Day Problems," *Access to Insight* (BCBS Edition), November 30, 2013, http://www.accesstoinsight.org/lib/authors/desilva/wheel337.html.
47. *Dīghajāṇu Sutta* (AN 8.54), trans. Thanissaro Bhikkhu, Sutta Central, https://suttacentral.net/an8.54/en/thanissaro.

48. Bodhi, "Walking Even Amidst the Uneven."
49. In Buddhism, these are referred to as "the four requisites."
50. de Silva, "One Foot in the World." In the aforementioned *Sigālovāda Sutta* (DN 31), the Buddha advises that wealth be divided into four parts: one part to be enjoyed, two parts to be invested in work, and the fourth to be set aside in case of future misfortune.
51. P. A. Payutto, *Buddhist Economics: A Middle Way for the Market Place*, trans. Dhammavijaya and Bruce Evans (Bangkok: Buddhadhamma Foundation, 1994), 32.
52. In Buddhist thought, the mental factor of *chanda* is the wish to achieve some particular goal. As such, it is ethically neutral. It may be wholesome or unwholesome, depending on the person's state of mind or motivation.
53. Payutto, *Buddhist Economics*, 25.
54. Payutto, *Buddhist Economics*, 23, 41.
55. R. Skidelsky, and E. Skidelsky, *How Much Is Enough? Money and the Good Life* (New York: Other Press, 2012), 13.
56. de Silva, "One Foot in the World."
57. Walter E. Williams, "Defense against Demagogues," *Townhall*, January 28, 2015.
58. Payutto, *Buddhist Economics*, 25.
59. Payutto, *Buddhist Economics*, 23.
60. Payutto, *Buddhist Economics*, 32.
61. Smith, *Theory of Moral Sentiments*, 212. Subsequent references appear parenthetically in the text as TMS followed by page number.
62. On this point, see James R. Otteson, *Adam Smith's Marketplace of Life* (Cambridge: Cambridge University Press, 2002), 3–4.
63. Dennis C. Rasmussen, "Adam Smith on What Is Wrong with Economic Inequality," *American Political Science Review* 110, no. 2 (2016), 342.
64. Simon Blackburn, "Love, Vanity, and Wealth," *Transformation* (October 25, 2013): https://www.opendemocracy.net/transformation/simon-blackburn/love-vanity-and-wealth.
65. On this point, see Georgios Halkias, "The Enlightened Sovereign: Buddhism and Kingship in India and Tibet," in *A Companion to Buddhist Philosophy*, ed. Steven M. Emmanuel (Malden, MA: Wiley-Blackwell, 2013), 494–95.
66. Rasmussen, "Adam Smith on What is Wrong with Economic Inequality," 351.

67. Peter Hershock, "Poverty Alleviation: A Buddhist Perspective," *Journal of Bhutan Studies* 11, no. 11 (2004): 44.
68. Hershock, 44.
69. Steven Pearlstein, "Is Capitalism Moral?," *Washington Post*, March 15, 2013.
70. Payutto, *Buddhist Economics*, 47.

BIBLIOGRAPHY

Blackburn, Simon. "Love, Vanity, and Wealth." *Transformation*, October 25, 2013. Accessed from https://www.opendemocracy.net/transformation/simon-blackburn/love-vanity-and-wealth.

Bodhi, Bhikkhu. "Walking Even Amidst the Uneven," *Access to Insight* (Legacy Edition), June 5, 2010. Accessed from http://www.accesstoinsight.org/lib/authors/bodhi/bps-essay_33.html.

Coase, R. H. "Adam Smith's View of Man." *Journal of Law and Economics* 19, no. 3 (1976): 529–46.

Den Uyl, Douglas J., and Douglas B. Rasmussen. "Adam Smith on Economic Happiness." *Reason Papers* 32 (2010): 29–40.

Easterlin, Richard A. "Does Economic Growth Improve the Human Lot? Some Empirical Evidence." In *Nations and Households in Economic Growth: Essays in Honor of Moses Abramovitz*, ed. P. David and M. Reder, 89–125. New York: Academic Press, 1974.

Easterlin, Richard A. "The Economics of Happiness." *Daedalus* 133, no. 2 (2004): 26–33.

Emmanuel, Steven M., ed. *A Companion to Buddhist Philosophy*. Malden, MA: Wiley-Blackwell, 2013.

Fleischacker, Samuel. *On Adam Smith's* Wealth of Nations: *A Philosophical Companion*. Princeton, NJ: Princeton University Press, 2004.

Friedman, Milton. *Capitalism and Freedom*. Chicago: University of Chicago Press, 1962.

Friedman, Milton, and Rose Friedman. *Free to Choose: A Personal Statement*. New York: Harcourt, 1990[1979].

Gombrich, R. F. *How Buddhism Began: The Conditioned Genesis of the Early Teachings*. London: Athlone, 1996.

Griswold, Charles. *Adam Smith and the Virtues of Enlightenment*. Cambridge: Cambridge University Press, 1999.

Halkias, Georgios T. "The Enlightened Sovereign: Buddhism and Kingship in India and Tibet." In *A Companion to Buddhist Philosophy*, ed. Steven M. Emmanuel, 491–511. Malden, MA: Wiley-Blackwell, 2013.

Hanley, Ryan Patrick. *Adam Smith and the Character of Virtue*. Cambridge: Cambridge University Press, 2009.

Helliwell, John, Richard Layard, and Jeffrey Sachs. *World Happiness Report 2017*. New York: Sustainable Development Solutions Network, 2017.

Hershock, Peter D. "Poverty Alleviation: A Buddhist Perspective." *Journal of Bhutan Studies* 11, no. 11 (2004): 33–67.

Hirschman, A. O. *The Passions and the Interests*. Princeton, NJ: Princeton University Press, 1977.

Hont, Istvan, and Michael Ignatieff. "Needs and Justice in the *Wealth of Nations*." In *Wealth and Virtue: The Shaping of Political Economy in the Scottish Enlightenment*, ed. Istvan Hont and Michael Ignatieff, 1–44. Cambridge: Cambridge University Press, 1983.

Kahneman, Daniel. *Well Being: The Foundations of Hedonic Psychology*. New York: Russell Sage Foundation, 2003.

Kahneman, Daniel, and Angus Deaton. "High Income Improves Evaluation of Life but Not Emotional Well-Being." *Proceedings of the National Academy of Sciences* 107, no. 38 (2010): 16489–93.

Kahneman, Daniel, Alan B. Krueger, David Schkade, Northert Schwarz, and Arthur A. Stone. "Would You Be Happier If You Were Richer? A Focusing Illusion." *Science* 312, no. 5782 (2006): 1908–10.

Keynes, John Maynard. "Economic Possibilities for Our Grandchildren." In *Essays in Persuasion*, vol. 9, *The Collected Writings of John Maynard Keynes*, 358–73. London: Macmillan, 1972.

Layard, Richard. *Happiness: Lessons from a New Science*. New York: Penguin, 2005.

Makransky, John. "Compassion in Buddhist Psychology." In *Wisdom and Compassion in Psychotherapy*, ed. Christopher K. Germer and Ronald D. Siegel, 61–74. New York: Guilford Press, 2012.

Meek, R. L., D. D. Raphael, and P. G. Stein, eds. *Adam Smith: Lectures in Jurisprudence*. Indianapolis: Liberty Fund, 1982.

Nicole, Pierre. "De la Grandeur" (1670). Quoted in Rudi Verburg, "The Rise of Greed in Early Economic Thought: From Deadly Sin to Social Benefit." *Journal of the History of Economic Thought* 34, no. 4 (2012): 515–39.

Otteson, James R. *Adam Smith's Marketplace of Life*. Cambridge: Cambridge University Press, 2002.

Payutto, P. A. *Buddhist Economics: A Middle Way for the Market Place*. Trans. Dhammavijaya and Bruce Evans. Bangkok: Buddhadhamma Foundation, 1994.

Pearlstein, Steven. "Is Capitalism Moral?" *Washington Post*, March 15, 2013.

Progressio Populorum [Encyclical Letter of His Holiness Pope Paul VI]. Vatican City: Vatican Polyglot Press, 1967.

Rasmussen, Dennis C. "Adam Smith on Commerce and Happiness: A Response to Den Uyl and Rasmussen." *Reason Papers* 33 (2011): 95–101.

Rasmussen, Dennis C. "Adam Smith on What Is Wrong with Economic Inequality," *American Political Science Review* 110, no. 2 (2016), 342–52.

Rasmussen, Dennis C. "Does 'Bettering Our Condition' Really Make Us Better Off? Adam Smith on Progress and Happiness." *American Political Science Review* 100, no. 3 (2006): 309–18.

Rasmussen, Dennis C. *The Problems and Promise of Commercial Society: Adam Smith's Response to Rousseau*. University Park: Pennsylvania State University Press, 2008.

Rollert, John Paul. "Greed Is Good: A 300-Year History of a Dangerous Idea." *The Atlantic*, April 2014. https://www.theatlantic.com/business/archive/2014/04/greed-is-good-a-300-year-history-of-a-dangerous-idea/360265.

Sen, Amartya. *Development as Freedom*. New York: Oxford University Press, 1999.

de Silva, Lily. "One Foot in the World: Buddhist Approaches to Present-day Problems." Access to Insight (BCBS Edition), November 30, 2013. Accessed from http://www.accesstoinsight.org/lib/authors/desilva/wheel337.html.

Sivaraksa, Sulak. "The Religion of Consumerism." In *Seeds of Peace: A Buddhist Vision for Renewing Society*, 3–9. Parallax, 1992.

Skidelsky, Edward. "The Emancipation of Avarice." *First Things: A Monthly Journal of Religion & Public Life* (May 2011), https://www.firstthings.com/article/2011/05/the-emancipation-of-avarice.

Skidelsky, Robert, and Edward Skidelsky. *How Much Is Enough? Money and the Good Life*. New York: Other Press, 2012.

Smith, Adam. *An Inquiry into the Nature and Causes of the Wealth of Nations*. 2 vols. Ed. R. H. Campbell and A. S. Skinner. Springville, UT: Liberty Press, 1976[1776].

Smith, Adam. *The Theory of Moral Sentiments*. Ed. Knud Haakonssen. Cambridge: Cambridge University Press, 2002[1759].

Thera, Nyanaponika, and Helmuth Hecker. *Great Disciples of the Buddha: Their Lives, Their Works, Their Legacy*. Boston: Wisdom, 2003.

Thera, Piyadassi. *The Buddha's Ancient Path*. Pariyatti Editions. Kandy, Sri Lanka: Buddhist Publication Society, 2017[1998].

Verburg, Rudi. "The Rise of Greed in Early Economic Thought: From Deadly Sin to Social Benefit." *Journal of the History of Economic Thought* 34, no. 4 (2012): 515–39.

Williams, Walter E. "Defense against Demagogues." *Townhall*, January 28, 2015, https://townhall.com/columnists/walterewilliams/2015/01/28/defense-against-demagogues-n1948304.

8

WHAT DO WE OWE FUTURE GENERATIONS?

Compassion and Future Generations: A Buddhist Contribution to an Ethics of Global Interdependence

PETER D. HERSHOCK

We do not live in the childhood world of our grandparents. As the global urban population increased from 224 million people in 1900 to the current total of 3.5 billion people, and as the number of cities with over 1 million inhabitants increased from just 12 to more than 450, vast tracts of forest have been cleared, rivers have been redirected, lakes have been drained, and hills have been leveled. Over the same period, wars, decolonization, and intensifying globalization have dramatically reconfigured political, economic, and social landscapes; advances in transportation and communication technology have made concerns about distance virtually obsolete; medical science has rendered impotent diseases that once killed millions; life expectancies have risen worldwide; and options regarding what to eat, what to wear, where to live, and what communities to call our own have reached levels that few could even have imagined a century ago.

Changes of similar magnitude and rapidity might plausibly be argued as having been part of the human experience at least since the advent of agriculture. Change is natural, and without it, there is neither life nor culture. But contemporary change dynamics are unique. For the first time, the scale and scope of human activity are such that it is altering planetary processes like climate. Because of this, the extension of justice concerns to future generations can no longer be seen as a purely academic exercise; it has become a global ethical imperative.

Prior to the advent of the environmental movement in the early 1960s, if any philosophical or policymaking consideration was given to future generations, it was generally done on the basis of assumptions that progress is inexorable and future generations will be the grateful beneficiaries of today's efforts to make the world a better place. These assumptions are no longer tenable. Present patterns of action (and inaction) will dramatically, unpredictably, and in all likelihood adversely affect future generations. The United Nations has estimated, for example, that between 50 and 350 million people will become climate migrants and refugees over the next thirty years, and that the number of people suffering the physical, cognitive, social, and economic costs of being chronically undernourished will rise well beyond the current global total of 800 million—roughly one out of every eight people.[1]

This raises important ethical and social justice questions. What duties do we have, if any, toward those who will live 50 or 100 years from now? Must we take their interests into account in utilitarian calculations aimed at minimizing suffering and maximizing human flourishing? Can necessarily voiceless future generations claim rights that we are nevertheless bound to honor? And is there any concrete meaning to caring for people whose existence, in even the most minimal sense, is merely potential?

Those who would answer such questions positively have, perhaps expectedly, encountered substantial philosophical and political resistance, and nearly twenty years after the Kyoto Protocol to the United Nations Framework Convention on Climate Change was drafted, there is still no globally binding commitment to address either the causes or likely consequences of anthropogenic climate variability. In response to this resistance, I want to build on recent efforts to craft an ethics of global justice around the social emotion of compassion, using Buddhist conceptual resources to argue that working effectively for intergenerational justice requires questioning the ontological primacy of the individual and working out from within an irreducibly relational worldview to envision a global ethics in which justice is delinked from fictions of equality and autonomy, and indexed instead to achieving equity-enhancing and systemically sustained diversity.

SOURCES OF RESISTANCE

The predominant sources of philosophical resistance to according future generations both moral and practical consideration is neatly encapsulated in Emmanuel Levinas's claim that ethics originates in confronting the face of another whose difference is present to us as an infinity that we cannot fit within the self-defining confines of our own totality.[2] Those who will live in 50 or 100 years have no faces. In less imagistic terms, there are three major obstacles to granting moral consideration to future generations: nonexistence, indeterminacy, and asymmetry. Those who will live in future generations do not exist now; their identities and interests are unknowable; and although we can change the circumstances of those in future generations for good or ill, they have no reciprocal ability to alter ours.

Stated in more pointedly ethical terms, future generations cannot call us to moral attention because they are not subjects or agents toward whom we could have duties or with whom we could enter into social contracts; they cannot express their needs and aims, so they can neither be factored into nor take part in hedonic calculations; they cannot deliberate with us about the meanings of and means to a just and flourishing community; and although concern for future generations might be forwarded as a virtue or mark of good character, it would be a purely abstract virtue, entirely lacking in actionable content. It may be true—as John Rawls has suggested—that "heads of households" have an emotional investment in caring about their immediate descendants, but the grounds for extending the temporal horizons of either "familial rationality" or "care" to include more distant generations are tenuous at best.[3] After all, even in the resolutely family-centered role of ethics expressed in Confucian traditions, in which ritually enacted familial concern is extended back seven generations—the memory horizon of our great-grandparents recalling their own great-grandparents—no ritual or theoretical considerations are granted to those with whom one has no prospect of actually relating.[4]

Many of the assumptions informing these conceptual challenges also underlie the obstacles to translating concern for future generations into action in policymaking and politics. The unborn are neither capable of determining the outcomes of elections nor of assessing (and perhaps contesting) the legitimacy of the state and its institutions. Future generations lack political agency. And while it is true that framing policies as responses to the needs of children and near-future generations does have considerable rhetorical force, doing so is much more effective in the theater of electoral suasion than it is in that of policy formulation and implementation; there, present-generation needs remain paramount. Indeterminacy regarding the needs of far-distant-future generations is tantamount to political invisibility, while apparent certainty regarding their lack of agency seals their political irrelevance. Future generations may be dramatically affected by current politics and policy decisions, but they have no reciprocal ability to affect current politics and policymaking.

As has become evident in recent political debates about climate change and variability, while indeterminacy about the needs and interests of far-distant-future generations has often served to legitimate their political invisibility, indeterminacy about their abilities has been used to grant them significant, albeit ironic, policy salience. While it is incontestable that we know nothing about the identities and interests of those in future generations, we also know nothing about their science and technology. We can already envision proactive adaptation based on existing science and technology that is capable of mitigating the negative impacts of climate change and variability.[5] If the production of scientific and technical knowledge continues at its current pace or further accelerates, it may be that in 50 or 100 years, many problems that are now insoluble and threats that are now apparently unavoidable will be dealt with simply as a matter of course. Given this, as well as the fact that, even if carbon emissions were curtailed entirely, we would not be able to avoid climate impacts that have already been set irreversibly in motion, it could be argued that the more rational course of action is to invest in science, technology, and industry and trust that future generations will have the epistemic and technical wherewithal to address challenges as they arise.

Finally, although future generations may or may not be able to offset the negative impacts of these changes and perhaps even profit from them by currently unimaginable means, the fact remains that these impacts are overwhelmingly the responsibility of those nations that industrialized first and that have enjoyed the benefits of fueling their economic growth through the use of cheap fossil fuels for nearly two centuries. Income, wealth, risk, and opportunity inequalities are the greatest they have ever been.⁶ And if nations are politically sovereign individuals that are fully within their rights to act in their own best interests, it is hard to imagine grounds on which newly industrializing countries like China, India, or Brazil would curtail their present use of fossil fuels when this almost certainly would consign their own future generations to living standards well below those already common in the already industrialized world.

STRUCTURAL CONSIDERATIONS

Uncertainties about future challenges and the identities, interests, and abilities of those who will face them are pivotal factors in persistent philosophical and political reservations about the rationality and effectiveness of acting on behalf of future generations. Ignorance is not a good foundation for effective policy-making and action. But using uncertainty to justify inaction in relation to future generations is morally plausible only if uncertainties about the nature and extent of threats, risks, and hazards that will be experienced by future generations are themselves *not* the foreseeable result of our own patterns of value-laden action and inaction. This, however, does not seem to be the case.

The computing and communications revolutions that resulted from market appropriations of Cold War research led to the displacement of the military-industrial complex by the military-industrial-communications complex, as well as a paradigmatic restructuring of global dynamics that Manuel Castells has referred to as the advent of "global informational capitalism" and the "network society." As dynamic structures, networks differ from hierarchies in two important ways. First, while the value of membership in a hierarchy is a function of distance from the center/top of the hierarchy, the value of network membership is a function of the quantity of nodes in the net and the informational quality of their connections to it. Second, network growth is not orchestrated from above; rather, it is shaped from within by the interplay of both negative (i.e., stabilizing) feedback and positive feedback, which accelerates interactions and amplifies differentiation. As has been made most strikingly evident in the financial sector, network growth is structurally sustained by internally generated *instability* and *volatility*.

This pairing of adaptive success and volatility is central to what Ulrich Beck, Anthony Giddens, and Scott Lash have referred to as "reflexive modernization"—the emergence of conditions in which it is no longer possible to externalize the environmental, social, and cultural costs of industrialization, and in which further growth entails producing unpredictable threats, risks, and hazards in the face of which responsible decisions must nevertheless be made.[7] Reflexive modernization is thus characterized by expanding "emancipatory" *freedoms of choice*, and by intensifying "disciplinary" *compulsions to choose* under conditions of disparately heightening ambiguity, uncertainty, and risk. The result is a blending of deepening interdependence with a progressive differentiation of globalization "winners" and "losers," not as a function of the failure of modern industrial-economic systems and institutions, but rather as a function of the successful globalization of their guiding values and purposes.

The onset of network-structured reflexive modernization, thus, signals an era-defining transition from the dominance of *problem-solution* to that of *predicament-resolution*. Here, problems can be understood as consisting in failures of existing practices as means to achieving current and abiding aims and interests. Problem-solution consists in developing new means for arriving at these aims and interests. The hybrid gas-electric automobile motor, for example, is a solution to the problem of automotive carbon emissions. In contrast, predicaments consist in awareness of conflicts among our own aims and interests. Predicaments cannot be solved, precisely because these conflicts prohibit establishing criteria according to which we could determine what would count as a solution. Climate change is, in these terms, not a problem but a predicament. We know, technically, what needs to be done to stop any further accentuation of climate change and variability. What stands in the way is not lack of scientific understanding or technical ability, but conflicts among political, economic, social, and cultural values and interests. Predicaments must be resolved, in which resolution entails both increasingly detailed *clarity* about how things have come to be as they are and deepening *commitment* to realizing new and aptly configured patterns of values and interests. In short, we are in the midst of an epochal shift from the centrality of the technical to that of the ethical.

Given the vibrant and yet volatile interplay of deepening interdependence and accelerating differentiation that characterizes contemporary globalization processes, the problem-to-predicament shift will necessarily be one of intensifying collisions both within and among value systems—collisions of the kind that will reveal and (at least initially) accentuate interclass and intercultural "fault lines." Resolving predicaments that enunciate class and cultural differences regarding, for example, the meaning of a "good" environment or "just" gender relations, will ultimately be—in Jean-Luc Nancy's philosophically pregnant terms—less a process of constructing *common* institutions than one of improvising *shared* structures of feeling that express sustainable new constellations of coordination-enriching values.[8]

THE CASE FOR COMPASSION

It is in the context of this need to improvise shared structures of feeling that efforts to build a global ethics of social justice around what Martha Nussbaum refers to as the "social emotion" of compassion gain both philosophical and political traction. In her book *Upheavals of Thought: The Intelligence of Emotions*, Nussbaum makes the case that compassion generates "a breadth and depth of ethical vision without which public culture is in danger of being rootless and hollow."[9] For her, compassion is not only a fact of individual psychology, it is also "embodied in the structure of just institutions," and it involves making three judgments: that some seriously bad things have happened to someone or some group; that these bad things were not deserved by those affected; and that the person or group that is undeservedly suffering is a significant element in one's own scheme of aims and interests.[10]

Working from within a broadly liberal set of assumptions about personhood and the rational bases of action, Nussbaum avers that knowing that we also might be affected by similar undeserved suffering motivates us to build institutions designed to mitigate conditions that stifle "human dignity and the capacity for action" or that create "social hierarchy and economic deprivation."[11] The anticipated end of building these institutions is a just society that guarantees its citizens certain core capabilities that include both cultivatable "intrinsic capabilities" for freely choosing what to do and who to be and "combined capabilities" that involve the functional merger of personal abilities and a supportive socioeconomic and political environment.[12] These core capabilities include the freedom to live a healthy life; to use one's senses and imagination; to think and develop emotional connections; to play; to affiliate with whomever one wants; and to exercise some measure of control over one's political and material environments.

Advocating the cultivation of compassion as a means to social justice challenges the widespread assumption that the

Hobbesian self-interest of individual agents is the natural and necessary cornerstone of civil society. Cultivating the "social emotion" of compassion is, at bottom, an affirmation of our mutual vulnerability and mutual relevance. But as it has been framed by Nussbaum around judgments of seriousness, nondesert, and mutual relevance, compassion does not seem to offer the help needed to break through conceptual and political resistance to actively pursuing intergenerational justice.

It is uncontroversially true that those who will live in future generations will not deserve the burdens and harms that they may have to bear as a result of threats like climate change that were caused by people living in their own relatively distant past. But as noted earlier, because those who will live in future generations do not yet exist and may enjoy technological capabilities far exceeding our own, it is impossible to know whether they will deem serious any burdens or harms that they will have to bear. The burdens and harms that we can imagine will result from current environmental policies may well be rendered trivial by technological and scientific advances made by intervening generations.

An even greater difficulty with Nussbaum's account of compassion is that because those who may live in distant future generations do not and may never exist, it is difficult (if not impossible) to see how they could be crucial to our own happiness and flourishing today. Barring an extreme extension of human life expectancy, interest and impact reciprocity between our own generation and that of our presumed great-grandchildren is unintelligible.

Finally, even if we allow that the primary function of cultivating compassion is to ensure that all members of a society have a basic set of capabilities or freedoms of choice, what—apart from blind faith in the rationality of self-interested choice—actually warrants the conviction that exercising individual freedoms of choice of the kind that Nussbaum sees as core capabilities will cumulatively serve to benefit future generations? It is, after all, a logical fallacy that actions that are good for any one of us will necessarily be good if undertaken by all of us.

It seems to me that Nussbaum is right to project compassion out of the psychological realm into that of the design of public institutions. As Maureen Whitebrook has argued, as a political virtue, compassion is not a matter of one-to-one charity.[13] A Good Samaritan can help someone in trouble, providing what is needed in the moment, without being motivated to identify structural or institutional causes of trouble and suffering, and without acting as needed thereafter to address these causes practically. But the strength of Nussbaum's projection, I think, is compromised by her allegiance to the individual as the basic unit of ethical analysis—an allegiance that leads her to entrain the alleviation of others' suffering with the pursuit of our own self-interest, and with guaranteeing equivalent capabilities for individual agency to all.

As Mervyn Frost has pointed out, knowledge about how and when to be compassionate is crucial both within communities or states and in the context of a global civil society in which all participants are understood as autonomous individuals constrained only by the requirement that they recognize and respect the rights and freedoms of others.[14] Otherwise, compassion runs the risk of triggering quick and ill-informed actions that overwrite the agency of others or have other unintended negative consequences. In political contexts, the effectiveness of compassion is to a significant degree a function of the depth of partnership among all involved. And it is not clear that securing the capabilities for acting in one's own interests affords the depth of partnership needed to address global predicaments like climate change, even if one does so "compassionately," in Nussbaum's terms, and judges ending others' suffering to be an element of achieving one's own aims and interests. If a primary driver for growing inequalities and suffering is indeed the reflexive pairing of risk and hazard production with amplifying compulsions to choose in conditions of structurally induced uncertainty and volatility, securing more individual freedoms of choice—no matter how compassionately motivated—seems most likely to serve as stabilizing feedback for the very systems responsible for and sustained by that pairing. Nussbaum's conception of freedom may simply be too self-centered to be useful in alleviating the structurally induced suffering that is an ironic product of economic and political systems devoted to industrially expanding the horizons of individual choice.

BUDDHIST COMPASSION

The Buddhist concept of compassion opens prospects for building on the intuition that compassion is a crucial element in realizing global social justice and extending ethical consideration to future generations. Although the notion of "global social justice" is relatively recent and not directly addressed in canonical Buddhist discourse, Buddhist teachings offer distinctive resources for developing a relational concept of justice that is critically consonant with an intergenerational politics of compassion.

To begin cashing out this claim, it is perhaps useful to note that Buddhism originated some 2,500 years ago in the context of dramatic rural-to-urban migration and the rise of industrial modes of production on the Indian subcontinent. Buddhist teachings and institutions spread quite rapidly, along with the expansion of regional (and eventually transcontinental) trade, facilitated by the Buddha's insistence that his teachings be conveyed in local vernaculars in ways that are accessible to different audiences. What we find in these teachings is a system of strategies for authoring one's own liberation from conflict, trouble, and suffering (*duḥkha*)—strategies that accord well with the needs of those immersed in the "predicament of culture"—the experience of at once being *in* a culture and having to look critically *at* it, making conscious and often uncomfortable decisions about which customs and identities to abandon and which to adopt.

In contrast with modern convictions about the ontological, ethical, and political primacy of the individual human being—the self-interested, rational agent—the core insight around which Buddhist teachings were first articulated is that all things arise interdependently, including persons. Relationality is ontologically primary, and what we take to be individually and independently existing things and beings ultimately are conceptually constituted abstractions from ongoing relational dynamics. *Duḥkha* is, accordingly, not understood as reducible to a subjective or psychological event, but rather as a function of relational distortion or interdependence gone awry. The central focus of early Buddhist practice is to examine the causes and conditions that bring about experiences of conflict, trouble, and suffering, particularly the impacts of actions undertaken on the basis of ignorance (of interdependence), habit formations (bodily, emotional, and cognitive), and craving forms of desire. With sufficient practice, it becomes clear that *duḥkha* is a function of our karma, our own "doing."

In contrast with pre-Buddhist uses of "karma" to refer to the operation of a cosmic moral law in which bad actions inexorably result in bad experiential consequences, the Buddhist teaching of karma stresses the crucial role of intentionality (*cetanā*). By paying close and sufficiently sustained attention, it becomes evident that a recursive consonance obtains between abiding patterns of values-intentions-actions and experiential opportunities and outcomes. Because our values, intentions, and actions are always open to change, so are our life circumstances and the relational dynamics occurring within them. That is, the meaning of interdependence is always open to revision. The conditions and causes of conflict, trouble, and suffering can be dissolved by changing why and how we conduct ourselves as we do—that is, by undertaking ongoing critiques both of our own values and intentions and of the constellations of values that are embodied in our cultural, social, economic, and political institutions and practices.

This process was traditionally understood as one of cultivating wisdom (*prajñā*), attentive mastery (*samādhi*), and moral clarity (*śīla*), especially through the practices of generosity (*dāna*) and various forms of meditation, including insight (*vipaśyana*), concentration (*samādhi*), calming (*śamatha*), and mindfulness (*satipaṭṭhāna*). Importantly, however, those faring well on the path of Buddhist practice were often described as suffusing their entire situation with the relational qualities of compassion (*karuṇā*), equanimity (*upekṣā*), loving-kindness (*mettā*), and joy in the good fortune of others (*muditā*).[15] That is, while subjective meditative experience was certainly understood as an important aspect of Buddhist practice, exemplifying what it means to be present in community with others as a personally manifest nexus of relational transformation was a crucial indicator of progress in attaining the fruits of Buddhist practice.

In early Buddhist traditions, compassion is almost invariably invoked as part of this suite of relational qualities, and it was understood to be a volitionally produced result of practice. As a meditative focus, compassion was not identified with the psychological event of "feeling-with" or "feeling-for" others, but rather with intentionally suffusing the entire world with awareness of suffering, the conditions that bring it about, and the meaning of and means of dissolving those conditions. As described by the early Theravāda Buddhist commentator Buddhaghosa (fifth century CE) in his *Visuddhimagga*, or Path of Purification (Chapter IX), compassion occurs when the suffering of others moves one's heart, when there is a firm intent to put an end to others' suffering, and when this intent is extended pervasively.

In contrast with the "apathetic" compassion of simply recognizing and wishing for the end of others' suffering—based, as Nussbaum suggests, on rational judgments that the suffering of others is serious, undeserved, and relevant to one's own happiness and flourishing—Buddhist compassion (*karuṇā*) involves active and transformative engagement based on caring insight into the interdependence and interpenetration of all things. In other words, compassion is not to be confused with the kind of sentimental sympathy that results in sorrow about the suffering of others—an experience that reinforces "cravings" and attachment to "self" (*atman*). Compassion in the Buddhist sense is predicated on being without-self (*anātman*).

In later, Mahāyāna Buddhist contexts, compassion came to be paired with wisdom (*prajñā*) and explicitly associated with an intergenerational intention to bring about the liberation of all sentient beings (*bodhicitta*). This *mahākaruṇā*, or "great compassion," was the defining characteristic of the ideal person in Mahāyāna Buddhism: the bodhisattva, or "enlightening being," who vows to remain immersed in the world of recursively engendered conflict, trouble, and suffering to work for the liberation of all—a vow that can be kept only because making and keeping the bodhisattva vow generate unlimited improvisation virtuosity, or "skillful means" (*upāya*). The practice of compassion is thus not a matter of simply caring about and caring for others; it involves realizing the capabilities for responding as needed in any situation to realize liberating/enlightening inflections of relational dynamics.

Bodhisattva action entails working out *from within* existing conditions in ways that are consistent with, and yet reconfigure, prevailing systems of values, aims, and interests. This is not action focused on arriving at some predetermined destination. Although the ostensible aim of all Buddhist practice is nirvana, the term simply means a "blowing out" or "cooling down" of the conditions for experiencing *duḥkha*. And while it might seem natural to identify the goal of practice with happiness (*sukha*)— the conceptual opposite of *duḥkha* —happiness only factors into discussions of the effects of engaging in calming and concentrative meditative techniques, not as a way of qualifying the culmination of Buddhist practice. Happiness is good, but it is not presented as a cardinal point for faring well on the Middle Path. Instead, those advancing well on the path of Buddhist practice are characterized as engaging in *kuśala* conduct, a term that is often translated as "skillful" or "wholesome," but which functions as a superlative. *Kuśala* conduct is not just good or effective or morally sound, it is virtuosic.

It is important that the bodhisattva vow is not formulated in such a way that the work of compassion is conceived as of finite duration. It is instead part of the vow to affirm that sentient beings in need of salvation from *duḥkha* are numberless, as are the teachings and responsive techniques needed to guide them toward enlightenment. By affirming the infinite inclusiveness of practicing *mahākaruṇā*, bodhisattvas explicitly extend the ambit of their concern beyond both the present generation and humanity. This is not, as might be expected, a universalist vow premised on the intrinsic equality of all beings. Rather, it is premised on the realization of the emptiness (*śūnyatā*) of all things—the ultimate reality (*paramārtha*) of being without any fixed or essential nature (*svabhāva*). But, as is affirmed in the Heart Sutra's concise statement of the "perfection of wisdom," this entails no denial of the uniqueness of each thing or being as a particular form or material presence (*rūpa*): form ultimately is emptiness; emptiness is ultimately form.

Rather than a universalist affirmation of the equality of all things or a monistic reduction of all things to a single kind or status of being, the bodhisattva vow involves an ongoing affirmation of the nonduality of all things. One of the key turning points in the history of Chinese Buddhism was the emergence of convictions that all beings have/are Buddha-nature (*fo-xing* 佛性): a propensity for realizing liberating patterns of relationality. But as the Chinese Buddhist thinker Fazang (643–712 CE) insisted, this should not be construed as a conviction that all beings are somehow the same. Realizing the nonduality entailed by the interdependence and interpenetration of all things is not an erasure of difference—it is a restoration of the ignorance-obscured mutual relevance and mutual nonobstruction of all things. As Fazang illustrates through his use of traditional Chinese building construction as a metaphor for the interrelatedness of all things, the nonduality of all things consists in the distinctiveness with which each thing differs meaningfully from and for every other. Ultimately, we only *are* what we *mean* for one another.

One implication of this ontological perspective is that our values-laden shaping and reshaping of the relational and experiential prospects of our own future selves are inseparable from shaping and reshaping those of future others. This is a familiar notion. But in addition, this nondualistic perspective, that all beings are what they mean for one another, implies that as future generations respond to the patterns of outcomes and opportunities that we have projected forward, they will also be continuously redefining what we *mean* for them, and thus who we ultimately *are*. Our relationships with future generations are not incidental to who we are—they are constitutive. Or, put in more metaphysically precise terms, our present selves are abstractions from patterns of relationality that encompass what we refer to as the past, present, and future. Ultimately, we are all *intergenerational beings*.

COMPASSION AND JUSTICE

Seeing ourselves as interdependent, interpenetrating, intergenerational beings has significant ramifications both for how we conceive a politics of compassion and for the means-to and meanings of intergenerational justice. At present, conceptions of justice fall into two broad categories, which I will characterize as "universalist" and "particularist."

Perhaps the single most influential universalist conception of justice is that of John Rawls. According to Rawls, justice is best achieved by making decisions about how best to organize society from behind an imagined "veil of ignorance" about what position we will have in the society that results from such deliberations.[16] Here, justice is linked to equality, not as a social and political result that we wish to achieve in society, but rather as a procedural safeguard woven into the very fabric of our policy-making deliberations. The expectation is that if we make policy decisions with no idea of where we will end up in society or with what endowments, we will do so in the most thoughtfully egalitarian way possible.

This procedural blueprint for justice has considerable appeal. By conceptually blending the universalist ideal of equality of opportunity with the liberal realism of rationally pursued individual self-interest, Rawls deftly circumvents the coercive potentials that are involved in prescriptive, utopian visions of the just society. However, both the veil of ignorance and the route to justice mapped out from behind it are products of imagination, and Rawls's theory has been subject to pointedly concrete feminist and postcolonial criticism. From these perspectives, imagining universal routes to justice is all well and good, but actually usable, socially and politically viable routes to justice have to be built in explicit and careful consideration of differences in historical experience, developmental topography, and identity. Whether these routes will or should converge on a singular, universal conception of justice is perhaps debatable. What is beyond question, though, is the particularity of conditions from within which we must embark en route to justice.

This insistence on particularity can be seen as an extension of the Aristotelean insight that there are instances when the universal application of laws and principles will result in injustice, and thus when concrete differences need to be taken into account—an insistence on the need to qualify the universal pursuits of justice with concrete considerations of equity. Implicit in feminist and postcolonial conceptions of justice, then, is an important recognition of needs for a more capacious conception of equity than is supported by the now-dominant identification of equity with equality of opportunity. As part of the process of realizing a just society, considerations of equity must begin in affirmations of particularity and difference, not in imagining their irrelevance. Nevertheless, these compensatory considerations of difference remain embedded within overarching commitments to equality and individual autonomy as core values. And while feminist and postcolonial emphases on caring relationships and power relations, respectively, do intimate that justice should be understood as a dynamic relationship rather than an achievable state of affairs, their ontological commitments to the individual—person, group, class, ethnic group, culture, gender, and so on—mean that this relationship must ultimately be understood as external and contingent rather than as internal or constitutive.

The brevity and breadth of these characterizations of universalist and particularist conceptions of the meaning of and means of achieving justice leaves them open to dismissal as caricatures. But they suffice, I think, to call attention to the poles toward which discussions about justice have been carried out in keeping with the assumption that the individual is the fundamental unit of justice concerns—an assumption that begs questions about the sociality invoked but left unspecified in appeals for social justice.

Buddhism offers a nondualistic middle way oblique to the polarization of universalist idealizations of equal opportunity and particularist demands for recognition, respect, and reparations for differences in identity and history. If these discursive poles are seen as analogous to the north and south poles of a planet, Buddhism can be seen as opening prospects for movement, not *on* the "planetary" surface of contemporary philosophical engagement with the means-to and meaning-of justice, but *off* it—movement away from the individual as the imputed center of justice-determining conceptual gravity. Buddhist recognition and affirmation of the interdependence and karmically qualified interpenetration of all things ultimately involves recognizing and affirming the mutual nonobstruction of self and society—or, more accurately stated, the mutual nonobstruction of the personal and the public as distinctive dimensions of human relationality. As an emergent relational ramification of *mahākaruṇā*, nondualistic justice consists in enhancing equity and diversity as relational qualities resulting from the committed and progressive embodiment of irreducibly social values, where *equity* is understood as a relational index of enhanced capacities-for and commitments-to furthering our own self-interests in ways deemed valuable by others; and where *diversity* is understood as a qualitative index of the degree to which differences are realized as dynamic openings for mutual contributions to sustainably shared flourishing.

Taken together, valuing equity and diversity shifts concern from *how much* we are different from each other to *how well* we are differing for one another. Nondualistic justice is neither a predetermined state at which we hope to arrive, nor a procedure for ensuring such arrival; it is a distinctive quality of relational dynamics oriented resolutely toward dissolving patterns of values, intentions, and actions that are conducive to the experience of *duḥkha*. Nondualistic justice consists in realizing *kuśala* qualities and patterns of relationality.

Universalist and particularist conceptions of justice have in common an ideal of nonexclusion and an association of freedom with individual agency—an ideal of realizing conditions in which everyone has equivalent opportunity to assert his or her own self-interest, making causally effective choices about who or what to do or be. In other words, they are consistent with compassionately securing Nussbaum's core capabilities. Injustice accordingly consists in any restriction of choice and assertive control. The ideal of nondualistic justice is irreducibly relational: compassionately realizing *kuśala* or superlative relational dynamics or arcs of change, while dissolving conditions for those that are *akuśala*. In keeping with this ideal, freedom is understood as appreciative and contributory virtuosity, and injustice as consisting in any attenuation of contributory capacities and commitments. From this perspective, ideological and institutional promotions of equality and rationally self-interested action may be effective at countering structural denials of agency to certain groups, but they are ultimately *akuśala*—that is, *relationally* unjust.

Resolving the predicament of human-induced climate change and other predicaments that are similarly profound and borderless will require significant, intercultural reconfigurations of the values that now structure global dynamics—new "software" for running the global network society. Placing compassion prominently among those values is, among other things, an important step in the direction of countering the hubris of the modern project of mastering nature. At the same time, valorizing compassion gives concrete focus to the pursuit of social justice as a quality of public and institutionally embodied relationality. Relational justice of this kind cannot be achieved as a summative effect of maximally unconstrained freedoms of choice exercised by self-defining, autonomous individuals. Valorizing choice, control, individual autonomy, and state sovereignty has been a defining feature of the karma driving the predicament-generating growth on which we have globally come to depend. The Mahāyāna personal ideal of the bodhisattva offers one alternative: resolute commitment to valorizing and realizing *shared* and *superlative* arcs of relational transformation.

Like liberally constructed universalist and particularist approaches to justice, a Buddhist conception of justice entails ending all forms of social, economic, political, and cultural exclusion. However, in addition, it entails appreciating—at once valuing and adding value to—*mutual inclusion*. Nondualistic justice mandates actively expanding the horizons of ethical consideration to encompass not only other species and ecological systems, but also future generations, and to do so in ways that continually enhance the *quality* of their inclusion.

Given the karmic origins of *duḥkha* and the emergence-prone kinds of complex interdependence that now characterize global dynamics, this ideal is not one that can be realized through acting in accord with fixed principles or constellations of values. A distinguishing feature of complex systems is that they are prone to behaving unpredictably, and yet in accord with their own structuring values.[17] They are characterized, in other words, by nonlinear change or emergence. Addressing predicaments that reach across cultures and generations in a world of complex interdependence requires both improvisational genius and ethical flexibility—a creative readiness to participate in jointly evaluating value systems, not as a task to be completed as quickly as possible but as an ongoing endeavor. Relational justice is a direction, not a destination. The bodhisattva practice of resolute commitment to being compassionately present as enlightening, intergenerational beings is ultimately a practice of realizing that regard for future generations is not some special or optional feature of justice. Ultimately, the means-to and meanings-of justice are irreducibly intergenerational.

NOTES

1. United Nations Report of the Secretary-General, *Climate Change and Its Possible Security Implications*, September 11, 2009, UN Doc A/64/350, http://www.unhcr.org/refworld/pdfid/4ad5e6380.pdf; United Nations Food and Agriculture Organization Report, *The State of Food Security in the World 2015*, http://www.fao.org/3/a-i4646e/index.html.
2. Emmanuel Levinas, *Totality and Infinity: An Essay on Exteriority*, trans. Alphonso Lingis (Pittsburgh, PA: Duquesne University Press, 1969).
3. John Rawls, *A Theory of Justice* (Cambridge, MA: Belknap Press, 1971), 128–29.
4. Roger T. Ames, *Confucian Role Ethics: A Vocabulary* (Honolulu: University of Hawaii Press, 2011).
5. Stanley E. Manahan, *Environmental Science and Technology: A Sustainable Approach to Green Science and Technology* (Boca Raton, FL: CRC, 2007).
6. Peter D. Hershock, "The Value of Diversity: Buddhist Reflection on More Equitably Orienting Global Interdependence," in *Value and Values: Economics and Justice in an Age of Global Interdependence*, ed. Roger T. Ames and Peter D. Hershock (Honolulu: University of Hawaii Press, 2015), 520ff.
7. Ulrich Beck, with Anthony Giddens and Scott Lash, *Reflexive Modernization: Politics, Tradition, and Aesthetics in the Modern Social Order* (Stanford, CA: Stanford University Press, 1994).

8. Jean-Luc Nancy, *Being Singular Plural*, trans. Robert Richardson and Anne O'Byrne (Stanford, CA: Stanford University Press, 2000).
9. Martha Nussbaum, *Upheavals of Thought: The Intelligence of Emotions* (Cambridge: Cambridge University Press, 2001), 403.
10. Nussbaum, *Upheavals of Thought*, 403.
11. Nussbaum, *Upheavals of Thought*, 413–414.
12. Nussbaum, *Upheavals of Thought*.
13. Maureen Whitebrook, "Love and Anger as Political Virtues," in *The Politics of Compassion*, ed. Michael Ure and Mervyn Frost (London: Routledge, 2014).
14. Mervyn Frost, "Compassion in International Relations," in *The Politics of Compassion*, ed. Michael Ure and Mervyn Frost (London: Routledge, 2014).
15. See, e.g., *Tevijja Sutta* (DN 13).
16. John Rawls, *A Theory of Justice* (Cambridge, MA: Belknap Press, 1971).
17. J. L. Lemke, "Discourse, Dynamics and Social Change," *Cultural Dynamics* 6, no. 1–2 (1993): 243–75.

BIBLIOGRAPHY

Ames, Roger T. *Confucian Role Ethics: A Vocabulary*. Honolulu: University of Hawaii Press, 2011.

Beck, Ulrich, with Anthony Giddens and Scott Lash. *Reflexive Modernization: Politics, Tradition, and Aesthetics in the Modern Social Order*. Stanford, CA: Stanford University Press, 1994.

Buddhaghosa. *Visuddhimagga*. Translated by Bhikkhu Ñāṇamoli as *The Path of Purification*. Kandy, Sri Lanka: Buddhist Publication Society, 2011.

Castells, Manuel. *The Rise of the Network Society*. Cambridge, MA: Blackwell, 1996.

Digha Nikāya. Translated by Maurice Walshe as *The Long Discourses of the Buddha*. Boston: Wisdom, 1995.

Frost, Mervyn. "Compassion in International Relations." In *The Politics of Compassion*, ed. Michael Ure and Mervyn Frost. London: Routledge, 2014.

Hershock, Peter D. "The Value of Diversity: Buddhist Reflection on More Equitably Orienting Global Interdependence." In *Value and Values:*

Economics and Justice in an Age of Global Interdependence, ed. Roger T. Ames and Peter D. Hershock. Honolulu: University of Hawaii Press, 2015.

Lemke, J. L. "Discourse, Dynamics and Social Change." *Cultural Dynamics* 6, no. 1–2 (1993): 243–75.

Levinas, Emmanuel. *Totality and Infinity: An Essay on Exteriority*. Trans. Alphonso Lingis. Pittsburgh: Duquesne University Press, 1969.

Manahan, Stanley E. *Environmental Science and Technology: A Sustainable Approach to Green Science and Technology*. Boca Raton, FL: CRC, 2007.

Nancy, Jean-Luc. *Being Singular Plural*. Trans. Robert Richardson and Anne O'Byrne. Stanford, CA: Stanford University Press, 2000.

Nussbaum, Martha. *Creating Capabilities: The Human Development Approach*. Cambridge, MA: Belknap Press, 2000.

Nussbaum, Martha. *Upheavals of Thought: The Intelligence of Emotions*. Cambridge: Cambridge University Press, 2001.

Rawls, John. *A Theory of Justice*. Cambridge, MA: Belknap Press, 1971.

United Nations Food and Agriculture Organization Report. *The State of Food Security in the World 2015*. http://www.fao.org/3/a-i4646e/index.html.

United Nations Report of the Secretary-General. *Climate Change and Its Possible Security Implications*. September 11, 2009. UN Doc A/64/350. http://www.unhcr.org/refworld/pdfid/4ad5e6380.pdf.

Whitebrook, Maureen. "Love and Anger as Political Virtues." In *The Politics of Compassion*, ed. Michael Ure and Mervyn Frost. London: Routledge, 2014.

CONCLUDING REMARKS

STEVEN M. EMMANUEL

In the closing chapter of his 1912 book *The Problems of Philosophy*, Bertrand Russell observed that the value of philosophy does not lie in producing "definite answers" to its questions, but rather in the effects that it has on the minds and lives of those who study it.[1] While it is true that philosophy aims primarily at gaining knowledge, the kind of knowledge it seeks "results from a critical examination of the grounds of our convictions, prejudices, and beliefs."[2] One of the most important functions of this critical activity is that it dissipates our sense of certainty about things. As Russell eloquently put it:

> The man who has no tincture of philosophy goes through life imprisoned in the prejudices derived from common sense, from the habitual beliefs of his age or his nation, and from convictions which have grown up in his mind without the co-operation or consent of his deliberate reason. To such a man the world tends to become definite, finite, obvious; common objects rouse no questions, and unfamiliar possibilities are contemptuously rejected. As soon as we begin to philosophize, on the contrary, we find . . . that even the most everyday things lead to problems to which only very incomplete answers can be given.[3]

By instilling in us a greater awareness of the uncertainty and partiality that underlie our claims to know things, philosophy fosters an intellectual humility which, from ancient times to the present, has been regarded as a mark of wisdom.

Yet even as philosophy diminishes our "feeling of certainty as to what things are," added Russell, "it greatly increases our knowledge as to what they may be" by expanding our imaginative purview of the world—enlarging our conception of what is possible.[4] The desire to get at the truth of things keeps philosophers searching for answers to the enduring questions about ultimate meaning and purpose, mind and matter, right and wrong, good and evil.[5] Although we may never reach a consensus regarding the answers to these questions, Russell insisted that it was part of the business of philosophy to take them up with seriousness and rigor—to examine all the different ways in which earlier philosophers have approached them, to scrutinize the various answers that have been proposed, to explore new ways of thinking about them, and perhaps most important of all, "to keep alive that speculative interest in the universe which is apt to be killed by confining ourselves to definitely ascertainable knowledge."[6]

Russell's observations on the value of philosophy are worth recalling here as we reflect on what we have gained from the present study. As noted at the outset, the aim of the volume was to expand and enrich our thinking on some perennially important questions in philosophy through a comparative study of Buddhist and Western thought. In addition to putting us in unfamiliar cultural and linguistic territory, our engagement with the Buddhist tradition challenged us to take a critical look at some of the central ideas, theories, and assumptions underlying the Western approach to answering the big questions—to acknowledge that there are other ways of thinking about philosophical problems. But the value of comparative study lies precisely in this challenge, for the point of cross-cultural engagement, to quote Julian Baggini, "is not to reach some kind of warm, ecumenical mutual understanding," but rather to "open up new vistas," so that we might "see our familiar intellectual territory in a different light."[7]

In the course of this study, we have been introduced to some radically different approaches to understanding the nature of reality, truth, and knowledge, as well as the ethical underpinnings of a good life and a just society. In the opening chapter by Stephen J. Laumakis, we saw how Buddhism combines normative ethical teachings with a practice of mental and moral training that grounds our ethical understanding of how we should live, and also provides the proper motivation for moral action. Moreover, by emphasizing the cultivation of wisdom and compassion, as well as the importance of using skillful means to address whatever suffering is at hand, Buddhism presents us with a unique and compelling model of philosophy as a way of life. In the next chapter, by Douglas Duckworth, we saw that Buddhist epistemology, while broadly empiricist in its approach, recognizes sources of knowledge that go beyond the five senses to include mental perception, self-awareness, and a form of "yogic perception" associated with a carefully prescribed form of meditation.

Next, Jan Westerhoff presented a Buddhist theory of nonfoundationalism which, remarkably, has no significant parallel in Western metaphysics. Dan Arnold's reading of prominent Buddhist idealists suggested a new way of conceptualizing the so-called "hard problem" in philosophy of mind, and Rick Repetti sketched out an effective response to Western free will skeptics based on the Buddhist conception of an "agentless agency." Amber D. Carpenter's comparative discussion of the problem of evil showed that Buddhism puts forward a compelling account of the causes of suffering—one that does not invoke the notions of blame and deserts, and perhaps more surprisingly, does not regard the ubiquity of suffering as something that even requires explanation. Turning to matters social and political, in chapter 7 we saw that Buddhism presents a robust challenge to the valorization of greed in Western libertarian accounts of prosperity, offering instead a model of economic progress in which the pursuit of wealth is compatible with moral and spiritual growth. And finally, with regard to the well-being of future generations, Peter D. Hershock showed how the conceptual resources of Mahāyāna Buddhism can be used to construct a relational conception of social justice that supports an intergenerational politics of compassion.

One point that comes through clearly in these chapters is that Buddhist philosophers do not approach their metaphysical and epistemological inquiries as mere theoretical exercises. All Buddhist discussions of the big questions of life are tied in one way or another to the basic task of articulating and inculcating a way of life that leads to greater happiness and peace. Some scholars have noted similarities between the Buddhist approach and that of the Hellenistic and Roman philosophers, for whom, as Pierre Hadot has shown, the pursuit of wisdom involved a "transformation of the individual's way of being."[8] According to Christopher Gowans, this comparison naturally suggests itself, insofar as both traditions operate with a wider conception of philosophical inquiry that includes various "spiritual exercises" aimed at cultivating wisdom, moral virtue, and serenity.[9]

Contemporary philosophers, especially those who work in the analytic tradition, do not speak much of wisdom, or of the ways in which philosophy promotes a virtuous and happy life. Indeed, philosophers nowadays (at least in the Anglophone world) very often focus on theoretical questions that seem to have little or no relevance to the actual lives of people. Such is the view of Robert

Frodeman and Adam Briggle, who note that philosophy, as an academic discipline, "has largely become a technical enterprise," a specialized field of research in which progress is measured by a scientific model of knowledge production. On one hand, this has helped fuel concerns about the perceived lack of progress in philosophy compared to the sciences, while on the other, it has robbed philosophy of one of its most important historical tasks (namely, to improve the lives of those who study it):

> Lost is the once common-sense notion that philosophers are seeking the good life—that we ought to be (in spite of our failings) model citizens and human beings. Having become specialists, we have lost sight of the whole. The point of philosophy now is to be smart, not good.[10]

It is true that analytic philosophers tend to distinguish sharply between the theoretical search for truth and the practical goal of moral or spiritual development. As Scott Soames bluntly puts it, "The goal in analytic philosophy is to discover what is true, not to provide a useful recipe for living."[11] In direct response to Frodeman and Briggle, Soames contends that philosophy has in fact made laudable progress in expanding our theoretical understanding of the world, particularly in those areas where philosophical inquiry overlaps with the sciences and mathematics; and while advances in ethics and political philosophy have admittedly been "less impressive," progress in these areas has been accelerating since the 1970s.[12]

Still, it seems reasonable to ask whether such a hard distinction between theory and practice is warranted. Have we not, as Frodeman and Briggle suggest, lost something vitally important by disparaging the practical goal of living wisely and well as a proper motivation for doing philosophy? It is salutary to recall in this connection that Russell, unlike many of his intellectual heirs in the analytic tradition, believed that the basic tasks of philosophy have remained essentially the same from ancient times to the present. "Philosophy," he wrote, "has a certain perennial value, which is unchanging except in one respect: that some ages depart from wisdom more widely than others do."[13] In his 1946 essay "Philosophy for Laymen," written in the shadow of World War II and the looming threat of nuclear holocaust, Russell spoke of the need to recover the original sense of philosophy as the love of wisdom. It is wisdom that we need more than ever, he urged, "if the new powers invented by technicians, and handed over by them to be wielded by ordinary men and women, are not to plunge mankind into an appalling cataclysm."[14] Russell's words may strike a chord with contemporary readers, who, in addition to the threat of mass destruction by nuclear war, must now confront the real prospect of the mass extinction of life brought on by the effects of global warming.

For his own part, Russell was well aware that the philosophical inquiries of academic "specialists" were somewhat removed from the concerns and problems of daily life. But he was adamant that if philosophy is to play "a serious part" in the lives of those who are not specialists, "it must not cease to advocate some way of life."[15] In the aforementioned essay from 1912, Russell pointed to the way that philosophy helps us develop qualities of mind that contribute to the creation of a better, happier life and a more peaceful world: "Apart from its utility in showing unsuspected possibilities, philosophy has a value—perhaps its chief value—through the greatness of the objects which it contemplates, and the freedom from narrow and personal aims resulting from this contemplation."[16] Echoing a central idea in Buddhist thought, he noted that there is something "feverish and confined" about the life of a person who is narrowly preoccupied with the satisfaction of private interests and instinctive wishes—who regards the outer world merely as a means to an end, as something alien and hostile, something to be feared and controlled. For those who view themselves and the world in this way, there can be no peace, only "a constant strife between the insistence of desire and the powerlessness of will." If we are to have a life that is "great and free," insisted Russell, we must find a way to escape the prison of the ego.[17]

Philosophic contemplation[18] provides a means of escape by giving impersonal breadth and scope to our view of the world and the ends of life. In its "widest survey," observed Russell, a philosophic contemplation "does not divide the universe into two hostile camps—friends and foes, helpful and hostile, good and bad—it views the whole impartially."[19] The largeness of this impersonal, disinterested outlook gives us a proper measure of ourselves; it enables us to see things "calmly" and "dispassionately," without the distortion of personal "hopes and fears," without "the trammels of customary beliefs and traditional prejudices."[20] Russell added that the freedom and impartiality of this perspective is the proper basis for action: "The impartiality which, in contemplation, is the unalloyed desire for truth, is the very same quality of mind which, in action, is justice, and in emotion is that universal love which can be given to all, and not only to those who are judged useful or admirable."[21] By enlarging the objects of our thoughts, philosophic contemplation increases our capacity to act with wisdom and compassion—it makes us "citizens of the universe, not only of one walled city at war with all the rest."[22]

Over the course of his long career as a public philosopher, Russell repeatedly returned to the theme of his 1912 essay. The general view that emerges from these writings, briefly stated, is this: through philosophy, we are able to develop a more objective and impartial way of thinking and feeling—one that frees us from the tyranny of dogmatism, prejudice, and fear; that helps us overcome the emotional bias that gives rise to "almost all the major evils in human life";[23] that produces "a lessening of fanaticism" and an "increasing capacity of sympathy and mutual understanding";[24] that alleviates the "anxieties and anguish" of life; and that "makes possible the nearest approach to serenity that is available to a sensitive mind in our tortured and uncertain world."[25] Russell noted that this way of thinking and feeling was perhaps most fully embodied by Spinoza, whom he regarded as a model of the philosophical life:

> Spinoza . . . remained completely calm at all times, and in the last day of his life preserved the same friendly interest in others as he had shown in days of health. To a man whose hopes and wishes extend widely beyond his personal life there is not the same occasion for fear that there is for a man of more limited desires. . . . I do not pretend that such a man will always be happy. It is scarcely possible to be always happy in a world such as that in which we find ourselves, but I do think that the true philosopher is less likely than others are to suffer from baffled despair and fascinated terror in the contemplation of possible disaster.[26]

The expansive view of philosophy presented by Russell in these writings is striking in the way that it aligns the quest for truth with the ideal of wisdom. Not unlike the Buddhist approach, it is a profoundly humanistic conception of philosophy that speaks to the deepest moral and existential concerns of human beings. It is a philosophy that teaches us how to live without certainty, "without the comforting support of fairy tales"[27] or religious dogma. It gives us some glimmer of hope that we can be happy, that we can experience at least some measure of serenity in this turbulent and uncertain world.

The study of Buddhist philosophy is valuable for the very same reasons that Russell thought the study of Western philosophy was valuable—not least because it expands the horizons of our thought, enriches our intellectual imagination, and liberates us from the tyranny of custom and the arrogant dogmatism that constitute "the greatest of the mental obstacles to human happiness."[28] It reminds us that there are different ways of conceiving of philosophy—ways that bring this activity into closer register with our actual lives.

The big questions of philosophy have endured precisely because they continue to have the same moral, spiritual, and existential urgency that they have had for human beings throughout history. Comparing the ways that Buddhist and Western thinkers have engaged these questions is not merely an intellectual exercise, but an opportunity to deepen our understanding of ourselves and our place in the world, and to gain new conceptual tools, methods, and insights that we can use in our pursuit of a good and happy life.

NOTES

1. Bertrand Russell, *The Problems of Philosophy* (London: Williams & Norgate, 1912), 242.
2. Russell, *The Problems of Philosophy*, 239.
3. Russell, *The Problems of Philosophy*, 242–43.
4. Russell, *The Problems of Philosophy*, 243.
5. Russell, *The Problems of Philosophy*, 242.
6. Russell, *The Problems of Philosophy*, 241–42.
7. Julian Baggini, "What Is the Self? It Depends," *New York Times*, February 8, 2016, https://opinionator.blogs.nytimes.com/2016/02/08/the-self-in-east-and-west/.
8. Pierre Hadot, *Philosophy as a Way of Life*, ed. Arnold I. Davidson, trans. Michael Chase (Oxford: Blackwell, 1995), 265.

9. Christopher W. Gowans, "Buddhist Philosophy as a Way of Life: The Spiritual Exercises of Tsongkhapa," in *Buddhist Philosophy: A Comparative Approach*, ed. Steven M. Emmanuel (Malden, MA: Wiley-Blackwell, 2017), 11–28.
10. Robert Frodeman and Adam Briggle, "When Philosophy Lost Its Way," *New York Times* January 11, 2016, https://opinionator.blogs.nytimes.com/2016/01/11/when-philosophy-lost-its-way/.
11. Scott Soames, *Philosophical Analysis in the Twentieth Century*, vol. 1 (Princeton, NJ: Princeton University Press, 2005), xiv.
12. Scott Soames, "Philosophy's True Home," *New York Times*, March 7, 2016, https://opinionator.blogs.nytimes.com/2016/03/07/philosophys-true-home/.
13. Bertrand Russell, "A Philosophy for Our Time," in *Portraits from Memory and Other Essays* (New York: Simon and Schuster, 1956), 178.
14. Bertrand Russell, "Philosophy for Laymen," in *Unpopular Essays* (London: George Allen & Unwin, 1950), 36.
15. Russell, "Philosophy for Laymen," 45.
16. Russell, *The Problems of Philosophy*, 244.
17. Russell, *The Problems of Philosophy*, 244–45.
18. By "contemplation," Russell meant a kind of reflection that transcends one's personal interests and desires and is not tied to the particularities of one's own time and place. The degree to which we are able to transcend our individuality depends on the development of certain intellectual virtues, chiefly the virtue of impartiality, which Russell declared "the source of all that is best in philosophic thought and feeling." See Bertrand Russell, "Mysticism and Logic," in *Mysticism and Logic and Other Essays* (London: Longmans, Green and Co, 1918), 26.
19. Russell's description is redolent of the ancient ideal of the sage, who, as Hadot explains, "thinks and acts within a cosmic perspective. He has the feeling of belonging to a whole which goes beyond the limits of his individuality" (*Philosophy as a Way of Life*, 273). This practice of viewing the world and ourselves with objective detachment—the "view from above"—can bring about a transformation in our consciousness that "changes our value judgments on things: luxury, power, war . . . and the worries of everyday life become ridiculous" (*Philosophy as a Way of Life*, 207).
20. Russell, *The Problems of Philosophy*, 248.

21. Russell, *The Problems of Philosophy*, 249.
22. Russell, *The Problems of Philosophy*, 249. In the essay " 'Useless' Knowledge," he observed that "action is best when it emerges from a profound apprehension of the universe and human destiny," adding that it is "from large perceptions combined with impersonal emotion that wisdom most readily springs." See Bertrand Russell, *In Praise of Idleness and Other Essays* (London: George Allen & Unwin, 1935), 42, 45.
23. Russell, "A Philosophy for Our Time," 182.
24. Bertrand Russell, *A History of Western Philosophy* (New York: Simon and Schuster, 1945), 864.
25. Russell, "Philosophy for Laymen," 49.
26. Russell, "A Philosophy for Our Time," 184.
27. Russell, *A History of Western Philosophy*, 11.
28. Russell, "Philosophy for Laymen," 42.

BIBLIOGRAPHY

Emmanuel, Steven M., ed. *Buddhist Philosophy: A Comparative Approach*. Malden, MA: Wiley-Blackwell, 2017.

Hadot, Pierre. *Philosophy as a Way of Life*. Ed. Arnold I. Davidson. Trans. Michael Chase. Oxford: Blackwell, 1995.

Russell, Bertrand. *A History of Western Philosophy*. New York: Simon and Schuster, 1945.

Russell, Bertrand. *Mysticism and Logic and Other Essays*. London: Longmans, Green and Co., 1918.

Russell, Bertrand. *Portraits from Memory and Other Essays*. New York: Simon and Schuster, 1956.

Russell, Bertrand. *In Praise of Idleness and Other Essays*. London: George Allen & Unwin, 1935.

Russell, Bertrand. *The Problems of Philosophy*. London: Williams & Norgate, 1912.

Russell, Bertrand. *Unpopular Essays*. London: George Allen & Unwin, 1950.

Soames, Scott. *Philosophical Analysis in the Twentieth Century*. Vol. 1. Princeton, NJ: Princeton University Press, 2005.

FOR FURTHER READING AND STUDY

GENERAL WORKS ON BUDDHISM

Bechert, Heinz, and Richard Gombrich, eds. *The World of Buddhism*. London: Thames & Hudson, 1984.

Carrithers, Michael. *The Buddha: A Very Short Introduction*. New York: Oxford University Press, 1983, 1996.

Crosby, Kate. *Theravada Buddhism: Continuity, Diversity, and Identity*. Chichester, UK: Wiley Blackwell, 2014.

de Bary, William Theodore. *The Buddhist Tradition in India, China and Japan*. New York: Modern Library, 1969.

Gethin, Rupert. *The Foundations of Buddhism*. New York: Oxford University Press, 1998.

Gombrich, R. F. *How Buddhism Began: The Conditioned Genesis of the Early Teachings*. London: Routledge, 2006.

Harvey, Peter. *An Introduction to Buddhism: Teachings, History, and Practices*. 2nd ed. New York: Cambridge University Press, 2013.

Rahula, Walpola. *What the Buddha Taught*. New York: Grove, 1974.

Williams, Paul. *Buddhist Thought: A Complete Introduction to the Indian Tradition*. London: Routledge, 2000.

SELECT STUDIES IN INDIAN BUDDHIST PHILOSOPHY

Anālayo, Bhikkhu. *A Comparative Study of the Majjhima-Nikāya*. Taipei: Dharma Drum, 2011.

Blumenthal, James. *The Ornament of the Middle Way: A Study of the Madhyamaka Thought of Śāntarakṣita*. Boston: Snow Lion, 2004.

Carpenter, Amber D. *Indian Buddhist Philosophy*. London: Routledge, 2014.

Collins, Steven. *Nirvana and Other Buddhist Felicities*. Cambridge: Cambridge University Press, 1998.

Collins, Steven. *Selfless Persons: Imagery and Thought in Theravāda Buddhism*. New York: Cambridge University Press, 1990.

Dunne, John D. *Foundations of Dharmakīrti's Philosophy*. Boston: Wisdom, 2004.

Frauwallner, Erich. *The Philosophy of Buddhism*. Delhi: Motilal Banarsidass, 2007.

Ganeri, Jonardon. *Attention, Not Self*. Oxford: Oxford University Press, 2017.

Garfield, Jay L. *Empty Words: Buddhist Philosophy and Cross-Cultural Interpretation*. New York: Oxford University Press, 2002.

Garfield, Jay L. *Engaging Buddhism: Why It Matters to Philosophy*. New York: Oxford University Press, 2015.

Garfield, Jay L., and Jan Westerhoff, eds. *Madhyamaka and Yogācāra: Allies or Rivals?* New York: Oxford University Press, 2015.

Gethin, Rupert. *The Buddhist Path to Awakening*. Oxford: Oneworld Publications, 2003.

Gold, Jonathan C. *Paving the Great Way: Vasubandhu's Unifying Buddhist Philosophy*. New York: Columbia University Press, 2015.

Goodman, Charles. *Consequences of Compassion: An Interpretation and Defense of Buddhist Ethics*. New York: Oxford University Press, 2009.

Gowans, Christopher W. *Buddhist Moral Philosophy: An Introduction*. New York: Routledge, 2015.

Gowans, Christopher W. *Philosophy of the Buddha: An Introduction*. New York: Routledge, 2003.

Hamilton, Sue. *Early Buddhism: A New Approach: The I of the Beholder*. Richmond, UK: Curzon, 2000.

Hamilton, Sue. *Indian Philosophy: A Very Short Introduction*. New York: Oxford University Press, 2001.

Harris, Ian. *The Continuity of Madhyamaka and Yogācāra in Indian Mahāyāna Buddhism*. Leiden, Netherlands: E. J. Brill, 1991.

Harvey, Peter. *An Introduction to Buddhist Ethics*. New York: Cambridge University Press, 2000.
Harvey, Peter. *The Selfless Mind: Personality, Consciousness and Nirvana in Early Buddhism*. Abingdon, UK: Routledge, 1995.
Heim, Maria. *The Forerunner of All Things: Buddhaghosa on Mind, Intention, and Agency*. New York: Oxford University Press, 2014.
Huntington, C. W. *The Emptiness of Emptiness: An Introduction to Early Indian Mādhyamika*. Honolulu: University of Hawaii Press, 1999.
Keown, Damien. *The Nature of Buddhist Ethics*. New York: Palgrave Macmillan, 2001.
Kochumuttom, Thomas A. *A Buddhist Doctrine of Experience*. Delhi: Motilal Banarsidass, 1982.
Rahula, Walpola. *What the Buddha Taught*. New York: Grove, 1979.
Ronkin, Noa. *Early Buddhist Metaphysics: The Making of a Philosophical Tradition*. London: RoutledgeCurzon, 2005.
Siderits, Mark. *Buddhism as Philosophy: An Introduction*. Indianapolis, IN: Hackett, 2007.
Siderits, Mark, Evan Thompson, and Dan Zahavi, eds. *Self, No Self? Perspectives from Analytic, Phenomenological, and Indian Traditions*. Reprint ed. New York: Oxford University Press, 2013.
Stcherbatsky, F. Th. *Buddhist Logic*. Mineola, NY: Dover, 1962.
Webster, David. *The Philosophy of Desire in the Buddhist Pali Canon*. Abingdon, UK: RoutledgeCurzon, 2005.
Westerhoff, Jan. *The Golden Age of Indian Buddhist Philosophy*. New York: Oxford University Press, 2018.
Westerhoff, Jan. *Nāgārjuna's Madhyamaka: A Philosophical Introduction*. New York: Oxford University Press, 2009.
Williams, Paul. *Mahāyāna Buddhism: The Doctrinal Foundations*. New York: Routledge, 1989.

ANTHOLOGIES

Anacker, Stefan. *Seven Works of Vasubandhu: The Buddhist Psychological Doctor*. Delhi: Motilal Banarsidass, 1998.
Bodhi, Bhikkhu. *In the Buddha's Words: An Anthology of Discourses from the Pāli Canon*. Boston: Wisdom, 2005.

Edelglass, William, and Jay Garfield, eds. *Buddhist Philosophy: Essential Readings*. New York: Oxford University Press, 2009.
Holder, John J. *Early Buddhist Discourses*. Indianapolis, IN: Hackett, 2006.
Rarhakrishnan, Sarvepalli, and Charles A. Moore, eds. *A Source Book in Indian Philosophy*. Princeton, NJ: Princeton University Press, 1957.
Shaw, Sarah. *Buddhist Meditation: An Anthology of Texts from the Pāli Canon*. New York: Routledge, 2006.

ENCYCLOPEDIAS, DICTIONARIES, AND HANDBOOKS

Buswell, Robert E., and Donald S. Lopez. *Princeton Dictionary of Buddhism*. Princeton, NJ: Princeton University Press, 2014.
Keown, Damien, and Charles S. Prebish, eds. *Encyclopedia of Buddhism*. New York: Routledge, 2007.
Powers, John. *A Concise Encyclopedia of Buddhism*. London: Oneworld Publications, 2000.
Thera, Nyanatiloka. *Buddhist Dictionary: Manual of Buddhist Terms and Doctrines*. Kandy, Sri Lanka: BPS Pariyatti, 2019.

DIGITAL ARCHIVES OF BUDDHIST TEXTS

There are a number of excellent online resources that support study and research. The following is a short list of stable and well-maintained websites containing archives of original texts, translations, commentaries, study aids, glossaries, and online dictionaries.

Buddhist Studies WWW Virtual Library, http://www.ciolek.com/WWWVL-Buddhism.html.
One of the largest online collections of Buddhist literature, maintained by Australia National University. This site contains many links to other useful resources.

Sutta Central: Early Buddhist Texts, Translations, and Parallels, https://suttacentral.net.
This site contains a full library of texts from across the Buddhist traditions, with translations from Pāli, Sanskrit, and Chinese.

Access to Insight: Readings in Theravāda Buddhism, https://www.accesstoinsight.org.
This site provides translations of Pāli suttas, commentaries, scholarly articles, and Pāli-language study aids.

84000: Translating the Words of the Buddha, https://84000.co.
This is an ongoing scholarly project aimed at translating into English all the Tibetan translations of the Buddha's teachings (Kangyur) and works written by Indian Buddhist masters (Tengyur).

LEXICOGRAPHIC RESOURCES

A Compendium of Sanskrit and Pāli Words (https://www.nichirenlibrary.org/en/dic/Appendix/A). The Nichiren Buddhism Library.

A Critical Pāli Dictionary (https://cpd.uni-koeln.de). Maintained by the Data Center for the Humanities at the University of Cologne.

A Glossary of Pāli and Buddhist Terms (https://www.accesstoinsight.org/glossary.html). Maintained by the Access to Insight website.

The Pāli Text Society's Pāli-English Dictionary (https://dsal.uchicago.edu/dictionaries/pali/). University of Chicago's Digital Dictionaries of South Asia.

Nyanatiloka Thera, *Buddhist Dictionary: Manual of Buddhist Terms and Doctrines*. A searchable digital version is available at https://www.budsas.org/ebud/bud-dict/dic_idx.htm.

CONTRIBUTORS

Dan Arnold is associate professor of philosophy of religions at the University of Chicago Divinity School. He is the author of *Buddhists, Brahmins, and Belief: Epistemology in South Asian Philosophy of Religions* (2005), which won an American Academy of Religion Award for Excellence in the Study of Religion; and *Brains, Buddhas, and Believing: The Problem of Intentionality in Classical Buddhist and Cognitive-Scientific Philosophy of Mind* (2012), which won the Numata Book Prize in Buddhism. He is currently working on an anthology of original translations from India's Madhyamaka tradition of Buddhist philosophy.

Amber D. Carpenter is associate professor of philosophy at Yale-NUS College. Her research interests span the ancient Greek and Indian philosophical traditions. She is the author of *Indian Buddhist Philosophy* (2014); "Persons Keeping Their Karma Together," in *The Moon Points Back: Analytic Philosophy and Asian Thought*, ed. Koji Tanaka, Yasuo Deguchi, Jay L. Garfield, and Graham Priest (2015); "The Unhappiness of the Great King," in *Rereading Ancient Philosophy: Old Chestnuts, Sacred Cows*, ed. Verity Harte and Raphael Woolf (2018); "Reason and Knowledge on the Path: A Protreptic Approach to the *Bodhicaryāvatāra*," in *Readings of*

Śāntideva's Guide to Bodhisattva Practice (Bodhicaryāvatāra), ed. Jonathan C. Gold and Douglas S. Duckworth (Columbia, 2019); and "Transformative Vision: Coming to See the Buddha's Reality," in *Buddhist Literature as Philosophy, Buddhist Philosophy as Literature*, ed. Rafal K. Stepien (2020).

Douglas Duckworth is professor and director of graduate studies in the Department of Religion at Temple University. His latest works include *Tibetan Buddhist Philosophy of Mind and Nature* (2019) and *The Profound Reality of Interdependence* (2019), a translation of an overview of the Wisdom Chapter of the *Way of the Bodhisattva* by Künzang Sönam. He also is the coeditor, with Jonathan Gold, of *Readings of Śāntideva's Guide to Bodhisattva Practice (Bodhicaryāvatāra)* (Columbia, 2019).

Steven M. Emmanuel is professor of philosophy and dean of the Susan S. Goode School of Arts and Humanities at Virginia Wesleyan University. His research interests lie mainly in the history of philosophy (both East and West), with an emphasis on moral and religious thought. In addition to his work on major figures in the modern European tradition, he is the editor of *Buddhist Philosophy: A Comparative Approach* (2018) and *A Companion to Buddhist Philosophy* (2013). He also produced and directed an award-winning, feature-length documentary, *Making Peace with Viet Nam* (2008), which examines the challenges of reconciliation in the aftermath of war.

Peter D. Hershock is director of the Asian Studies Development Program at the East-West Center in Honolulu. His philosophical work uses Buddhist conceptual resources to address contemporary issues of global concern. He has authored or edited more than a dozen books on Buddhism, Asian philosophy, and contemporary issues, the most recent of which are *Valuing Diversity: Buddhist Reflection on Realizing a More Equitable Global Future* (2012); *Public Zen, Personal Zen: A Buddhist Introduction* (2014); *Value and Values: Economics and Justice in an Age of Global Interdependence* (edited, 2015); and *Philosophies of Place: An Intercultural Conversation* (edited, 2019). His current project, initiated while he was a 2017–2018 Fellow of the Berggruen Institute in China, is a monograph on *Ethical Virtuosity in the Age of Intelligent Technology: Learning from Buddhism and Classical Philosophy*, a reflection on the personal and societal impacts of the attention economy and artificial intelligence.

Stephen J. Laumakis is professor of philosophy and former director of the Aquinas Scholars Honors Program at the University of St. Thomas in St. Paul, Minnesota. Among his publications are articles in the *Modern Schoolman, American Catholic Philosophical Quarterly, Journal of Markets & Morality, Journal of the Philosophy of Sport,* and *Journal of Dialogue Studies*. He is the author of *An Introduction to Buddhist Philosophy* (2008) and "The Philosophical Context of Gotama's Thought," in *A Companion to Buddhist Philosophy*, ed. Steven M. Emmanuel (2013).

Rick Repetti is professor of philosophy at CUNY Kingsborough. His publications on free will include *Buddhism, Meditation, and Free Will: A Buddhist Theory of Mental Freedom* (2019), the edited collection *Buddhist Perspectives on Free Will: Agentless Agency?* (2017), and *The Counterfactual Theory of Free Will: A Genuinely Deterministic Form of Soft Determinism* (2010), as well as numerous articles and book chapters, including "Freedom of the Mind: Buddhist Soft Compatibilism," *Philosophy East and West* 70, no. 1 (2020); "Symposium on *Buddhist Perspectives on Free Will: Agentless Agency?*," *Journal of Buddhist Ethics* 25 (2018);

"Buddhist Meditation and the Possibility of Freedom," *Science, Religion & Culture* 2, no. 2 (2015); "Meditation and Mental Freedom: A Buddhist Theory of Free Will," *Journal of Buddhist Ethics* 17 (2010); and "What Do Buddhists Think About Free Will?," in *A Mirror Is for Reflection: Understanding Buddhist Ethics*, ed. Jake Davis (2017).

Jan Westerhoff is professor of Buddhist philosophy at the University of Oxford; a fellow of Lady Margaret Hall, University of Oxford; and research associate at the School of Oriental and African Studies, University of London. His publications include *The Non-Existence of the Real World* (2020), *The Golden Age of Indian Buddhist Philosophy* (2018), *The Dispeller of Disputes: Nagarjuna's Vigrahavyavartani* (2010), and *Nagarjuna's Madhyamaka: A Philosophical Investigation* (2009).

INDEX

Abhidharmakośa (*Treasury of Abhidharma*) (Vasubandhu), 103–4
Abhidharma tradition, 108–9; on causal conditions, 113–14, 125n20; on dharmas, theory of, 92; Vasubandhu on, 103–4; Yogācāra philosophers and, 125n16
abhijjhāvisamalobhābhibhūtena (covetousness and unrighteous greed), 231
acquaintance, knowledge by, 75n12; Four Noble Truths and, 71; knowledge about versus, 58, 67–68; knowledge that versus, 58, 66–69; self-awareness and, 66–69, 73
Ādittapariyāya Sutta (fire sermon), 218
adosa (nonhatred), 221
Africa, Asia, and the History of Philosophy (Park), ix
agentless agency, 16, 144, 152–53, 277
agent/self, Buddhism rejecting, 144–46, 150
aggregates, 39, 54n19, 219–20

Ālambanaparīkṣā ("Critical Analysis of the *Ālambana*") (Dignāga), 113–14
ālayavijñāna (store-house consciousness), 125n16, 125n19
alobha (nongreed), 221
amoha (nondelusion), 221
analytic tradition, of philosophy, 3, 8, 278–80
anaṇasukha (happiness of being debtless), 225
Anaṇa Sutta, 225
Anāthapiṇḍika, 224, 244n40
anātman (being without-self), 264
anavajjasukha (happiness of being blameless), 225–26, 233–34
Anaxagoras, 179
anger, 198n37; *Dhammapada* on, 180–83, 199n41, 199n43; justice and, 199n43
Aṅguttara Nikāya, 40, 197n30
apatheia, 212
apperception, transcendental unity of, 75n10

INDEX

appicchatā (limited desires), 227
Aputtaka Sutta, 244n44
Aquinas, Thomas, 192n6
arahant ideal, 41, 43
Aristotle, 166; Buddhist thought compared with, 47; free will and, 132, 147; on good human life, 25, 27–30, 32, 47, 52n2; on justice, 268; virtue theory of, 25, 29–30, 32, 47, 52n2
Aronson, Harvey B., 149, 156n27
atman (self), 264
atomism, 115; Greek, 131–32; Manorathanandin on, 108; Vasubandhu on, 83, 105–6, 108, 114, 124n9
attachment: greed and, 218–19; self and, 219–22; as *upādāna*, 218–20
atthisukha (happiness of having material wealth), 225
Augustine, Saint, 132, 145, 154n3
Austin, J. L., 115
autonomous agent/self, Buddhism rejecting, 144–46

Bactria, 148, 168
Baggini, Julian, 277
Bandhula (fictional character), 177–79, 183–84
Beck, Ulrich, 256
being without-self (*anātman*), 264
benevolence, 234
Bentham, Jeremy, 30, 52n2
Bernasconi, Robert, ix
bhogasukha (happiness of enjoying material wealth), 225

bīja (seeds), 117–19, 125n16
Blackburn, Simon, 236
blamelessness, Buddhist concept of, 225–26, 233–34
bliss (*sukha*), 225, 265
Block, Ned, 125n21
block-universe account, 95n5
Bodhi, Bhikkhu, 223, 226–27
bodhicitta, 42–43, 264
bodhisattva: intergenerational ethics of, 264–65, 272; *mahākaruṇā* of, 20, 264–65; Mahāyāna Buddhism on, 20, 21n19, 42–43, 47, 52, 264–66, 271; nonduality affirmed by, 266; relational justice and, 271–72; Six Perfections of, 43
Briggle, Adam, 278–79
Brothers Karamazov, The (Dostoyevsky), 165, 189, 191n5, 201n54
Buddha, vii, 244n38; accessibility emphasized by, 261–62; Anāthapiṇḍika and, 224, 244n40; in *Commentary on the Dhammapada*, 184–86, 198n40; Devadatta and, 169; in *Dhammapada*, 40, 176, 181–82; on economic development, 238–39; on Eightfold Path, 37–40, 46, 149–50; on Four Noble Truths, 37–40, 46, 149, 218; free will and, 145–47, 149–53, 154n3; on good human life, 35, 37–38, 45–51, 55n28; on greed, 216–18, 231; on happiness, four kinds of, 225–26; idealism and, 97, 104, 106–7;

Indian thought, classical, and, 32, 34–36; Kālāmas and, 50–51; karma and, 36, 147, 171–72, 175, 185–86, 194n17; on liberation, path to, 222–23; on Middle Way, 37–39; in *Milindapañha*, 168–72, 194n16, 196n26; on moderation, benefits of, 228; nirvana and, 36, 38, 144, 149–50, 222; in Pāli canon, discourses of, 170; on "Parable of the Arrow," 48–50; on person, five parts of, 83; post-Vedic thought and, 32, 34–35; on samsara, 36, 169; on self, 40, 83, 144, 173; on *skandhas*, 83; on skillful conditions, 230; soteriological focus of, 11, 146; suffering and, 11, 168–71, 173, 187, 194n13, 218–19, 222; *Sutta Piṭaka* of, 35, 37; Three Baskets of, 35, 37; on Three Marks, 37–38, 40, 80–81; on untimely death, 170–71, 194n16; Vasubandhu on, 97, 104, 106–7; on wealth, acquisition of, 18–19, 216–17, 223–25, 245n50. *See also* Siddhārtha Gautama

Buddhaghosa, 264

Buddha-nature, 42–44, 266

Buddhist Economics (Payutto), 227–28

burning house, parable of, 72

Cakkavattisīhanāda Sutta, 237–38

Candrakīrti, 198n37

capabilities: compassion and, 258–61; core, 258–60, 270; intrinsic and combined, 258

capitalism: Buddhism on, 230; consumerism in, 226–27, 229–30; economists, modern, on, 208–10; Friedman on, 209–10; global informational, 255; happiness and, 216, 243n24; Keynes on, 216, 243n24

Cartesian dualism, 100–101

Castells, Manuel, 255

Categorical Imperative, 30, 47

causal conditions: Abhidharma tradition on, 113–14, 125n20; Dignāga on, 113, 115–17, 119; free will and, 134–35, 148; *hetupratyaya*, 113–14, 125n16; *pratyaya*, 113–14

cause, 86, 126n22; of cognition, Dharmakīrti on, 112–13; of cognition, Dignāga on, 113–20, 122; final, 188

cetanā: as intentionality, 197n30, 262–63; as thought, 104, 123n7; as volition, 147, 197n30

Chadha, Monima, 195n19, 200n48

Chalmers, David: on consciousness, hard problem of, 14, 98–100; on philosophy, progress of, 2–4

chanda (desire), 227–28, 230, 245n52

change dynamics, contemporary, 250–51

Chinese, Sanskrit texts translated into, viii

Chinese Buddhism: Buddha-nature in, 266; Huayan school, 96n10

Chinese philosophy, x–xi, 166

choice, freedoms and compulsions in, 256, 261

chronically undernourished, global population of, 251
Cicero, 179
cities, growth of, 250
climate change, 270, 280; adaptation to, technological, 254, 259; climate migrants, UN on, 251; future generations facing, 251–52, 254–55, 259; globally binding agreement on, lacking, 251–52; inequality and, 254–55; predicament-resolution, dominance of, and, 256–57; problem-solution and, 256
cognition: cause of, 112–20, 122; Dharmakīrti on, 107–13; Dignāga on, 15, 113–20, 122
combined capabilities, 258
Commentary on the Dhammapada (Dhammapada-aṭṭakathā), 177
common, shared and, 257
communications revolution, 255
comparative philosophy, 5–6; dialogue in, 8–9; philosophy, value of, and, 276–77; philosophy curriculum, diversifying, and, 10; traditional, criticisms of, 7–8
compassion: Buddhist, 6, 20, 261–67, 269; Buddhist, relational dynamics of, 20, 262–64, 266–67, 269; capabilities, freedoms, and cultivating, 258–61; craving and, 264; individual and, 260–61; institutions and, 258, 260–61; intergenerational ethics and, 259–61, 278; justice and, 6, 20, 260–61, 267–72; justice and social emotion of, 19, 257–59; *karuṇā*, 51, 263–64; *mahākaruṇā*, Mahāyāna Buddhism on, 20, 264–65, 269; Nussbaum on, 19, 257–61, 264; social emotion of, 19, 257–59; suffering and, 51, 258, 260, 262, 264–65

Compatibilism: Buddhist, wiggly, 148; Frankfurt on, 140–42; Semi-Compatibilism, 142–43, 148–49; Soft, 140, 148. *See also* incompatibilism
compulsions to choose, 256, 261
computing revolution, 255
conceptual knowledge: Buddhism on, 62–66, 73; Dignāga on, 62–63; perceptual versus, 58, 62–66, 73, 75n10
Confucian traditions, 253
consciousness: Buddhist debates on, 146; causal conditions of, 113–17, 119, 125n16, 125n20; Dharmakīrti on, 15, 98–100, 116; Dignāga on, 15, 98–100, 113–22; explanatory gap of, 125n21; first-person perspective on, 14–15, 114, 119–22; neuroscience and skepticism on, 143; seeds of, 117–19, 125n16; store-house, 125n16, 125n19; third-person perspective on, 14–15, 114, 117–18, 120–22
consciousness, hard problem of, 123n2; Buddhist idealism and, 15, 98–100, 277; Chalmers on, 14, 98–100; Dignāga and, 113–14, 121–22; physicalism and, 120–22, 126n22; subjectivity and, 99, 122

Consequence Argument, 129, 136, 138–39, 143
consequentialism: deontological theory and, 31–32; God and, 31; on good human life, 25, 30–32, 52n2
consumerism, 226–27, 229–30
consumption, mindfulness of, 228
contemplation, 280, 284nn18–19
contentment: Buddhist, 227, 230; economists on, 229–30; *santuṭṭhi*, 227
covetousness and unrighteous greed (*abhijjhāvisamalobhābhibhūt ena*), 231
Crane, Tim, 126n22
craving (*taṇhā*), 231; compassion and, 264; consumerist, 226–27, 229–30; ending, 222; in Four Noble Truths, 218; self and, 219–22; suffering and, 218
"Critical Analysis of the *Ālambana*" (*Ālambanaparīkṣā*) (Dignāga), 113–14
Critique of Practical Reason (Kant), 30
cross-cultural study: dialogue in, 9–10; fusion philosophy, 8; philosophical, 5–10, 276–77; traditional, criticisms of, 7–8
curriculum, philosophy, diversifying, x–xi, 10

Dalai Lama, viii
dāḷiddiya (poverty), 237
dāna (generosity), 221, 223–24, 263
deception, economics and, 215

deontological theory: consequentialism and, 31–32; on good human life, 25, 29–32, 52n2
dependent origination, 11
Descartes, René, 100–101
desire (*chanda*), 227–28, 230, 245n52
determinism, 15, 135, 140–42, 154n5; Buddhist, wiggly, 147; Consequence Argument on, 129, 136, 143; Hard, 136, 148; Manipulation Argument on, 129, 136, 143; Optimist's Dilemma and, 133–34, 143
Devadatta, 169
Dhammapada, 201n52; on anger, hatred, 180–83, 199n41, 199n43; Buddha in, 40, 176, 181–82; first and second wife story in, 180–83, 198n40, 199n41, 199n43; karma in, 177–83, 185–86, 198n35, 199n42, 199n45 Sākiyas, slaying of, in, 184–86; suffering in, 180, 182, 199nn41–42; Three Marks in, 40
Dhammapada-aṭṭakathā (*Commentary on the Dhammapada*), 177; Buddha in, 184–86, 198n40; Kāyāyana in, 183–84; Mallikā in, 177–80, 183–84, 198n35; Pasenadi in, 177–79, 183; Viḍūḍabha in, 183–86
Dharmakīrti, viii, 12; on cognition, 107–13; on cognition, cause of, 112–13; on consciousness, 15, 98–100, 116; empiricism and, 108–11; idealism of, 97–98, 102–3, 107–13; on perception, 13, 65–66, 70, 73, 109–10; on rebirth, 15, 98, 102–3, 123n5; on yogic perception, 13, 65, 70

dharmas, theory of: Abhidharma, 92; as ontology, 84–85
Dīghajāṇu, 244n38
Dīgha Nikāya, 41
Dignāga, viii, 13; atomism and, 114–15; on cognition, 15, 113–20, 122; on conceptual knowledge, 62–63; consciousness, hard problem of, and, 113–14, 121–22; on consciousness, 15, 98–100, 113–22; "Critical Analysis of the *Ālambana*," 113–14; on epistemology, 61; idealism of, 97–98, 108–9, 114, 116–17, 121; on perception, 112, 114–16; on *pramāṇa*, 61
Dispelling Disputes (Nāgārjuna), 60
diversity, 269–70
Doṇapāka Sutta, 228
Dostoyevsky, Fyodor, 165, 189, 191n5, 201n54
dualism: Buddhist, 100–103; Cartesian, 100–101
duḥkha (suffering), 262, 265, 270–71
dukkha (suffering), 40, 44, 46, 50, 218

economic liberalism, 208–9
economics: on contentment, 229–30; deception and, 215; development, Buddha on, 238–39; on greed, modern, 208–11, 229; happiness and, Buddhism on, 225–31; happiness and, contemporary research on, 214; soteriology, Buddhist, and, 239. See also Smith, Adam

ego, prison of, 280–81
Eightfold Path: Buddha on, 37–40, 46, 149–50; free will and, 149; in Theravāda Buddhism, 37–40, 44
empiricism, 114; Dharmakīrti and, 108–11; idealism and, 108; rationalism and, 63–64
emptiness: form and, 266; knowledge and, Buddhism on, 60; Madhyamaka theory of, 83–87, 93–94, 95n8; nonfoundationalism and theory of, 83–87, 93–94; *śūnyatā*, 265–66; Yogācāra school on, 86–87
Engaging Buddhism (Garfield), 7–8
environmental movement, 251
epistemology: Buddhism and, 13, 58–66, 73–74; Buddhist, conceptual and perceptual in, 62–66; good human life, metaphysics, and, 53n7; Mahāyāna Buddhism and, 13, 59–60; *pramāṇa*, 61
equity, 267–70
ethical conduct (*sīla*), 221
ethics, 53n8, 257, 277; Levinas on, 252; metaethics, normative ethics and, 45; Rawls on, 253; relational, 20, 252, 262–64, 266–67, 272, 278
ethics, intergenerational, 6, 19; bodhisattva, 264–65, 272; Buddhist compassion and, 259–61, 278; Confucian, 253; family-centered, 253; global justice and, 251–52, 261;

nonduality in, 266–67, 272, 278;
relational, 20, 252, 266–67, 272, 278
event-based ontology, Buddhist, 101
experience, subjective, 14–15
Eze, Emmanuel Chukwudi, ix

family, intergenerational ethics
and, 253
Fazang, 266
feedback, 256
feminism, 268
final cause, 188
fire sermon (*Ādittapariyāya Sutta*), 218
Fischer, J. M., 142
five aggregates, 39, 54n19
Five Precepts (*pañcasīla*), 244n39
Flanagan, Owen, 132
form (*rūpa*), 266
foundationalism, 13–14, 62, 150
Four-Case Argument, 136, 143
Four Noble Truths: Buddha on, 37–40, 46, 149, 218; knowledge and, 71–72; liberation and, 39–40, 71; suffering in, 39–40, 46, 71, 187; *taṇhā* in, 218; in Theravāda Buddhism, 37–40, 44
fo-xing (Buddha-nature), 266
Frankfurt, H., 140–42
freedoms of choice, 256
free will: agentless agency and, 16, 144, 152–53, 277; Aristotle and, 132, 147; Augustine on, 132, 145, 154n3; Buddha and, 145–47, 149–53, 154n3; Buddhism on, 130, 144–53; Buddhism on, historical, 145–51;

Buddhist counterargument on, possible, 151–53; causal conditions and, 134–35, 148; Compatibilism on, 140–43, 148–49; Compatibilism on, Buddhist, 148; Consequence Argument on, 129, 136, 138–39, 143; Eightfold Path and, 149; Four-Case Argument on, 136, 143; God and, 132–33; Impossibility Argument on, 129–30, 139–40, 143; incompatibilism on, 136–38, 140–42, 147–48, 150, 154n7; libertarian indeterminism on, 137–38, 141–42, 150, 154n7; Mahāyāna Buddhism on, 150–51; Manipulation Argument on, 129, 136, 138–39, 143; Mind Argument on, 129, 137–39, 143; neuroscience and skepticism on, 143–44; Optimist's Dilemma of, 129, 133–34, 136, 138–40, 143; prephilosophical understanding of, 130–31, 137, 142; quantum indeterminism of, 133–34, 137–38, 154n5; self and, 16, 146, 149–50; Semi-Compatibilism on, 142–43; Semi-Compatibilism on, Buddhist, 148–49; soteriology and, 149–50; Theravāda Buddhism on, 150–51; two-truths distinction and, 148–49, 151, 156n27; Western problem of, 15, 129–33, 145, 154n3
Friedman, Milton, 209–10
Frodeman, Robert, 278–79

Frost, Mervyn, 260
fuel (*upādāna*). *See* attachment
fusion philosophy, 8
future generations, 6; asymmetry with, 252; bodhisattva and, 264–65, 272; Buddhist compassion and, 259–61, 278; climate change facing, 251–52, 254–55, 259; family and, 253; global hunger facing, 251; indeterminacy of, 252–54; intergenerational justice for, 19–20, 251–52, 259, 261, 267, 271–72; moral consideration for, obstacles to, 252–53; nonduality and, 266–67, 272, 278; nonexistence of, 252, 259; policymaking, politics for, 251–54; relationality for, 20, 252, 266–67, 272, 278; structural considerations on, 255–57

Garfield, Jay L., 7–9, 132
Gendün Chöpel, 61
generosity (*dāna*), 221, 223–24, 263
Gethin, Rupert, 219–20
Gettier, Edmund, 69
Giddens, Anthony, 256
global antirealism, of Madhyamaka school, 90–94
globalization: differentiation characterizing, 256–57; global informational capitalism, 255
global justice. *See* justice
global populations: undernourished, 251; urban, 250

God: as consequentialist, 31; free will and, 132–33. *See also* problem of evil
gods, Greek, 165
good human life: Aristotle on, 25, 27–30, 32, 47, 52n2; Buddha on, 35, 37–38, 45–51, 55n28; Buddhist, philosophical benefits of, 52; Buddhist, real-world benefits of, 48–52; Buddhist and Western approaches to, 12, 44–48, 53n8; consequentialism on, 25, 30–32, 52n2; Eastern and Western philosophical roots and, 24–25; epistemology, metaphysics, and, 53n7; happiness and, 23–25, 30, 36; Hesiod, Homer on, 25–26; Indian thought, classical, on, 32–35; Kant on, 25, 29–32, 47, 52n2; Mahāyāna Buddhism on, 25, 41–44, 51–52; Mill on, 25, 30–32, 47–48, 52n2; Plato on, 27–28; post-Vedic thought on, 33–35; pre-Socratic philosophers on, 25–26; Socrates on, 24, 27–28; Sophists on, 26–27; Theravāda Buddhism on, 25, 32, 35–44; virtue theory on, 25, 29–32, 47, 52n2; Western philosophy, contemporary, and, 278–79. *See also* ethics
Goodman, C., 144
government, Buddhism and, 237–40
Gowans, Christopher, 278
great compassion (*mahākaruṇā*), 20, 264–65, 269

greed: *abhijjhāvisamalobhābhibhūtena*, 231; attachment and, 218–19; Buddha on, 216–18, 231; in Buddhist thought, concept of, 216–22, 231; consumerist, 226–27, 229–30; *dāna* as antidote to, 223; defenses of, 18–19, 205–6, 208–11, 229, 278; economists, modern, on, 208–11, 229; Friedman on, 209–10; hatred and, 231; *lobha*, 217; *rāga*, 218; Smith and, 18, 206–8, 211–16; *taṇhā* and, 218, 226–27, 229–30; vanity and, 211–12, 215, 232, 235
Greed with John Stossel (news special), 210
Greeks: atomism of, 131–32; on gods, archaic, 165; philosophy originating with, myth of, viii–x
Griswold, Charles, 216

Hadot, Pierre, 278, 284n19
Hallisey, Charles, 198n35
Hanley, Ryan Patrick, 216
Hansen, Anne, 198n35
happiness: Buddha on four kinds of, 225–26; in Buddhism, wealth, acquisition of, and, 225–32, 238–39; capitalism and, 216, 243n24; delusion about, Buddhism on, 231; Eastern and Western philosophical roots and, 24–25; economics of, contemporary research on, 214; good human life and, 23–25, 30, 36; monastic, 227; Smith on, 212–16, 231–33,

239–40, 242n18; as subjective well-being, 23, 25; *sukha*, 225, 265
happiness of being blameless (*anavajjasukha*), 225–26, 233–34
happiness of being debtless (*anaṇasukha*), 225
happiness of enjoying material wealth (*bhogasukha*), 225
happiness of having material wealth (*atthisukha*), 225
Hard Determinism, 136, 148
Hard Incompatibilism, 140, 148
Hard Indeterminism, 148
hard problem of consciousness. *See* consciousness
Harvey, Peter, 44
hatred, 198n37; *Dhammapada* on, 180–83, 199n41, 199n43; greed and, 231; nonhatred, 221
Heart Sutra, 265–66
Heim, Maria, 199n42
Hershock, Peter, 238
Hesiod, 25–26
hetupratyaya (causal conditions which are causes). *See* causal conditions
higher knowledge (*prajñā*), 59
Hindu tradition: karma in, 171, 191n4, 195n19, 200n48; problem of evil and, 171, 192n7, 195n19, 200n48; Weber on, 164, 191n3, 192n7
Homer, 25–26, 165
Honderich, T., 154n5
Horner, I. B., 194n16
How Much Is Enough? (R. Skidelsky and E. Skidelsky), 229
Huayan school, 96n10

human flourishing: Buddhism on, 233–34, 237–39, 269; Smith on, 231–37, 239–40
Hume, David, 144
hunger, world, 251

idealism: Buddha and, 97, 104, 106–7; of Dharmakīrti, 97–98, 102–3, 107–13; of Dignāga, 97–98, 108–9, 114, 116–17, 122; empiricism and, 108; epistemic case for, 107–11; hard problem, of consciousness, and, 15, 98–100, 277; Kantian, 92–93; reductionism and, 15, 97–98; Vasubandhu on, 95n7, 97, 103–9, 123nn6–7; of Yogācāra school, 92, 95n6
impartiality, 281
Impossibility Argument, 129–30, 139–40, 143
inclusion, mutual, 271
incompatibilism, 136, 147; Hard, 140, 148; libertarian, 137–38, 141–42, 150, 154n7
indeterminacy, of future generations, 252–54
indeterminism, 15; Buddhism and, 147–48; Consequence Argument and, 129, 138–39, 143; Hard, 148; libertarian, 137–38, 141–42, 150, 154n7; Mind Argument on, 129, 137; quantum, 133–34, 137–38, 154n5
Indian Buddhist philosophers: cross-cultural study and, 8–9; first millennium CE, tradition of, 11–12, 21n20; on free will,

early, 146; idealism of, 97, 100; reductionism of, 97–98
Indian thought, classical: Buddha and, 32, 34–36; on good human life, 32–35; Indian Way, 32; on knowledge, 59; post-Vedic thought, 32–35; pre-Vedic thought, 33–34; Vedic thought, 33–34
individual: Nussbaum emphasizing, 260–61; questioning, 252; Russell on transcending, 280–81, 284n18; social justice focusing on, 267–69, 271
inequality: climate change and international, 254–55; modern defenses of, 209–10; Smith on, 18, 207–8, 236–37
inference, 13, 61–62, 70, 110
Inquiry into the Nature and Causes of the Wealth of Nations, An (Smith). See *Wealth of Nations, The*
instability, network, 256
institutions, public, 258, 260–61
intentionality, 123n2, 197n30, 262–63
intergenerational beings, 20, 267, 272
intergenerational ethics. See ethics, intergenerational
intergenerational justice. See justice
international inequality, 254–55
intrinsic capabilities, 258
invisible hand, metaphor of, 207–8, 236
Inwagen, Peter van, 4

Jaina Sūtras, 197n30
James, William, 67–68

Jansenism, 205
Job (biblical character), 164–65, 171, 186, 188, 195n18
justice: Aristotle on, 268; bodhisattva and relational, 271–72; Buddhist compassion and global, 6, 20, 261; Buddhist nondualistic, 269–70; Buddhist relational, 20, 269–72; compassion, social emotion of, and, 19, 257–59; compassion and, 6, 20, 260–61, 267–72; feminist and postcolonial conceptions of, 268; individual as focus of social, 267–69, 271; intergenerational, 19–20, 251–52, 259, 261, 267, 271–72; karma and, 171, 185–86; particularist, 268–71; Rawls on, 267–68; relational, 20, 261, 269–72, 278; restorative and retributive, 199n43; suffering and, 189, 201n54, 270; universalist, 267–71

Kālāmas, 50–51
Kamalaśīla, 51
kamma. *See* karma
Kane, Robert, 138, 154n7
Kant, Immanuel: on apperception, transcendental unity of, 75n10; Categorical Imperative of, 30, 47; *Critique of Practical Reason*, 30; on good human life, 25, 29–32, 47, 52n2; Kantian idealism, 92–93; on receptivity, 109; virtue theory compared with, 30–31

Kapstein, Matthew, 11–12
Karamazov, Ivan (fictional character), 165, 189, 191n5, 201n54
karma (*kamma*), 9, 200n47; Buddha and, 36, 147, 171–72, 175, 185–86, 194n17; in Buddhism, Hinduism compared with, 171, 195n19, 200n48; Buddhist discomfort with, 171–72; in *Dhammapada*, 177–83, 185–86, 198n35, 199n42, 199n45; in Hinduism, 171, 191n4, 195n19, 200n48; intentionality and, 262–63; justice and, 171, 185–86; karma-result structure, Buddhism and, 172–76, 196nn26–27, 197n28, 197n30; nonfatalistic, 147; no-self and, 174–75; problem of evil and, 17, 164, 171, 175–76, 191n3, 194n17, 195nn18–20; rebirth and, 174; suffering and, 17, 167–75, 191n4, 200n49, 262; Vasubandhu on, 103–5, 123n7; Weber on, 164, 191n3, 194n17
karuṇā (compassion). *See* compassion
Kaufman, Whitley, 195n19
Kāyāyana (*Commentary on Dhammapada* character), 183–84
Kelley, David, 210
Keynes, John Maynard, 216, 243n24
Khmer Rouge, 199n43
Khuddakapāṭha, 196n26
King, Winston, 195n18

knowledge: by acquaintance, 58, 66–69, 71, 73, 75n12; conceptual, Buddhism on, 62–66, 73; conceptual versus perceptual, 58, 62–66, 73, 75n10; Dharmakīrti on, 12–13, 65, 70; Dignāga on, 61–63; emptiness and, 60; Four Noble Truths and, 71–72; Indian thought, classical, on, 59; knowing how and yogic perception, 70–74; knowing that versus knowing how, 58, 70–74; knowledge about versus knowledge by acquaintance, 58, 67–68; knowledge that versus knowledge by acquaintance, 58, 66–69; Mahāyāna Buddhism on, 12–13, 59–60; Nāgārjuna on, 60–61; nirvana and, 71–72; perceptual, 58, 63–66, 73, 75n10; perceptual and inferential, 13, 61–62, 70, 110; *prajñā*, 59; *prajñā-pāramitā*, 59–60; *pramāṇa*, 61; propositional versus knowing how, 58, 70–74; Russell on, 58, 67, 75n12; self-awareness, 65–69, 73, 75n10; soteriology and, 73; of things versus self-knowledge, 58; yogic perception, Dharmakīrti on, 13, 65, 70; yogic perception and, 13, 62, 65, 70–74, 277. *See also* cognition

kuśala (skillful, wholesome) conduct, 265, 270

Kūṭadanta Sutta, 238–39

Kyoto Protocol to the United Nations Framework Convention on Climate Change, 251

Ladyman, James, 80
Lash, Scott, 256
latent disposition (*vāsanā*), 117–19
Layard, Richard, 214–15
Levinas, Emmanuel, 252
liberalism, economic, 208–9
liberation: Buddhist path to, 221–23; Four Noble Truths and, 39–40, 71
libertarianism, philosophical, 137–38, 141–42, 150, 154n7
limited desires (*appicchatā*), 227
lobha (greed), 217
Lotus Sūtra, 72

Madhyamaka school, 79; on emptiness, theory of, 83–87, 93–94, 95n8; global antirealism of, 90–94; mereological reductionism of, 81–83; nonfoundationalism in, 14, 80–81, 83–87, 91–94, 96n10; nonfoundationalism in, consistency of, 87–89; nonfoundationalism in, Indian criticisms of, 87–88; ontology and, 13–14, 84–93; on parts and wholes, 81–84; soteriological, 94; on truth, 88–94; Yogācāra concepts combined with, 86–87, 95n8

mahākaruṇā (great compassion), 20, 264–65, 269

Mahāsudassana Sutta, 41
Mahāyāna Buddhism, 72, 278; on
  bodhisattva, 20, 21n19, 42–43,
  47, 52, 264–66, 271; on free will,
  150–51; on good human life, 25,
  41–44, 51–52; on knowledge,
  12–13, 59–60; on *mahākaruṇā*,
  20, 264–65, 269; on suffering,
  172; Theravāda and, 32, 42–44,
  150; Yogācāra school, 15, 86–87,
  92, 95n6, 95n8, 125n16. *See also*
  Madhyamaka school
Majjhima Nikāya, 195n20
Mallikā (*Commentary on
  Dhammapada* character):
  Kāyāyana contrasted with,
  183–84; retribution and, 178, 184;
  story of, 177–80, 183, 198n35
Mandeville, Bernard, 205–6
Manipulation Argument, 129, 136,
  138–39, 143
Manorathanandin, 107–8
material presence (*rūpa*), 266
mathematics: philosophy of,
  structuralism in, 80; set theory,
  89, 91
McDermott, J. P., 194n13, 194n17,
  197n28, 197n30
McDowell, John, 109
McGinn, Colin, 4
meditative concentration (*samādhi*),
  221–22
Mellor, D. H., 126n22
Menander (Milinda) (king), 148–49,
  168–70, 172
mental events, rebirth and, 101–2

mental perception, Buddhism on,
  65–66
mental phenomena, 87
mereological reductionism, 81–83
metaethics, 45
metaphysics, 28, 53n7; Buddhism
  and, 91–93; of Vasubandhu, 105–
  6, 114; Western, contemporary
  theories of, 92–93
Middle Way, 37–39
migrants, climate, 251
Milinda (Menander) (king), 148–49,
  168–70, 172
Milindapañha (*Milinda's Questions*)
  (*Questions to King Milinda*),
  197n30; Buddha in, 168–72,
  194n16, 196n26; suffering and,
  168–72, 194n13; translation of,
  194n16; two-truths distinction
  in, 148–49; on untimely death,
  170–71, 194n16
*Milinda's Questions. See
  Milindapañha*
military-industrial-communications
  complex, 255
Milken, Michael, 210, 242n16
Mill, John Stuart: deontological
  theory compared with, 31–32;
  on good human life, 25, 30–32,
  47–48, 52n2; virtue theory
  compared with, 31
Mind Argument, 129, 137–39, 143
mind-moments, 87
Missionaries of Charity, 242n16
moderation, Buddhist sense of,
  228–31

mokṣa. See samsara
momentariness, 85–86, 95n5
monastics, happiness of, 227
monism, 82
moral philosophy, 53n8; on good human life, 28–31; Kant on, 29–30; metaethics, normative ethics in, 45; Mill on, 31
Müller, Max, 194n16

Nāgārjuna, vii, 14, 60–61, 79
Nāgasena: suffering and, 168–71, 194n13; on two-truths distinction, 148–49; on untimely death, 170–71, 194n16
Nālandā (university), vii–viii
Nancy, Jean-Luc, 257
naturalist realism, 92–93
neo-Confucianism, viii
networks, 255–56, 270
neuroscience, 143–44
newly industrializing countries, 255
nibbāna (nirvana). *See* nirvana
Nicole, Pierre, 205
Nidhikaṇḍasutta, 196n26
nihilism, 82
nirvana *(nibbāna)*, 152, 196n26; bodhisattva forgoing, 43; Buddha and, 36, 144, 149–50, 222; knowledge and, 71–72; Pali attaining, 55n25; suffering and, 44, 71, 144, 172, 265
nondelusion *(amoha)*, 221
nonduality: bodhisattva affirming, 266; intergenerational ethics and, 266–67, 272, 278; relationality and, 266, 269–70

nonfatalistic karma, Buddhist, 147
nonfoundationalism, 150, 277; as consistent position, 87–89; emptiness, theory of, and, 83–87, 93–94; Madhyamaka, 14, 80–81, 83–87, 91–94, 96n10; Madhyamaka, consistency of, 87–89; Madhyamaka, Indian criticisms of, 87–88; in Western philosophy, 80. *See also* foundationalism
nongreed *(alobha)*, 221
nonhatred *(adosa)*, 221
nonself. *See* no-self
normative ethics, 45
no-self, 11, 60; Buddha on, 40; free will and, 16, 146, 149–50; karma and, 174–75. *See also* being without-self
Nussbaum, Martha: on compassion, 19, 257–61, 264; on core capabilities, 258–60, 270; individual emphasized by, 260–61; *Upheavals of Thought*, 258

Obeyesekere, Gananath, 198n40, 199n43
Obeyesekere, Ranjini, 198n40, 199n43
object, subject and, 67–68
O'Flaherty, Wendy Doniger, 194n17, 199n44
ontic structural realism, 80
ontology: dharmas, theory of, as, 84–85; emptiness, theory of, and, 84–85, 87; event-based, Buddhist, 101; Madhyamaka school

and, 13–14, 84–93; ontological
dependence, 13–15
Optimist's Dilemma: Consequence
Argument and, 129, 136,
138–39, 143; determinism,
indeterminism, and, 133–34,
143; Impossibility Argument
and, 139–40, 143; Manipulation
Argument and, 136,
138–39, 143
own-being (*svabhāva*), 83, 85, 87,
89–90, 265

Pāli canonical texts: suffering in, 17,
170; on wealth, acquisition of,
222–24, 244n44
pañcasīla (Five Precepts), 244n39
paññā (wisdom), 221
Papineau, David, 1
"Parable of the Arrow" (early
Buddhist story), 48–50
paramārtha (reality), 265
Pāramitās (Six Perfections), 42–43
Parfit, D., 144
Park, Peter K. J., ix
Parsons, Talcott, 192n7
particularist conceptions, of
justice, 268–71
parts, wholes and, 81–84
Pasenadi (king), 224; in *Commentary
on Dhammapada*, 177–79, 183; in
Doṇapāka Sutta, 228
Path of Purification. See
Visuddhimagga
Pattakamma Sutta, 231
Payutto, P. A., 227–31, 240
Pen Khek Chear, 199n43, 200n47

perception: conceptual versus
perceptual knowledge, 58, 62–66,
73, 75n10; Dharmakīrti on, 13,
65–66, 70, 73, 109–10; Dignāga
on, 112, 114–16; empiricism and
rationalism on, 63–64; inference
and, 13, 61–62, 70, 110; Kant
on, 109; mental, Buddhism
on, 65–66; self-awareness,
acquaintance, knowledge by,
and, 66–69, 73; self-awareness,
Buddhism on, 65–68, 75n10;
yogic, 13, 62, 65, 70–74, 277
Pereboom, Derk, 136, 143
perfection of knowledge (*prajñā-
pāramitā*), 59–60
Perrett, Roy, 19n4, 200n49
person, five parts of, 83
persons, Buddhist reductionism
of, 101
person-theorists (Pudgalavādins),
146, 149, 174
phenomenology, 67–68
philosophy, value of: analytic
tradition, contemporary, on,
278–80; Buddhist philosophy
and, 282–83; comparative
philosophy and, 276–77; Russell
on, 275–76, 279–83
philosophy departments, x–xi, 10
"Philosophy for Laymen"
(Russell), 280
physicalism, 15, 97–98, 100
Plato: on good human life, 27–28; on
problem of evil, 166
population growth, 250
postcolonial criticism, 268

post-Vedic thought, 32–35
poverty: Buddhism on, 230, 237–38; *dāḷiddiya*, 237; economists, modern, on, 209–10; Friedman on, 209; Keynes on, 216; Smith on, 216, 234–37
Powers, John, 21n19
pragmatic truth, 69–74
prajñā (higher knowledge), 59
Prajñākaragupta, 66
prajñā-pāramitā (perfection of knowledge), 59–60
pramāṇa (knowledge). *See* knowledge
pratyaya (causal conditions). *See* causal conditions
predicament-resolution, 256–57
pre-Socratic philosophers, 25–27
pre-Vedic thought, 33–34
problem of evil, 132; Aquinas on, 192n6; Aristotle and Plato on, 166; biblical, 164–65, 171, 195n18; in Chinese philosophy, 166; Hindu tradition and, 171, 192n7, 195n19, 200n48; karma and, 17, 164, 167, 171, 175–76, 191n3, 194n17, 195nn18–20; nontheistic, 17, 166–67; suffering and, 16, 165, 167, 171, 175–76, 188–89, 200n48, 277–78; Weber and, 164–65, 191n3, 192n7, 194n17
Problems of Philosophy, The (Russell), 275–76
problem-solution, 256–57
progress, philosophical, 1–4
property-particulars, 84–85

propositional knowledge, 58, 70–74
prosperity. *See* wealth, acquisition of
prudence, 232–33
Pudgalavādins (person-theorists), 146, 149, 174
punishment, 183, 199n44

qualia, 123n2
quantum indeterminism, 133–34, 137–38, 154n5
quantum science, 133–34, 154n5
Questions to King Milinda. See Milindapañha

rāga (greed), 218
Randomness Argument. *See* Mind Argument
Rasmussen, Dennis C., 216, 236–37
rationalism, 63–64
Rawls, John, 253, 267–68
reality (*paramārtha*), 265
reality, pre-Socratic philosophers on, 25–27
rebirth, 9, 21n19; Dharmakīrti on, 15, 98, 102–3, 123n5; karma and, 174; mental events and, 101–2; post-Vedic view of, 34
receptivity, 109
reductionism: idealism, physicalism, and, 15, 97–98; Indian Buddhist, 97–98; mereological, 81–83; of persons, Buddhist, 101
reflexive modernization, 256
refugees, climate, 251
relationality: bodhisattva, 271–72; Buddha-nature in, 266; of

Buddhist compassion, 20,
  262–64, 266–67, 269; in ethics,
  20, 252, 262–64, 266–67;
  intergenerational, 20, 252, 262–64,
  266–67, 272, 278; justice and, 20,
  261, 269–72, 278; nondualistic,
  266, 269–70; suffering and, 262
restorative justice, 199n43
retribution, 178, 184, 199n43
Ross, Don, 80
rūpa (form, material presence), 266
Russell, Bertrand, 285n22; on
  contemplation, 280, 284nn18–19;
  on individual, transcending,
  280–81, 284n18; on knowledge,
  58, 67, 75n12; on philosophy,
  value of, 275–76, 279–83;
  "Philosophy for Laymen,"
  280; *The Problems of Philosophy*,
  275–76; on Spinoza, 282
Ryle, Gilbert, 70

Saddharmaratnāvaliya, 181
sage, ideal of, 284n19
sahabhūhetu, 125n20
Sākiyas, 184–86
samādhi (meditative concentration),
  221–22
samsara, 34, 189–90; Buddha on, 36,
  169; *mokṣa*, 36
Sanskrit-language materials, in
  China, viii
Śāntideva, 198n37
santuṭṭhi (contentment), 227
Sapaṇ, 66
Schellenberg, J. L., 2, 4–5

scientific revolution, 133
seeds (*bīja*), 117–19, 125n16
self: agent/self, Buddhism
  rejecting, 144–46, 150; *atman*,
  264; attachment, craving, and,
  219–22; Buddha on, 40, 83,
  144, 173; Buddhism critiquing,
  81, 83, 144–46, 149–50, 152, 173,
  264, 269; disidentification
  from, 222; dualism and denial
  of, 100–101; free will and, 16,
  146, 149–50; Hume on, 144;
  Madhyamaka critique of, 81, 83;
  neuroscience and skepticism on,
  143–44; person, five parts of, 83;
  Pudgalavādins on, 146, 149, 174;
  suffering and, 173, 175, 219–22. *See
  also* agentless agency; no-self;
  individual
self-awareness: acquaintance,
  knowledge by, and, 66–69, 73;
  Buddhism on, 65–68, 75n10; as
  knowledge, 65–69, 73, 75n10
self-interest, 209
self-knowledge, knowledge of
  things versus, 58
self-love, 206
Sellars, Wilfrid, 64, 68, 148
Semi-Compatibilism, 142–43,
  148–49
set theory, 89, 91
shared, common and, 257
Siddhārtha Gautama, vii;
  soteriological focus of, 11;
  Theravāda Buddhism on, 37–38
Siderits, Mark, 8, 90, 148–49

Sigālaka, 223
Sigālovāda Sutta, 245n50
sīla (ethical conduct), 221
Silva, Lily de, 225, 227, 229
Sivaka Sutta, 170
Six Perfections (*Pāramitās*), 42–43
skandhas, 83–84, 92
Skidelsky, Edward, 229
Skidelsky, Robert, 229
skillful conditions, 230
skillful conduct (*kuśala* conduct), 265, 270
skillful means (*upāya*), 43, 51, 73, 264, 277
Smith, Adam, 241n5; on benevolence, 234; on deception, economics and, 215; greed and, 18, 206–8, 211–16; on happiness, 212–16, 231–33, 239–40, 242n18; on human flourishing, 231–37, 239–40; on inequality, 18, 207–8, 236–37; on invisible hand, 207–8, 236; on poverty, 216, 234–37; on prudent man, 232–33; responses to, 216; on Stoics, 212; on tranquility, 212, 232; on vanity, 211–12, 215, 232, 235; on wealth, acquisition of, 18, 206–8, 211–16, 232, 235–36; *Wealth of Nations*, 18, 206–7, 215, 239. See also *Theory of Moral Sentiments*
Soames, Scott, 279
social emotion, of compassion, 19, 257–59
social justice. *See* justice
Sociology of Religion (Weber), 192n7
Socrates, viii, 3, 24, 27–28

Soft Compatibilism, 140, 148
Solomon (king), 182
Song dynasty, viii, x–xi
Sophists, 26–27
Sophocles, 166–67, 188, 201n52
soteriology, 21n19, 123n6; Buddha focusing on, 11, 146; free will and, 149–50; knowledge and, 73; Madhyamaka, 94; social and economic views, Buddhist, and, 239
space, time and, 85
Spinoza, Baruch, 282
Sri Lanka, 177
Stages of Meditation, The (Kamalaśīla), 51
Stoic philosophy, 212
Stoljar, Daniel, 20n14
store-house consciousness (*ālayavijñāna*), 125n16, 125n19
Stossel, John, 210
Strawson, Galen, 68–69, 139
structuralism, 80
subjective well-being, happiness as, 23, 25
subjectivity, 123n2; consciousness, hard problem of, and, 99, 122; phenomenology on, 67–68; subjective experience, 14–15
suffering: attachment and, 219–20; Buddha and, 11, 168–71, 173, 187, 194n13, 218–19, 222; cessation of, 39–40, 71, 172–73, 189–90, 221–22, 265; compassion and, 51, 258, 260, 262, 264–65; craving and, 218; in *Dhammapada*, 180,

182, 199nn41–42; in Four Noble
Truths, 39–40, 46, 71, 187; justice
and, 189, 201n54, 270; karma
and, 17, 167–75, 191n4, 200n49,
262; Mahāyāna Buddhism on,
172; *Milindapañha* and, 168–72,
194n13; Nāgasena and, 168–71,
194n13; nirvana and, 44, 71, 144,
172, 265; Pāli canonical texts on,
17, 170; pragmatic truths ending,
73; problem of evil and, 16, 165,
167, 171, 175–76, 188–89, 200n48,
277–78; relationality,
interdependence, and, 262; self
and, 173, 175, 219–22
suffering (*duḥkha*), 262, 265, 270–71
suffering (*dukkha*), 40, 44, 46, 50, 218
sukha (bliss, happiness), 225, 265
śūnyatā (emptiness). *See* emptiness
Sutta Piṭaka, 35, 37
svabhāva (own-being), 83, 85, 87, 89–90, 265

taṇhā (craving, thirst). *See* craving
Teresa (Mother), 210, 242n16
Thales, 26
theism, problem of evil in, 16–17
theodicy. *See* problem of evil
Theory of Moral Sentiments (Smith), 241n5; on benevolence, 234; on deception, economic growth and, 215; on greed, 208, 211–15; on happiness, 212–15, 232–33, 239–40, 242n18; on invisible hand, 208; on poverty, 234–37; prudent man in, 232–33; on tranquility, 212, 232;
on vanity, 211–12, 215, 232, 235; on
wealth, acquisition of, 206, 208,
211–15, 232, 235–36
Theravāda Buddhism, 194n15;
on anger, justice and, 199n43;
Buddhaghosa, 264; on
compassion, 264; Eightfold Path
in, 37–40, 44; Four Noble Truths
in, 37–40, 44; on free will, 150–51;
on good human life, 25, 32, 35–44;
Mahāyāna and, 32, 42–44, 150;
Middle Way in, 37–39; Three
Baskets of, 35, 37
thirst (*taṇhā*). *See* craving
thought (*cetanā*). *See cetanā*
Three Baskets (*Tipiṭaka*), 35, 37
Three Marks, 37–38, 40, 44, 80–81
time: momentariness, 85–86, 95n5;
space and, 85
Tipiṭaka (Three Baskets), 35, 37
Trakakis, Nick, 195n19, 200n48
tranquility: Buddhist, 221–22; Smith
on, 212, 232
*Treasury of Abhidharma
(Abhidharmakośa)* (Vasubandhu),
103–4
truth, 3; global antirealism on,
90–94; Madhyamaka school on,
88–94; pragmatic, 69–74
Tsongkhapa, 68
two-truths distinction, 148–49, 151,
156n27

UN. *See* United Nations
undernourished, global population
of, 251

United Nations (UN), 251
universalist conceptions, of justice, 267–71
universals, 62–63
untimely death, 170–71, 194n16
upādāna (attachment, fuel). *See* attachment
upāya (skillful means), 43, 51, 73, 264, 277
Upheavals of Thought (Nussbaum), 258
Uppalavaṇṇā, 199n42
urban population, global, 250

Valberg, J. J., 109, 119
Vaṇijjā Sutta, 223
vanity, 211–12, 215, 232, 235
vāsanā (latent disposition), 117–19
Vasubandhu, 125n20; on atoms, 83, 105–6, 108, 114, 124n9; on Buddha, 97, 104, 106–7; on idealism, 95n7, 97, 103–9, 123nn6–7; on karma, 103–5, 123n7; metaphysics of, 105–6, 114; *Treasury of Abhidharma*, 103–4; *Vimśatikā*, 83, 95n7
Vedas, 33
Vedic thought, 33–34
veil of ignorance, 267
Vibhaṅga, 194n15
Vico, Giambattista, 205
Viḍūḍabha (*Commentary on Dhammapada* character), 183–86
Vimśatikā (Vasubandhu), 83, 95n7
virtue theory: of Aristotle, 25, 29–30, 32, 47, 52n2; on good human life, 25, 29–32, 47, 52n2; Kant compared with, 30–31; Mill compared with, 31
Visuddhimagga (Path of Purification) (Buddhaghosa), 264
volatility, network, 256
volition (*cetanā*). *See cetanā*

Watson, G., 141
wealth, acquisition of: Buddha on, 18–19, 216–17, 223–25, 245n50; Buddhism on happiness and, 225–32, 238–39; defenses of, 18–19, 205–8, 215; happiness and, contemporary research on, 214; Keynes on, 216, 243n24; Pāli canonical texts on, 222–24, 244n44; Smith on, 18, 206–8, 211–16, 232, 235–36; vanity and, 211–12, 215, 232, 235. *See also* greed
Wealth of Nations, The (Smith): on human flourishing, 239; on invisible hand, 207; on wealth, acquisition of, 18, 206–7, 215
Weber, Max, 164–65, 191n3, 192n7, 194n17
Whitebrook, Maureen, 260
Whitehead, Alfred North, 27
wholes, parts and, 81–84
wholesome conduct (*kuśala* conduct), 265, 270
wiggly determinism, 147
Williams, Walter E., 229
wisdom (*paññā*), 221
worthy one (*arahant*), 55n25

Xuanzang, viii

Yijing, viii

Yogācāra school, 15; Abhidharma tradition and, 125n16; on emptiness, 86–87; idealism of, 92, 95n6; Madhyamaka concepts combined with, 86–87, 95n8

yogic perception (*yogipratyakṣa*), 62, 277; Dharmakīrti on, 13, 65, 70; knowing how and, 70–74

Zahavi, Dan, 67

GPSR Authorized Representative: Easy Access System Europe, Mustamäe tee 50, 10621 Tallinn, Estonia, gpsr.requests@easproject.com